OLIVIA
NEWTON-JOHN

Don't Stop Believin'

G
GALLERY BOOKS
New York London Toronto Sydney New Delhi

G

Gallery Books
An Imprint of Simon & Schuster, Inc.
1230 Avenue of the Americas
New York, NY 10020

Text copyright © 2018 by Olivia Newton-John
Originally published in 2018 in Australia by Viking Australia
This edition published by arrangement with Penguin Random House Australia Pty. Ltd.

First Gallery Books trade paperback edition January 2021

GALLERY BOOKS and colophon are registered trademarks of Simon & Schuster, Inc.

For information about special discounts for bulk purchases, please contact Simon & Schuster Special Sales at 1-866-506-1949 or business@simonandschuster.com.

The Simon & Schuster Speakers Bureau can bring authors to your live event. For more information or to book an event, contact the Simon & Schuster Speakers Bureau at 1-866-248-3049 or visit our website at www.simonspeakers.com.

10 9 8 7 6 5 4 3 2 1

Library of Congress Cataloging-in-Publication Data is available for the hardcover edition.

ISBN 978-1-9821-2224-9
ISBN 978-1-9821-2225-6 (pbk)
ISBN 978-1-9821-2226-3 (ebook)

This book is dedicated to my darling daughter, Chloe, so that you may know more about my life before you were in it!
You are my world, and I love you
bigger than the universe.

Mama ♡

CONTENTS

I'LL NEVER STOP BELIEVIN'

It has been almost a year since I flew back from Oz, arriving in LA in a wheelchair. I spent the next ten months or so graduating from bed to a walker, from crutches to a walking stick, and now . . . "Look, Mum! No hands!"

I was thrilled to be back in Australia in the fall of 2019 to walk the Wellness Walk and Research Run for the ONJ. My extra excitement was because before that, John and I had gone on holiday to my very favorite place: my Gaia Retreat & Spa in the Byron Bay Hinterland. We enjoyed the most delicious food and the most nurturing treatments of any spa or healing facility in the world.

I am so proud that Gaia recently won World's Leading Retreat from World Travel Awards *for the fourth year in a row*. What an achievement for our magnificent team! Gaia continues to be honored with many hotel/spa awards, including, in 2018, the most prestigious of them all—Global Hotel of the Year from the World Luxury Hotel Awards. I was also incredibly touched to receive the Wellness Pioneer Award at the World Spa Awards held at the Armani Hotel in Dubai. I'm so grateful that the dream Gregg and I shared all those years ago is now everyone's dream place!

In February, Gaia Retreat & Spa released our skincare line, Retreatment Botanics. The natural, luxurious formulas are vegan and Australian made, contain powerful native extracts, and are certified palm oil free by the Orangutan Alliance. This was extremely important to us as the environment has always been of huge concern.

To add to my excitement, I received a special gift upon our departure from Los Angeles. As John and I were preparing to board our Qantas A380 to fly back to Australia, we ran into Father Jim Sichko, a delightful Roman Catholic priest I had met once before in Vegas, with Donny Osmond. He came to where we were sitting, and sweetly and ceremoniously handed me a beautiful silver cross. Father Jim proceeded to tell us an intriguing story about how he'd serendipitously had an unexpected meeting with Pope Francis at the Vatican. The Pope then asked him to become one of his emissaries, which involves traveling the globe and spreading the word of love and kindness.

I was deeply moved to learn that my cross was one of fifty blessed by the papal leader and given to Father Jim to bestow upon those he believed needed them. It was especially meaningful because just before leaving the Olivia Newton-John Wellness & Research Centre to head to the airport after being a patient there last year, I was given a very beautiful Jerusalem cross by Dennis, our palliative-care counselor. So, I guess you could say that I was "double-crossed" in a beautiful way!

Over the past year, as I grew stronger in body and spirit, I found myself gaining even more gratitude for each and every day. Every moment is truly a gift, and joys are waiting around every corner. This year marked the US release of my memoir, and I was so delighted when *Don't Stop Believin'* debuted at #12 on the *New York Times* bestsellers list, and I was blown away that it made the top ten at number #7 on *Publishers Weekly*'s bestsellers list! Thank you to everyone who helped make that happen!

In June, I was so proud to be awarded a Companion of the Order of Australia (AC) that I fondly refer to as my "Air Conditioner Award"! It is the highest honor you can receive in Australia, and it was an exceptional and meaningful day at the home of Chelsey Martin, the Australian Consul-General, in Los Angeles with Chloe, John, and close friends on hand to witness my investiture by Joe Hockey, the Australian ambassador to the US. Thank you, Chelsey and Joe!

I must say that 2019 was a really extraordinary year. And why not? I've always believed that good things can come out of difficult times. I'll never forget how the 2018 Wellness Walk & Research Run was so difficult for me as I couldn't walk and had to fake it. My way to embrace life fully again was this year's Wellness Walk, which was a huge success both for me personally and for the ONJ. For me, the 2019 event was truly special because, to add to my joy of being able to walk some of it, my darling Chloe came to walk with me, along with my wonderful husband, John, who has been such an integral part of my healing. By the way, we raised over a million dollars and had the best walker participation *ever* of over five thousand people. And many of them brought their dogs—my favorite part!

*

And now a few words about my husband, John.

Being a plant medicine man, over the last year he has grown and produced medicinal cannabis for me that has changed my life. I weaned myself off morphine (which I had been taking for intense pain while at the ONJCWRC) with high doses of cannabis. This had been extremely important for me to do, as I had heard so much about opioid addiction. I had decided before I'd even started the morphine that I would wean myself off it as soon as possible. I had to wait until my fracture healed, but slowly I titrated (the cool word for "weaned") off the drug that had been such a huge help to me in my crisis of intense pain.

I was relieved to learn from John that no one has died of cannabis use, unlike opiates, which are killing thousands of people a year. I had to have my lungs drained only once, and I continue taking my antiestrogenic medications and multiple supplements, herbs, and, of course, tinctures of specific cannabis strains that John lovingly grows just for me and friends who are in need. We hope one day to be able to make them available to everyone in need.

I never would have dreamed, even a couple of years ago, that I would be speaking to the world about using cannabis as one of my pathways to help heal from my breast cancer metastases.

Yet, here I am. Each day is a new chance to share.

*

Twenty-seven years ago, I was nervous to speak about my breast cancer, but looking back I realize it was very important that I put my voice out there. It has put me on a healing track and inspired me to speak out again now to help make medicinal cannabis easily available for all people in pain and those who are suffering.

John and I, along with my ONJ research team, have been to Parliament House in Canberra to talk to the Australian Government about offering easier patient access to cannabis. I'm also excited to be launching a cannabis research program at my ONJ Cancer Research Institute.

I believe plant medicine is the future of healing, as we realize the need to return to the natural world for answers. Our bodies are now rejecting many of the synthetic drugs and becoming resistant to them. Above all, I want to help find kinder treatments for cancer patients. I believe in a holistic approach, combining different modalities of healing. I believe this is the answer. It certainly has been and continues to be *my* answer.

In 1992, during my first bout with cancer, I had surgery and chemotherapy. The second time around, over twenty years later, I relied on natural therapy. And this most recent time, I chose targeted radiation, estrogen blockers, bone strengtheners, and a wide array of herbs, supplements, and daily tinctures of cannabis as my "team" of healing choices.

Everyone has to make their own decisions on their healing journey.

I also believe in living each day to the fullest and laughing and loving as much as possible!

I am delighted that Greg Hunt, the Australian Minister of Health, has announced that he is appropriating three million dollars toward cannabis research. This is a huge step in the right direction for Australia and a way to learn the science behind the thousands of anecdotal testimonies. I'm very hopeful that in the not-so-distant future, all Australians will have easy access to medicinal cannabis.

*

This has been a very exciting year, all the way around.

I'm feeling great, my mobility is back, and I just sold my *Grease* jacket and pants, the ones I wore an unbelievable forty-one years ago. Yes, those are the special pants, broken zipper and all, that I shimmied into at the end of the movie when Sandy #2 tries to "get her man"! I was thrilled to auction off these iconic pieces along with many other items and memorabilia from my life and career to raise funds for the wellness and research programs at the ONJ. It's very satisfying to know that someone bought these items and will enjoy them. Luckily for me, I will always have the memories and a gorgeous catalog of photos that Julien's Auctions provided.

I just learned that my skintight black pants were "won" by Sara Blakely, the inventor and CEO of Spanx. I sang at her wedding in 2008, and she wanted her first dance with her husband to be to the *Grease* songs. How serendipitous that she now has those pants—she is the perfect new owner as they really are the original Spanx!

My life keeps getting fuller, and I'm happier and more thankful than ever!

As I was writing this note for the paperback edition, John Travolta and I were planning our celebration of forty-two years of friendship by joining together at the yuletide season for a few *Grease* appearances featuring a sing-along version of the movie. We met some of our fans in what we called a "Meet 'n *Grease*" and after the special screening conducted a Q and A with the audience with us and three of the T-Birds, Barry Pearl, Michael Tucci, and Kelly Ward. We encouraged the audiences to dress up as their favorite Greasers. Our director, Randal Kleiser, was part of this celebration, too. Sadly, my longtime Frenchy friend, Didi Conn, was doing a pantomime in London and wasn't able to be with us.

It was so much fun!

I'm still amazed that after forty-one years, new generations are discovering *Grease*. When I was on tour and then in Las Vegas for a three-year residency, I would meet grandparents who had just introduced the film to their grandchildren. It's such a timeless movie!

*

The holiday season is a perfect time to celebrate life and its many blessings. My favorite gift ever was to see Chloe's one-year-old face on her first Christmas. I can still see her playing with that sparkly wrapping paper under the tree. She liked that better than any other gift!

Memories like this remind me that I've been so blessed in my life. I have a beautiful daughter and a loving husband, amazing family and friends, plus an extended human and animal family that reaches far and wide across the planet. I have also enjoyed an exceptionally long and diverse career, for which I'm thankful. Whether you are new to my world or a longtime supporter, I welcome you and thank you for all of your kindness and love. I am forever grateful. This has been—and continues to be—an incredible life.

However, I still have a long to-do list! It begins this way:

I will help find kinder cancer treatments.

I will see an end to cancer in my lifetime.

I will look up at my Olivia Newton-John Cancer Wellness & Research Cancer Centre sign and watch as they remove the word "Cancer" from the building.

Yes! Goodbye!

*

PS: I'm so happy to share that I'm living extremely well with cancer! My recent MRI and medical tests show that my metastases are either gone, smaller, or have stayed the same! No progression of the disease! This really strengthens my belief in my holistic approach to it. "Holistic" in this case means using the best of all available options to heal myself.

It also reinforces my message: Don't Stop Believin'.

*

PPS: Okay, I have to tell you another story—or two!

An unbelievable thing happened a few days ago, just as I was sending this off to the publisher: I was shown one of the greatest acts of kindness ever! "Surprised" doesn't begin to cover my emotions when I was told that my "#1 fan" (who wishes to remain anonymous) gave me back my *Grease* jacket, which he had purchased at the auction.

"Olivia," he said, "I believe this belongs with you."

Completely blown away, the tears streamed down my face. I couldn't believe that anyone would do something that generous for me! Thank you again, my mystery man. You have given me a beautiful opportunity to display my jacket in the ONJCWRC for all to enjoy!

When it comes to human kindness, I remain a true believer.

One last thing . . .

I didn't think anything more extraordinary could happen to me in 2019! Then, just before the new year, I received high honors from the British government and Queen Elizabeth when I was named a dame, the female equivalent of a knight. I was recognized for both my singing and my charitable work supporting cancer research.

I am so honored by this acknowledgment and find it hard to believe! As a woman born in Cambridge, I am very proud of my British ancestry and so appreciate being recognized in this way by the United Kingdom. I'm delighted beyond words to be included in such an esteemed group of women who have received this distinguished award before me.

I'd been lucky enough to have been presented with an OBE

(Officer of the Order of the British Empire) by Her Majesty the Queen in 1979. The thought of meeting her again, or another member of the royal family, is an exciting prospect. I so respect their service and all they do for charity around the globe.

By the way, *South Pacific* was always one of my favorite musicals when I was a child, and now I can sing "There Is Nothin' Like a Dame" with gusto!

I'll never stop believin'!

Love and Light,

Olivia

XOXO

AUTHOR'S NOTE

I am a private person living a very public life.

I therefore choose to only tell stories about my own life that I hope are entertaining or interesting—and that I still remember!

I am grateful for all the people on my life's journey, whether I have known you for a moment—a reason, a season, or a lifetime.

Know that you're in my heart.

Please forgive me if you don't get a mention, for I had only so many pages!

love + light

Olivia

INTRODUCTION

Olivia's dream was to have a wellness and research center that treats the person, not just the disease. The Olivia Newton-John Cancer Wellness & Research Centre (ONJ Centre) was the first of its kind in Australia to bring together world-class clinical treatment, breakthrough research and education, and complementary wellness therapies.

Today the ONJ Centre continues to provide leadership in the benefits of complementary support and therapies by recognizing cancer diagnosis and treatment is a physically and emotionally demanding time. The wellness center is a beautifully restored building that provides space for people and their caregivers to be away from the clinical setting and relax in a tranquil environment.

The Olivia Newton-John Cancer Research Institute laboratories sit alongside patient treatment facilities so our researchers and clinicians can work together. The ONJ Centre is currently involved in nearly three hundred clinical trials, and our passionate researchers are working to use significant scientific discoveries from the laboratory to improve clinical practice. This means ONJ Centre patients have more timely access to potential new treatments and targeted therapies.

The ONJ Centre is a partnership where patients and their families, scientists, doctors, nurses, and therapists collaborate to provide the best possible person-centered treatment to make constant improvements to cancer care.

Cancer research and wellness therapies provided rely solely on donations. You can support Olivia and people going through cancer treatment by making a donation at onjcentre.org.

Every year thousands of people who are touched by cancer come to the Olivia Newton-John Cancer Wellness and Research Centre. They face the challenge of a lifetime with hope because they receive the best care guided by the latest research delivered with passion, love, kindness, and understanding. Patients, their loved ones, researchers, and staff are all hugely grateful for what Olivia has helped build and sustain: a truly unique cancer center founded on her vision, with boundless enthusiasm and love.

—Professor Jonathan Cebon, Medical Director,
Olivia Newton-John Cancer Wellness & Research Centre

PROLOGUE

Don't stop believin', you'll get by
Bad days will hurry by.

May 30, 2017

My favorite time of day is "magic hour," when the sun takes a dive behind the craggy mountain ranges and the sky is painted a stunning purple-pink. I'm sitting during magic hour right now on a weathered stone bench, allowing the day to wash over me, surrounding myself with love and light.

I smell the early-summer roses and smile as our energetic German shepherd, Raven, brings me her ball for yet another toss. My wonderful husband, John, should be pulling up in the driveway any moment. It's a beautiful life and remains so, even though I told the world a few hours ago that my cancer has returned.

Yesterday I went in to be measured. When you have photon radiation therapy, you must be in exactly the same position every single time, so they give you small dot tattoos to make sure your body is lined up properly in the machine.

"I guess this will be the fun part," I told the technician as he poked a small, needlelike pen through flesh to mark my hips.

When I saw that what he'd created was no more than tiny circles, I asked, "Can't you give me something a little more interesting?"

John and I have matching tattoos on our left ankles—a spiral pattern we designed when we were in Australia on our fifth anniversary.

"Hey, I thought I was only going to get a tattoo once in my life!" I joked. "Not fair to John now that I'll have an extra one."

We had a good laugh.

Being positive isn't always easy, but we always have that choice.

This is my third journey with cancer, which might come as a surprise. The previous one was five years ago and I kept it private, and luckily it remained so, which isn't always easy when you live your life in public.

In May 2013, John and I were rear-ended in our Prius on Highway 101 in heavy Los Angeles traffic. We were on the way to my sister Rona's house. My niece Tottie and her daughter, Layla, had been visiting us and they were in the back seat. Raven, our new puppy, was in a crate in the back. That poor baby was surrounded by shattered glass, we were hit that hard. For months afterward, Raven was nervous every time I even *looked* at the car.

The accident was only part of what was a tough time for our family. My beloved Rona was very ill and died a short time later, on May 24, of a brain tumor. And soon my own health would be called into question.

The day we had the accident, the seat belt hit me very hard in my right shoulder. It wasn't long before I noticed a lump had formed there.

I ended up at Rona's local doctor, who wasn't overly concerned.

"It's most likely from the accident," she said. She did an X-ray but didn't find anything.

As time passed, I couldn't lift my arm easily, which was chalked up to a slight fracture. But why wouldn't the pain subside? In my gut, I knew it wasn't that simple and kept asking and digging. It was my body, and my instincts told me to find the real answer.

I insisted on additional testing and found that the bump was actually a recurrence of my breast cancer.

My immediate healing plan was immune-boosting IVs at a clinic in Georgia where they help people deal with illness in a natural way without prescription drugs. I did this along with continuing on a healthy diet that included many of my husband's Amazonian herb formulas. And I also consulted with my oncology team at the Olivia Newton-John Cancer Wellness & Research Centre in Melbourne. With their advice, including taking an antiestrogenic pill, I felt I was on the right track.

I didn't tell my family or anyone else at the time, except for John, of course. There was too much going on with the loss of my sister.

When I went back for a second CAT scan, the tumor had reduced and we decided to keep an eye on it.

Life went on.

Three years ago, I was playing tennis at my close friend Pat Farrar's birthday party. I hadn't played in a while and was out on the court for three hours of nonstop fun. I had a blast, sat down for lunch, and absolutely couldn't get up afterward. This could've been because of very sore muscles since I hadn't played in months, but I had trouble even standing and wobbled when I forced myself upright. What followed were months and months of excruciating, sleep-depriving, crying-out-loud pain.

Night after night, I hobbled onstage in Las Vegas, where I was doing a residency at the famed Flamingo Hotel. The crippling back pain would flare up at the worst times but would occasionally die down—thank goodness! During a good period, a friend of mine, Joanne, who is a great tennis player, said the magic words.

"Come on over, Liv. We'll have a gentle hit."

I was on the court for about half an hour before a sciatic attack had me seeing stars. Despite the pain, I refused to cancel any of my shows because of a lifelong discipline instilled in me at the tender age of fifteen.

No matter what—the show must go on!

But would I be able to go on? Some nights, after the last curtain call, I would limp backstage and gingerly lie down on my dressing-room floor, crying in agony. It felt like I was being tortured with hot pokers that were being stabbed into my side, causing searing pain to jolt up and down my left leg.

In my prone position backstage with tears running through my makeup, I wasn't sure how I would ever get up. But . . . *the show must go on, and it isn't over*. I still had to do my fan meet and greet, with all the proceeds going to my Olivia Newton-John Cancer Wellness & Research Centre. I only allowed myself exactly five minutes to rest and then my husband would pull me to my feet.

My checklist was as follows:

1. Wipe away the tears.
2. Fix my face.
3. Go back out there and do the meet and greet backstage for the fans.

These lovely people had waited sometimes an entire year just to say hello, and I wouldn't let them down. Somehow, I held it all together while I smiled and took a few pictures. It was the least I could do for this kind of loyalty.

My last show of 2017 before my diagnosis was a concert for those who served in the military and had been awarded a Purple Heart for their bravery. I had my *Liv On* collaborators and dear friends Amy Sky and Beth Nielsen Chapman by my side and we honored, among others, my father-in-law, Tom, a Purple Heart recipient.

It should have been a beautiful night that I would never forget—and it was. The pain was cruel, relentless, and agonizing, and I found it almost impossible to walk. This was no longer about just pulling myself up but facing the fact that I could not do it any longer.

The next day, John's niece Corrine, an upper cervical and spinal expert, did a thermogram of my whole body at her clinic. It showed some hot spots in my sacral area, and she suggested a seated MRI. This revealed something rather suspicious pressing on the nerves in my sacrum. No one recommended a biopsy because of the sensitivity of the area. But in my heart, I knew.

Something wasn't right.

I believe it's crucial to *always* listen to your body and trust your instincts. I can't say this enough: no one knows your body like you do.

Corinne and John insisted that I give this my immediate attention, so I postponed the rest of my tour, which was very difficult for me because of that work ethic I mentioned earlier. But now I had no choice. I drove to the clinic in Georgia for two weeks of diagnostics and natural IV therapies. Within a week, my pain level went from a ten to a one, which was very encouraging.

And then came the news.

My ONCOblot test was in. It showed breast cancer—again.

This time it had metastasized into my sacrum.

They had found a mass.

I put out a press release because I wanted my fans to hear this from me and not the rumor mill.

For Immediate Release
OLIVIA NEWTON-JOHN POSTPONES JUNE
CONCERT DATES

    May 30, 2017—Las Vegas, NV—Olivia Newton-John is reluctantly postponing her June U.S. and Canadian concert tour dates. The back pain that initially caused her to postpone the first half of her concert tour has turned out to be breast cancer that has metastasized to the sacrum.

That day, after those words were released to the world, I sat on my stone bench as the sun sank behind the mountains. In the hours that followed, the outpouring of goodwill touched my heart in ways that I will never forget. There were phone calls, emails, messages, and even flowers wishing me well.

I sat there knowing that this was going to be another challenging journey, but I would never stop believing that I would be okay. I knew I had so much living and loving to do.

I sat, visualizing myself many years in the future, happy and healthy, and I began reflecting on my incredible life.

ONE

Sail into Tomorrow

If a ship of dreams bid me come,
Would I board it?

I am a young girl racing home from school across the grass on
the grounds of Ormond College in Melbourne, Australia. I'm
running home to the music of nature. Birds are serenading me—
kookaburras, parrots, crows, and those magpies with the large
wings and scary beaks that hover and hide in the trees. Oh, those
magpies! Sometimes I would have to cover my small blond head
with my schoolbooks as those huge, striking black-and-white birds
swooped down on me. I can still hear the sound of the brisk wind
in their feathers that brushed so close to my ears as I walked under
the gum trees that held their nests. Magpies become very protective
in the spring, guarding their homes and families.

Music was a big part of my home and family as well. My mum
said I could carry a tune as young as two years old, and soon I knew
the words and would sing harmonies to every song on the radio. I
believe I got this gift from my father, Brinley "Brin" Newton-John,

who was Welsh and had a beautiful bass-baritone singing voice. He could have been an opera singer but chose to become an academic because he was so critical of himself and didn't think he was good enough. He had one recording of himself on an old black acetate disc but destroyed it because there was one bad note in it. (I wonder where I got my perfectionism from?)

My mum, Irene Helene Born, was the daughter of Nobel Prize–winning Max Born, a German physicist and mathematician who was one of the founders of quantum mechanics. Albert Einstein was a close friend, and when my mother was a young girl, Einstein spent many evenings in her family house playing the violin while my grandfather played piano. My mother would later translate a book of letters between Albert Einstein and Max Born called *The Born–Einstein Letters*. My German grandfather was the first person to sign an antinuclear proliferation treaty because he was strongly opposed to war. He was also a good friend of J. Robert Oppenheimer, the physicist credited with being the father of the atomic bomb, but my grandfather refused to collaborate with him on anything that was destructive or would hurt people. In 1933, my Jewish grandfather fled from Germany with his wife, Hedwig, to escape Hitler's regime. He was not only a brilliant mind but also a humanitarian who helped Jews escape Germany. I'm extremely proud of my peace-loving grandfather.

My uncle Gustav, who sadly died recently at age ninety-six, listened to his father, who advised him to become a doctor because "you won't have to kill people, and you're less likely to be killed."

As if that's not enough family history, I was thrilled to learn that way back on my mother's side of the family tree is Martin Luther, who created the Lutheran Church. (No wonder I've always been fascinated with different religions and belief systems.) And there's a Spanish king in our family history somewhere, too.

A lot to live up to!

One of the few regrets I have in my life is that I never met my grandfather. Even when I moved from Australia to the UK as a teenager starting my singing career, there was no time—or so I thought. My mother would say, "You must come see Grandfather." I was always too busy, but I learned an important lesson.

You make the time.

My father, Brin, came from far more humble beginnings. He was born to a middle-class family in Wales, where his father, Oliver John, worked as a carpenter. His mother, Daisy, was a very strict Quaker woman who would wash my dad's mouth out with soap if he ever swore or said anything close to blasphemy.

Dad's innate intelligence won him a scholarship to the University of Cambridge. He was a brilliant man who spoke French and German fluently. In fact, his German was so perfect that, when he became a wing commander and later an intelligence officer for the Royal Air Force, he spoke *Hochdeutsch* (high or perfect German) and interrogated German prisoners of war. (Future warning: I would never be able to hide anything from him!) He even worked on the Enigma project at Bletchley Park during WWII, cracking the German codes, and later helped bring Nazi deputy führer Rudolf Hess into custody.

Dad would wine and dine infamous prisoners, generally the higher-ranking officials in the Third Reich, in order to pry information out of them. One day, he took Hess to a fancy hotel in

London for afternoon tea and the discussion turned to weapons. Dad apologized to Hess for carrying only a simple pistol.

"Use mine," Hess said, offering Dad a Luger that he had hidden in his clothing! Of course, it didn't set off any metal detectors in those days.

A different time!

My parents might have never met at Cambridge if my mum didn't have such a keen ear for beautiful music—the kind that could melt your heart. One day, she heard a man singing in a deep baritone voice and she couldn't take another step. She actually followed the voice. Mum always said she fell in love with the voice first before she even saw him. They were the same age, seventeen—young and full of dreams. Mum was brunette, classically beautiful, and carried herself in the most elegant way. Dad was six foot three, fair-haired, with movie-star good looks and that beautiful aristocratic voice. Need I say more? What a beautiful couple.

You could call it love at first listen, and then sight. It wasn't too long after that they were married, and in a blink, my brother Hugh (destined to be a doctor), was born, and then my stunning sister Rona (future model, actress, and singer). I was the youngest of the three, born eight years after Rona, and apparently the "try to save the marriage" baby—but more on that in a moment.

Before I was born, my mother went through some very difficult times. My father was away, serving in World War II at Bletchley Park, working on the Enigma project, and she was left alone with two young children. She was a beautiful German woman, and the villagers were suspicious of her. Two kind Quaker women would bring eggs and vegetables to her doorstep to help her and the children. They were her only friends. In turn, Mum would speak kindly with the German prisoners of war. One of the many things my mother taught me was that no matter what you're going through in life, kindness is what will sustain you.

Not everyone was kind, though. Later, Rona would tell me that our father had an affair while he was in the air force. One day, a woman came knocking on my mother's front door to tell her about it. It left my mother insecure and untrusting, not to mention brokenhearted, as she had loved my father since she was seventeen.

To her credit, she stayed in the marriage and tried to make it work for the good of the entire family. Forgiveness was another thing she would teach me, the makeup baby, who would be her last child.

My father was charming, charismatic, and devilishly handsome, and demanded the best from himself and his family. A "well done" was a compliment of the highest order from him, and not easily attained. Dad believed in hard work, discipline, and doing things on your own merits. For example, he could have easily arranged for my brother to get a free pass into university, but he insisted that Hugh excel at his exams and earn his own place. And, of course, Hugh was amazingly brilliant and did it. My brother, in fact, graduated as a doctor with honors. He went on to be a specialist in infectious diseases and invented the first portable iron lung. As I'm writing this I'm thinking, *Lucky I can sing!* Thanks, Dad, for the musical genes.

When I was a little girl, Dad would sing out loudly in church, but I was embarrassed by it because I didn't want to be noticed. He had a wonderful sense of humor and would tease me by pretending to be a really old man, crinkling his fingers and speaking in a creaky voice. I laughed and laughed.

I adored my father and think more about him now than ever before, especially when I hear classical music, which was always playing loudly in our house. I close my eyes and see my father busily conducting each note as he smiled and drank his evening sherry.

For many years after they divorced, I couldn't even listen to classical music and neither could my mum—it would make both of us cry. Years later, I would find my mother sitting in a chair with beautiful classical music on the radio and tears in her eyes. I knew she was thinking of my father. She was in her eighties at the time.

I'll never forget when she turned seventy. Dad, who had been married twice more since their union, sent her seven bunches of violets, one for each decade.

They were her favorite flower.

When I was a young child, we lived in England, where my father was headmaster of King's College in Cambridge. I have very few memories of that time besides crawling around on a thick blue carpet between my parents' twin beds in their bedroom. The sleeping situation was quite the norm for those days. They were like the English Lucy and Ricky!

Of course, I was a young child and full of energy, so there were a few unfortunate moments, including when I swallowed a bunch of sleeping pills by mistake. I had to have my stomach pumped, and the whole experience was so mortifying and memorable that no wonder drugs of any kind have never interested me again.

I was perfectly willing to go on other types of adventures,

though. When I was quite little, I stood on a stool in front of the bathroom mirror with a thermometer in my mouth because I suddenly needed to take my own temperature for reasons unknown. Not knowing what to do, I bit straight through the glass and soon found the mercury rolling around my tongue. It was at that point that I decided to involve a responsible adult, and my actions caused my parents a good deal of alarm, though I was no worse for wear.

Most of the time I was a good little girl, except for the occasional misstep. Later, when I went to school in Australia, we had a weekly bank day where we would take money to school and they would put it in the bank for us. It was a lovely discipline, and I did take money to school, but instead of saving it I used it for a *current need*: to buy everyone a lolly. I thought I was being kind! Sadly, the headmaster at my school had other ideas. In quite a stern voice, he called me up to the front of the class and embarrassed the hell out of me.

"Olivia Newton-John!" he boomed. "Where is your money to put in the bank? What about your future?"

What future? I was five!

I put my hand in an empty pocket of my little pink dress and explained the "lollies situation." This wouldn't be my only punishment. On my way home that day, the big force of nature and former MI5 agent that was my dad intercepted my tricycle and pulled me the rest of the way home. (Oh, big, big, big trouble was brewing!)

My headmaster had called him, and Dad was very upset, but not for long. Thank goodness my big sister, Rona, was always a beautiful free spirit who defied authority—she made for a perfect diversion.

That night, she took the heat off my foolish "crime" with her own antics. She had been expelled from school for wearing her school uniform skirts too short and bleaching her hair. She also skipped school to meet with boys.

I was off the hook!

In the early fifties, our lives took a dramatic turn, one that would mold my psyche. We were migrating to Melbourne because my father had accepted the coveted position of master of Ormond College at the University of Melbourne. He was the youngest man, at only forty, to ever receive a position of this kind. I was five years old when my parents, Hugh, Rona, and I boarded a massive ship called the *Straithard* to cross the ocean to Australia.

Even at that young age, I was so very proud of my father because he was up against older and more experienced academics for this important position. Dad had written a letter to the dean, explaining how he wanted to introduce his family to the amazing country of Australia—and he got the job.

That can-do spirit runs deep in the Newton-John family.

Professionally, it was the chance of a lifetime for my father, and personally, it was an opportunity for my parents to create a new chapter in their life together. They were fighting a lot before we moved and thought a change of scenery could provide a fresh start.

My only memory of the ocean voyage from Cambridge to our new life in that place called Melbourne was losing my favorite teddy bear, Fluffy. I was brokenhearted because I loved Fluffy, but my parents replaced it with a stuffed penguin named Pengy (so creative!) that they found in the ship's store. It was never quite the same, though. Some things are irreplaceable, as I would soon find out in much bigger ways.

It wasn't long before we were in a new country and unpacking boxes at our fantastic new home on campus, a beautiful stone mansion with endless bedrooms and our own housekeeper. I couldn't believe my eyes as I navigated those long hallways that were perfect for hide-and-seek. There were so many big rooms to explore, and it all fed my imagination. One day, I was a princess in the castle; the next, an explorer. There were no limits.

We were required to live on the Ormond College grounds so that my father was accessible both day and night. No one minded because it was such a safe and lively atmosphere and, in many ways, I considered it a giant playground. Ormond was a place of old vine-covered buildings and rolling green lawns that gave me plenty of exercise. And I never got lost because there was a steep clock tower in the middle of campus that served as my compass.

As a little girl, I loved watching the students find the fun in their college days. I remember "water bagging," where the undergrads would drop bags of water out the windows of their bedrooms onto the unsuspecting heads of the people walking below. If you looked up, you'd get a face full of cold liquid, right between the eyes. I probably got hit by accident, but then again, I liked the excitement and the dare of looking up!

"You're soaking wet!" Mum would say when I walked in the door from a day at the Melbourne Teachers' College training school (where we literally had new teachers practice on us every month).

"Yes, Mum, I am!" I said with glee.

At night, I could hear the young men who had won their rowing competitions banging their spoons on the solid wooden tables in the huge dining room as they enjoyed their meal, looking up at the gorgeous stained glass windows. The dining hall was adjacent to our house. Years later, when I visited Ormond to see my father's oil portrait hanging there, I saw all those spoon dents from years of celebrations—it brought back great memories.

My favorite activity was sitting outdoors on the steps of a beautiful old stone building where I would wait for my father to finish work for the day. There I was, a six-year-old girl in her school uniform—a blue-and-white-checked dress with little brown shoes and white ankle socks. I'd visit with the birds and trees, smell the fresh blooms, and write poetry while waiting to slip a small hand into his bigger one.

Our home had a huge drawing room where my parents would entertain important university types, such as visiting professors or other university presidents or even government officials who helped raise money for the school. I'd hide in a little alcove halfway up the stairs, watching the beautiful people arrive for lavish, catered cocktail parties.

From my vantage point, I could see my mother in a gorgeous red velvet evening dress with hundreds of tiny covered buttons up the back. It was so glamorous and exciting. She would greet each person in her refined and regal way, and then she and my father both always made time to come upstairs to kiss me good night.

If I was allowed downstairs, I'd go to work lighting people's cigarettes. For some reason, I liked the smell of the sulfur of the match and the burning tobacco and paper. My father used to smoke when he was reading me a bedtime story, so I must have associated comfort with smoke, although now I know cigarettes and secondhand smoke are toxic for your health. No one really worried or knew about it in those days, of course. In fact, doctors would tell you that smoking was relaxing and good for your health. (Can you even imagine?)

One of my parents obviously had a sixth sense about future discoveries. One night, Mum saw me lighting cigarettes at a university function and pulled me aside.

"Well, darling, why not try a whole one?" she suggested, handing me an entire package of cigarettes.

I was nine and thought this was a splendid idea. How amazing that Mum would allow me this "treat" at my age! I sparked up a cigarette.

"Why don't you take a deep puff?" Mum instructed.

I was excited and complied—only to cough violently for what seemed like forever. "I never want to smoke again!" I cried.

Yes, she was a really smart mum.

Years later, when my friend Pat and I were living in London and singing together, I would try to take up smoking again. We had a crazy notion that smoking would give us sultry singing voices like our favorite singer, Julie London. Alas, sultry wasn't in the cards for me because I was still that nine-year-old in her pj's. Later in my life, in my Sandy nightie, I would try to smoke on-screen in *Grease* and became that little girl again, hacking away.

Art imitating life!

I can still remember my father's smoke lingering on the sleeves of my pink cotton pj's. I'd go to sleep smelling him with my nose pressed to my pajama sleeve, which was sadly an experience I wouldn't have for long.

Our home looked perfect from the outside, but inside was another story. When the newness of moving to another country turned into sameness, my parents' marriage began to deteriorate again. I knew because Mum and Dad took separate holidays, although they tried hard not to make an issue of it.

I remember nature-loving Mum taking us children camping in Mallacoota in a field near the beach. One afternoon, we went out to fish for our dinner and a few runaway cows wandered over to our tent and trampled everything—except a can of condensed milk with a cow's face on it! Mum could only laugh, and we were crying tears because it was so funny. Mum had a keen sense of humor and could find anything amusing. I loved her spirit! She even managed to laugh when I was being taught how to fish and accidentally caught my brother's mouth with the hook!

When I was about nine, my parents announced that they were designing a beautiful new house for us to live in on the Ormond property. Sadly, we would never sleep a night in it. One evening after school, my father calmly told me, "Your mother and I are going to live separately, and you will go and live with her."

"What about the new house?" I asked through a veil of tears. "Are you . . . ?"

I didn't want to say the words.

I didn't want to believe it.

"Yes," he said. "We're getting a divorce."

"But I want to live with you," I pleaded as tears raced down my cheeks. It was the most painful moment of my young life, made worse when my father shook his head with a finality that indicated my living conditions had already been settled.

"You can't live with me," he said. "It's better if you live with your mother. But you can still see me every day."

In a blink, my young life was turned upside down. Mum and I

did move, to an apartment not far away, in Parkville. It was going to be harder to see my father now.

It got worse. Eventually, Dad was asked to leave his post at the college because the administration was strict about needing a married man at the helm. He was no longer traditionally "married with children."

It was so sad because Dad loved Ormond College, and he'd made the school coeducational, allowed alcohol for the first time on campus, and was a very popular headmaster. But rules were rules, and they made him leave because he was now a divorced man, which was strictly forbidden. Given no choice, Dad moved to Newcastle, a two-hour flight away, where he worked as a vice-chancellor and taught German. This marked the end of any hope of even weekly or monthly visits, as they were too expensive on his academic salary.

My heart was broken.

Mum wouldn't be around as much during the days, either, as she had to support us on her own for the first time in her life. In those days, women didn't fare very well in divorce settlements, and watching my mother struggle financially taught me how strong women rally to take care of themselves and their children. Mum had never worked outside the home, but she was funny, witty, and intelligent. She had other valuable skills, too. She wrote beautiful poems and would regularly write letters to the editor of our newspaper about local issues.

It makes me sad now because my mother was always very interested in science but was dissuaded from following that path. Women weren't encouraged to go into academia in those days, and this was a particular shame, given her father's scientific past.

Luckily, Mum quickly got a job, located in the tallest structure in Melbourne at the time, called the ICI House. It was Australia's first skyscraper, and it felt exciting when she left each day for her work as a receptionist. We were all proud of her for making ends meet—Dad didn't have a lot of money to spare, but he sent what he could scrape up to help the two of us. My siblings were out of the house by now and Rona was even married.

It was just us two.

We could only afford for me to see my father at Christmas. During those two months off, I spent as much time as possible with him and the three daughters of his best friend, a Welsh professor, Harry Jones. One of them, Shahan, brought some much-needed joy to my life because she had a beautiful chestnut horse with white socks named Cymro, which means "friend" in Welsh. It was sheer bliss for me to ride every day with her. My father even rented me a horse of my own so we could ride together.

Oh, how I loved my beautiful shaggy pony named Flash. He was anything but just a loaner. I adored him.

Mornings when my father was busy meant Shahan and I could ride to our hearts' content, followed by picnics with her sisters and then swimming with the horses at the beach and in the lagoon. Tired, but happy, I would come home and tell my father that I didn't want to take a shower that night.

"I want to smell like my horse!" I informed him.

My fondest wishes in those days were that my father would return home and that I could bottle that musty scent of my horse laced with the worn leather of the saddle.

I loved those summers and cherished every moment, including when my father fell in love with a wonderful woman named Val, who was the university librarian and a very accomplished pianist.

She would play piano, and Dad would sing. They eventually married, which gave me a loving new brother, Toby, and new sister, Sarah. From the start, I adored them all.

I've never liked the prefix "step" when attached to family members. It has a bad connotation—like Cinderella or something!

One of the most beautiful lessons I learned at this time was from my mum, who combined kindness with forgiveness. When my dad had children with his new wife, she sent gifts for the babies.

I missed my father when I couldn't see him but loved and respected my mother for working so hard for us. Soon she was able to put a down payment on a house in Jolimont, far from University High School, where I was a student. Before that, we lived near the Melbourne Zoo and the move meant I would miss my former "clocks": dawn was welcomed by the beautiful song of the exotic birds, while in the evening I would hear the roar of the lions.

Talk about natural background music.

My clever mum made the move and kept us financially sound. She even transformed the bottom half of the house into an apartment, which she rented out to help pay the mortgage and give us some additional funds. I never knew Mum was so good with math. Thanks, Grandpa!

As for me, I wasn't the studious type. Maybe it was because I missed my father, or the fact that I wasn't that academic, but I wasn't enjoying school. I felt as if everyone else was getting it and I wasn't. I scored very high on intelligence tests but had trouble concentrating on my lessons. Looking back, I think I was much more affected by the divorce than I realized. I just couldn't retain what my teachers were teaching me, which was stressful because I still wanted to make my family proud. It didn't help that the headmistress of my school was extremely strict.

"There will be no patent leather shoes," she insisted. "Boys will be able to see the reflection in those shoes and be able to look up your dresses!"

It's funny to mull over what passed as important morals of the day. For instance, we could *never* wear red because it was just "too exciting" for the males in the vicinity. If only they knew I would someday record a song called "Physical"!

Luckily for me, singing didn't require a degree, although it did require a little good fortune and a big break. When I was fourteen, I thought I'd found that break when I met three girls (and still dear friends), Carmel, Freya, and Denise, who would visit a cute boy who lived in a loft opposite my upstairs-bedroom window. The girls would constantly see me sitting alone in my room doing homework and it wasn't long before I left the bookwork and started talking to them through my window. Mum was at work, and, as a latchkey kid, I was bored and welcomed any human contact.

They were sweet girls who lived to sing (like me), so we started a singing group that we called the Sol 4. Our wardrobes consisted of denim jeans, hessian jackets, and black turtlenecks. At the time, we were all quite stylish and modern with our long beatnik hair, imitating our favorite folk and jazz musical icons.

Soon, we were "working" together as a group and booking ourselves into local jazz spots. It wasn't the safest of jobs. After one show, the audience threw pennies at us. We didn't know if it was a tip or a message to get off the stage! Another time, there was even a gang war between the "jazzers" like us and the "rockers." One of my girlfriends was thrown on the road by one of the rockers. There was no provocation. They just shouted: "You should like rock and roll!"

Believe me, I did!

Soon my mother felt like I was spending way too much time singing and not enough time studying, so she put an end to it—or so she thought. My sister Rona, now the mother of three young children, was married to a man named Brian Goldsmith, who owned a local coffee shop. Brian had a folk singer in his restaurant on the weekend, Hans Gorg, and I was allowed to go watch him perform, with Rona keeping a close eye on me. I remember sitting at the edge of the stage and singing harmonies.

One day, Hans invited me onstage to actually sing *with* him and his guitar. *Heaven*. Pieces clicked into place. I had found my everything.

Well, not quite my everything, but that was about to happen! Rona had met a talented young singer/entertainer named Ian Turpie and wanted to introduce him to me even though I was only fifteen.

Ian watched me sing with Hans and this led to us singing together—and then dating. He was my first boyfriend and my first love.

Not long after, Rona introduced me to something else that would be wonderful and life-changing. There was a show on Saturday morning on Australian TV called *Kevin Dennis Auditions*, hosted by a famous local car dealer. Someone would sing, dance, or do something strange (often with questionable talent), and a panel of judges would either give them a thumbs-down, or a gong, which was a thumbs-up. You prayed for the sound of that gong, a ringing endorsement that you were indeed worthy.

One day, Rona asked me the magic question: Did I want to go on the show?

I asked Ian if he could accompany me on guitar (he was a wonderful guitar player) for one of my favorite songs, "Summertime."

We turned up at eight in the morning, and I faced a panel that looked like they would be tough. I stepped on their stage for the first time, mustered my confidence, and sang.

Gong!

Gong!

Gong!

It was the best score one could get! As a result, Evie Hayes, one of the judges and a famous American TV personality in those days, phoned my mom to ask if she could manage my career. *What career?* All I had was a dream, three gongs, and a live studio audience that gave me a round of applause!

Mum was always fast when it came to protecting her young. "Oh, *vell*, I'm managing Olivia at *ze* moment, *sank* you very much," she said.

All of a sudden, just like that, I had a career *and* a manager, *sank* you very much.

TWO

Trust Yourself

You know all the answers
You know what is right.

Mum would often tell me that, as a little girl, I sang perfectly in tune. "You sing like an angel," she said. I always made my mother and my sister cry when I sang, but in a good way (hopefully). By the time I was three, if you sang to me or played a song, I could sing it right back to you in perfect pitch. We had a big radio in the kitchen, and I'd listen for hours, memorizing the words of my favorite songs and then insisting on putting on mini concerts for my family. These were "professional" concerts despite the venue, the zero cost of admission, and the wardrobe being whatever I could steal from Mum's closet.

Although I loved singing, I was shy—I found it difficult to perform randomly in public and would perform only for my family. I would have to learn to conquer my stage fright. One of my first public performances was as Lady Mary, the lead in the school play *The Honorable Mr Crichton*. I did it, it was a bit painful, I loved it.

As for becoming a professional singer, though, it wasn't in my early plans. I thought I'd do something with animals, like become a mounted police officer who would get paid to ride horses. The only problem was women weren't allowed to be mounted police in those days. Years later, when I was on tour for *The Main Event* with John Farnham and Anthony Warlow, I was invited by the Adelaide mounted police to ride with them. I was finally able to live that dream! Another plan was to become a veterinarian, but that didn't work, since I failed math at school—which was hysterical considering who my grandfather was. Well, they say math and music are related, so thank goodness one of them worked for me. If all else failed, I figured I'd muck out horse stables (something I do now with my little Harry and Winston, my miniature horses).

Amazingly, I also failed music in high school, earning an F for the sight-reading part of it. I'm embarrassed to say I'm still not that good at it. The main issue back then was that I was thinking about other things and couldn't focus after my parents split. I could learn music by ear, but, with my mind wandering, my heart just wasn't in it.

That was only a sign of things to come when it came to my relationship with high school. It's hard to focus when you're emotionally upset, and our family being scattered left me feeling uncertain.

I always found my peace in music and writing poetry. It wasn't long before my poems turned into songs. The first song I ever wrote was with my godmother Pearl's daughter Cara. I was around twelve years old.

Why, oh, why did you go away from me?
It seems like years to me.

Why does it have to be?
My heart is a-breaking
'Cause you've been a-taking
The love you said was meant for me.
And, darlin', love ain't meant for three.

Looking back, those are pretty heavy lyrics for twelve!

At age fifteen, most young girls have a life that revolves around school, boys, and the occasional argument with their mothers. I didn't have time for all that conventional teenage angst—apart from the arguments with Mum, of course. After my success on *Kevin Dennis Auditions*, I was hired as a temporary stand-in on a TV program called *The Happy Show*, where I played the part of Luv'ly Livvy—replacing Luv'ly Ann, who was getting married over the Christmas holidays. I told stories, sang, danced, and gave out prizes with my cohorts, Princess Panda, Happy Hammond, and Cousin Roy. It was make-believe, joyous fun, and I never wanted that gig to end.

Forget about any stage fright. The kids in the audiences were enthusiastic and adorable, plus it was exciting to film at a real TV studio. When the real Luv'ly Ann returned from her honeymoon to take her part back (darn it), I didn't have time to be sad about hanging up my Livvy costume.

In a blink, I was offered a full-time job of my own on a show called *Time for Terry*, hosted by an Irishman named Terry O'Neill, where I was also able to sing with my new boyfriend, Ian.

A quick word about boyfriends: My father *never* wanted me to date, while my mother was a bit more lenient. She was still against me going out with someone, but I was at that age where limits were going to be tested.

A boyfriend wasn't the only sign I was growing up. My boundaries were allowed to stretch when I hit the road and traveled to Sydney to take part in another talent show that I had auditioned for in Melbourne called *Sing, Sing, Sing*, hosted by none other than Johnny O'Keefe, who was known as the Elvis Presley of Australia. His hits included "The Wild One" and "Shout!" Johnny had dramatic curly blond hair pushed back on his forehead and a wide, wild smile that made all the young Aussie girls swoon and scream.

I was nervous to meet Johnny, let alone sing for him. And back in those days, it wasn't considered odd or dangerous to try out in places other than the TV studio. Ian came with me to Johnny's hotel room, where I would audition in front of the Aussie Elvis and his producer. Ian played guitar, and I sang a well-rehearsed "Summertime."

When it was over, Johnny said, "Yes, you got it."

The thing I remember most is that he ordered these turkey sandwiches slathered with sweet cranberry sauce for all of us. They were incredible, and I've loved them ever since that first bite.

A few months later, it was arranged that I'd go to a recording studio to sing the song for the first show, which would be filmed in Sydney.

I stepped into a recording studio, where Johnny shook my hand and pointed to the spot in the center of the room where they had a little sound booth set up with a microphone. A breath later and the room went silent. (No pressure!)

I sang an age-appropriate Liza Minnelli song from the musical

Best Foot Forward, called "What Do You Think I Am?" It was fitting because I stood at a mic in my starched school uniform and softly crooned a song about a young girl asking someone (defiantly) if they thought she was just a baby. Part of the lyrics even asked the audience to (wink, wink) see if I was all grown up because I was using Maybelline mascara now. The truth in real life: yes, yes, yes, I was just a baby!

My nerves jumped when Johnny put up a hand midsong, which meant I was to stop singing. *Didn't he like my voice? Did I do something wrong?* My heart sank all the way down to my polished black Mary Jane shoes.

"Livvy, stop right there," Johnny commanded. "Not everyone in the world knows what Maybelline is. Why don't you sing, 'What do you think I'm using Vaseline for?'"

Sweet relief. All he wanted was a lyric change. I could do that!

I was so naive—I did it, and all the guys fell down laughing as I sang about that good old Vaseline. In the end, Johnny was just pulling a good-natured prank and being a bit naughty. That big smile went wide, and he doubled over cackling as I continued to sing my little heart out. I don't even know if I finally got it! I was mortified, and my skin turned bright pink.

Welcome to the music business.

I was thrilled when I made the final cut of Johnny's talent contest singing my favorites by Dionne Warwick. (Little did I know then that later in my life, I would actually sing with her on a TV special!) On that day, I crooned the hit "Anyone Who Had a Heart." To my amazement, I ended up winning the talent contest, and the grand prize was a trip to England by boat and some spending money.

This started the final struggle with Mum over my education. I had just finished *The Happy Show* over the summer holidays, and Mum wanted me to return to school to finish my studies. I took my dilemma to one of my favorite teachers, Mr. Hogan.

"What should I do?" I asked him.

In my heart, I wanted to jump straight into my future as a singer, even though I still had one year left of high school.

"Liv, if you're going to be thinking of singing and trying to get through this last school year at the same time, it's not going to happen. Follow your passion," he said.

Those were great words of wisdom—and he provided me with clarity. Thank you, sir!

Mum wasn't thrilled, but she understood that I was forging a path and doing something that I truly loved. As my manager, she was adamant that, if I wasn't going to finish school, the next step was to go to London and take my career seriously while going to the Royal Academy of Dramatic Art (RADA). Underneath it all, I think she was really trying to get me away from Ian. She felt I was too young to have a serious boyfriend.

Maybe that's why, all of a sudden, Mum was all in to go—but she had a few rules. She didn't want me to go to London just for a quick visit. If I wanted to become a singer, she knew that I—make that *we*—needed to move there for a decent period of time and really try to get my career off the ground.

Hang on! Move away from everything I know and my boyfriend? Not happening!

We fought; I cried; I begged. "I'm not going!" I yelled, with all my teenage hormones fueling my anger at being sent away for an extended period. It felt tragic! I couldn't understand why I had to leave now when I had a local TV show, a boyfriend, and a career. There'd even been a story about me in the local paper! Wasn't that enough?

"Go," Mum said. "If you want to sing, then take this chance. There might never be another."

I wish I could say that I started packing, but I was stubborn. Then life, like it often does, actually intervened and decided for me.

My prize of that free boat ticket was expiring soon (thank goodness), and having that date in mind cemented my future. It wasn't long before Mum and I were ready to set sail and Ian was crying on the dock. My heart was breaking as my boyfriend watched me sail away. I promised him I would be back in three months, but in adolescent years that was an eternity.

Teenage angst hit hard, and I was miserable the whole way to England. The only thing I remember was being named Queen Neptune at the equator line, which was a little boat celebration where the newly named King Neptune doused everyone with water. As queen, I just had to stand there and watch.

I'm frowning in the picture.

Swinging London in the 1960s was in the middle of a youth-driven cultural revolution, with a flourishing art, music, and fashion scene that influenced the entire world. Exports included the Beatles, and miniskirts worn by Twiggy and Jean Shrimpton. There was a new "mod" way of living, and music was at the forefront of the scene, thanks to the Who, the Kinks, and the Rolling Stones, to name a few.

What a time to grow up, and what a place to do it.

If only I felt that way. I forgot to mention that my boyfriend had given me a three-month ultimatum: if I wasn't back by then, he'd start dating other people.

It was my first heartbreak—with many more to come!

Mum and I were plunked right in the middle of what should have been an exciting new adventure as we settled into our new flat in Hampstead, but I remained sullen. Our new home was a teeny-tiny, one-bedroom place where I slept on a foldout couch in the living room. The cost was nine pounds a week, which we could afford since I had put some money away from my TV career at home. Thank goodness bank day had made quite an impression on me, so I remembered to save this time. (No more lollies for me!)

Mum and I still struggled with the issue of schooling. She wanted me to go to the Royal Academy of Dramatic Art; I didn't want to push a pencil or crack a book ever again. She wanted me to study acting; I only wanted to sing. In retrospect, I should have listened to her.

Chaperone Rona was also living in England now. She wasn't a bad influence, since I wasn't interested in the sixties' sex, drugs, and rock-and-roll lifestyle. I couldn't even stomach another cigarette. Instead, I lived out any wild instincts vicariously through Rona.

I wasn't exactly impressed with London—at least not at first.

"Everything is so old and dirty," I said in dismay. Looking back now, I can't believe I ever thought or said it! I love the beauty of those worn, lived-in buildings with such magical history. At sixteen, however, the lasting importance of architecture wasn't exactly on my mind.

What *was* on my mind was Ian. Much to Mum's dismay, I didn't forget about him, even though I knew he had his own life back in Australia and wasn't waiting for his long-distance girlfriend to return.

I must have been quite a handful, as my mum worked every day to make a living in London while I schemed and plotted a way to get back to Melbourne to be with Ian. I even secretly booked my passage several times, but Mum was one step ahead and always canceled my reservations.

The clock was ticking on those three months. I needed to go home, and Mum's making sure I was ticketless left me furious with her. I even went so far as to try to become a ward of the court so my mother wouldn't have jurisdiction over me. Denied!

All I wanted was to be with Ian, but my mother blocked it all from happening. What did I know at fifteen? Answer: absolutely nothing about real life or men. But try telling that to a teenager in love who was thousands of miles away from her boyfriend and crying her eyes out at night while reading the mushy letters we'd been writing each other almost every single day.

Eventually the "Dear John" came when he wrote: *Liv, you're not back, so I started seeing someone.* The truth was, Ian wanted a wife and a family, and I wasn't ready for either of those commitments. At one point, I asked him to come to London, but he refused to leave Australia. I wanted to stay in England, which was a huge turning point. I found out in that moment I wanted my career more than I realized.

Now, as a mother myself, I understand that Mum was doing the right thing by moving me to London. She wanted me to explore my talent and gave me every opportunity. And yes, Ian eventually married the lovely Jan, and it was the perfect relationship for him. I like Jan very much and we all remained friends despite his untimely death a few years ago.

In 1966, on Decca Records, I recorded my first single called "Till You Say You'll Be Mine" (with the B-side "For Ever"). I met these young guys who were producers, and they wanted to do a track with me. Unfortunately, the song sounded like it was cut in someone's bathroom. One of the reviews said I should "stick with a career as an airline hostess." It wasn't exactly a great production, but it was a start.

You have to learn to deal with criticism, and I was learning. It was hard at that time, though, because I didn't have the success to balance out the harsh words, so they would linger.

Our saving grace—mine and Mum's—came in the form of Pat Carroll, who had just arrived in London. I'd worked with Pat back in Australia on *The Go!! Show*, a teenage pop show hosted by Ian and featuring up-and-coming greats, including the Bee Gees.

"We became great friends straightaway," Pat remembers.

Pat was a well-known singer and dancer, and during our brief time on the show, she had helped me with a few pointers when it came to stage presence. She was also a lovely human being and we'd kept in touch. I was so excited when she won a radio award that got her to England in a major way. She'd signed a contract with a top agent, the Bernard Delfont Agency, and they had already booked her into several local clubs.

I met her at Heathrow Airport on a cold winter's day with the idea that I'd help her move into the flat her agent rented for her. Snow swirled through the frigid air as we took the bus to an incredibly sleazy part of town where the two of us walked a few dangerous blocks to a dilapidated apartment building. It could have defined the word "depressing." Inside, it was worse. We quickly left and stood on the street, staring up at the gloom.

"You can't stay here—even for one night," I said. "C'mon, you're staying with us."

Pat didn't need much convincing. "The original place was horrendous!" she said.

We turned around and left immediately. Grateful beyond words, she moved into our tiny one-bedroom flat, where she slept on the floor on a blowup mattress for the next year and all three of us shared a bathroom you could barely turn around in. We didn't have much space, but Mum was ecstatic, because Pat seemed to be the grounding force that I needed to establish a new life in London.

Mum was right—it was wonderful having Pat there with us. We quickly got into the swing of things with our hairpieces, false eyelashes, fake nails, and big black-rimmed eyes highlighted with liner and gallons of mascara (black, of course). We wore fantastic paisley-patterned dresses and very short miniskirts, and my cream patent leather boots were my favorites because I had to save up for them. All the London girls—or dolly birds—flashed their legs and didn't apologize for it.

At first, I went with Pat to her club dates around England as moral support, but it wasn't long before there were other ideas of how we could combine our mutual dreams.

Athol Guy, who played bass and sang with the extremely popular Australian pop quartet the Seekers, was a friend of ours and took us under his wing. One day he suggested, "Why don't you two join up as a double act? You can travel together."

"I was lonely working alone," Pat remembers now. "When a duo was suggested, it was perfect. One blonde. One brunette."

"What will your agents say?" I asked Pat.

They loved the idea, but there was one twist. They couldn't wrangle any more money, but that didn't matter: we'd split the fees, cut the expenses, and begin to conquer the world.

The billing: "Pat and Olivia."

A duo was born.

Years later, Pat would jokingly say to me, "Well, I split my fee with you back then. How about you share yours with me now?"

THREE

Power of Now

I believe in the power of now.

Our rehearsal studio was that cramped flat located in a pretty cobblestoned area of Hampstead. During the daytime, when Mum was at work, we'd practice, followed by an early dinner and then out the door to perform each night. Pat was a fantastic seamstress and made all our costumes like she was tailoring a major rock show. I was hopeless in this domestic art and was quickly tasked with the chore of hemming, which I happily did while I listened to my favorites on the radio.

It turns out clothing was the least of our issues.

Our first night at one of the local London clubs, we forgot that we had actual dance moves, which meant *moving*, and in those days microphones were attached to thick, black cords. During the middle of one of our sets onstage—in front of an audience at one in the morning—Pat went left and I went right. The cords tangled, and we were hopelessly entwined in each other to the point where neither of us could move. There is nothing like singing and suddenly hearing the audience burst into loud laughter. Little did we know that we were actually doing a comedy show! If I'd added a pratfall, I think we would have had a standing ovation from the ten people at the bar who were half listening.

Transportation also became an issue, and so Pat and I bought a car, even though I didn't know how to drive and was too young to get a license in England. Two years older, Pat had a license, so we bought this beat-up old thing, a Mini-Minor van, that cost us a whopping forty pounds. It was all we could afford.

Pat's father had always handled her business affairs, but we didn't tell him about the wheels because we were quite mature and certainly worldly enough to handle the negotiations—or so we thought.

There we were, two innocent young girls handing an older guy a wad of cold, hard cash and then catching the car keys from him as he tossed them into the air. We took off with no inspection, no pink slip, no registration, no insurance, basically no nothing. What did we know? We were just two dolly birds with wheels until a couple of very cute young bobbies stopped us and one asked, "Can I see your registration?"

"What registration?" we stammered.

"Step out of the car, ladies."

Our first major investment would soon meet a cruel fate. The car was sent to an impoundment lot, while those helpful and handsome officers drove us home. Just to be nice. And then for some reason, the officers kept showing up at our flat to ask questions about the car incident. They were huge flirts, and so were we. They even ended up selling the car for us despite the lack of paperwork.

Small favors from strangers were the tiny breaks that we needed to survive in those lean days. Eventually, we took off on a "tour" of England—a series of small-club dates, with fifty pounds to our names. That was a ridiculously low budget given that we needed to use that money for the two of us to eat, find lodging, and figure out transportation.

We lived on our dreams, once even taking a boat across the sea in the bitter cold to vacation in Ireland, where we got terribly lost. Whenever we asked one of the locals where something was located, they would twirl a hand in the air and say, "Oh, it's just a little bit down the road." Twenty miles later, we were still riding our bikes.

We did find a very special, sacred place and kissed the Blarney Stone for good luck. According to legend, kissing the stone not only bestows the kisser with the gift of the gab but also increases their humor and wit. The only problem was the way you had to kiss the stone. You had to climb to a castle's peak, lean over backward on the parapet's edge, tilt your head, and then place your lips on the stone. And this wasn't my only concern. *Ewwww*, my brain was screaming. I thought about putting a tissue between my lips and the rock, because God only knows who had kissed it before me.

Our trip was wonderful, even if a little frustrating for Pat, who expected to eat the leftovers of a delicious dinner for breakfast. I remember her frowning when I fed the entire contents of our bag to a needy horse. (And I would do it again today, and I do!)

On the old boat back to London, we had the cheapest tickets, plus Pat was feeling a little seasick, so we sat outside on the deck with the harsh, damp English winds slapping our red-raw faces. The captain saw that we were about to (literally) freeze in place, took pity on us, and let us sit inside his cabin, where we chattered our teeth and thawed out. Somehow, we stayed in one piece.

We weren't exactly the most experienced travelers, but we always survived by the grace of God.

Our budget jaunts included going to Zurich, where we met two charming American boys on the train. We knew they were American because they had such perfect white teeth! They invited us to have dinner with them, and, of course, we said yes because it was nice to have their companionship—plus, in reality, it was a free meal.

The guys took us to a fancy hotel restaurant overlooking a beautiful, crystal clear lake. We had a gorgeous meal and even stuffed a few dinner rolls in our purses for breakfast. Meanwhile, the men were hoping that our evening could continue with drinks at another location and . . . Well, that "and" part really frightened us!

Nervously, we piled into a cab with the men, who gave the driver the address of a local hotel. In a panic now, I kept glancing at Pat; she gazed back at me and looked like she wanted to jump out the window. We needed to make a quick move before this got out of hand. While the guys were paying the cabbie, we just ran for it, as fast as our feet could carry us, disappearing into the big and crowded hotel before the men could even figure out what had happened. It was as if we evaporated into thin air.

We didn't want to *be* dessert.

By the way, if these men are reading this now, we apologize—and thanks for dinner!

Once, when we had a week without work and twenty pounds to spare each, we decided to take the train through Europe, ending up in Paris. We had yesterday's bread for breakfast while we collected our loose change to buy two pieces of fruit for lunch and something for dinner (or not). On many days, we just had the bread and the fruit and considered it a nutritionally balanced day.

We stayed in places with hard, old beds that were ready for the garbage dump, with thin, worn blankets and horribly rough toilet paper. Maybe it was sandpaper because that was cheaper! There was very little heat on frigid nights, and I remember the freezing cold tiles that instantly turned our feet into ice if we dared to get up in the middle of the night to make a run to the bathroom. But we didn't mind one little bit. We were young, free, singing for our suppers, and having the time of our nomad lives.

Sometimes we'd go to afternoon movies in Paris and sleep through them because it was cheaper than getting a room for just half a day before our train left the station. We had somewhere warm to snooze, and occasionally the movie wasn't half bad, even if we didn't understand it.

When Pat and I got back to London, we continued to get club gigs and made enough money to live on. This was despite the fact that we were booked at some very strange places that were dangerous at worst and questionable at best.

I'll never forget the night we were booked somewhere we had never heard of called Raymond Revuebar. Pat and I arrived in our best pale blue minidresses with stylish marabou feathers along the edges that Pat had created and I had hand-hemmed to perfection. One last look in the backstage mirror, and I smiled because my little flicked-up hairdo was perfectly sprayed. Not a wisp was out of place.

As an accompanist, the club gave us their piano player, who pounded out a few notes as we came onstage. I did think it was a little odd that behind the stage, there was an enormous fish tank without a single fish in it. It was occupied by a half-naked girl!

The audience of all men—eight in number, including the cook and the waiter—looked at us strangely as we, in all our innocent youth, made our way to center stage. It turns out girls who looked like us rarely walked through *that* door. My eyes popped when I noted that more than a few of the men at tables were wearing raincoats—and it wasn't raining outside.

We sang "Soon It's Going to Rain," which turned out to be a tribute to the kind of club it actually was and the uniform of those lusty men. We had our sweet little choreography going— little moves right and left—while the men seemed a bit confused, as if they were waiting for something.

But the feathers stayed on us, as did all our clothing. Even my hair stayed secure, not one piece out of place.

A few numbers later and the owner of the club, Paul Raymond, met us backstage, shaking his head, but he wasn't really mad.

"Girls," he said, "I just don't think this is going to work out. Your agent misunderstood."

To his credit, he paid us off for the entire week. As we left, I glanced one more time back at the girl in the fish tank, hoping she didn't drown.

Even though we were working the nightclub scene, I never noticed any really bad stuff, or anything that would leave scars on my psyche. I never saw people do drugs or anything else that was illegal. Maybe I didn't see it because I wasn't into that scene and I wasn't really interested.

Or maybe it was the music.

We were constantly practicing our act and perfecting it. We saw ourselves on TV once and noted that I was in the habit of staring while Pat blinked naturally all the time. I was too robot-like, but Pat came to the rescue and tried to teach me how to dance. At home, in front of Mum when we were in London, we used hairbrushes for microphones. Then I learned the moves:

One, two, three, four.

Cross, two, three, four.

Back, two, three, four.

Turn, two, three, four.

It was a sixties' version of *So You Think You Can Dance*!

Soon we were performing for the troops, with a show that took us to American army bases in Germany and Cyprus. Those audiences of soldiers were incredible, warm, and welcoming. Once, we flew to Libya, where a few American GIs asked Pat and me if we wanted to have a ride with them in their tanks. A tank—in the Libyan desert—a pretty incredible memory.

This could have proven dangerous, but it wasn't. We wore camouflage and hard hats, and had a wonderful time with the guys, who were very sweet and respectful. I think being somewhat naive actually saved us from bad things, plus there was power in numbers. Pat and I always had each other's backs.

As time moved us along, I was always meeting new people, which would inevitably lead to new love. I met Bruce Welch, part of a very successful instrumental group called the Shadows, who were Cliff Richard's backing band for many years. They were a big deal in England, and Pat and I were very fortunate to have a gig opening for them, which was a thrill.

We shared a manager with Cliff in Peter Gormley, who also guided the early careers of artists such as Frank Ifield, the Seekers, Marvin, Welch & Farrar. Peter also founded Festival Records, where I would soon release my original studio albums in Australia.

Pat and I toured with Cliff on *The Cliff Richard Show*. We were hired as backup singers—although we didn't always stay strictly in the background.

"When Olivia and Pat were backing me, I did notice a little phenomenon happening," Cliff remembers. "All the men in the audience were looking past my left shoulder. One night during a performance, I looked over my shoulder and saw that Pat and Olivia were no longer their normal six or seven feet behind me. They'd moved up and were almost level with me. And they were doing these sexy little dances!

"The next night, I said to Peter, our manager, 'Do me a favor. Set the girls up behind the piano.' Then when I came out onstage, I had someone put the piano lid up so no one could see them at all! They knew I was just joking. We had such fun together then and later when we would sing duets together.

"You have to fall in love a little bit with the other singer in a duet, and that was so easy with Livvy," Sir Cliff says.

By age nineteen, I had long hair and bangs and wore little cotton shirts and tartan skirts that came from the children's department of Marks & Spencer. My clothes had to make it through several seasons and usually did. It was lucky I was good at economizing, because Pat and I were breaking out on our own. I loved Mum, but we needed more space, and she even encouraged us to get our own flat.

My first home out on my own was in a section of Central London in the borough of Kensington and Chelsea known as Earl's Court. It was also known as a home-away-from-home Aussie hangout. Freedom was expensive, so Pat and I roomed with two other Aussie girls, Geraldine and Gail.

Our living conditions weren't much more spacious than in the Hampstead flat with Mum: Pat and I shared a room, while sisters Gail and Geraldine had the other one. They were both talented actresses trying to make their way in London. Pat would later do a stage production of *Bye Bye Birdie* with Gail. We had single beds with a curtain across for some privacy, plus a little living room and tiny kitchen. Still, it was so much fun to be on our own without any rules. There was also an excitement of surviving by our own wits.

We were jolly dolly birds!

Frankly, we were lucky to get from one day to the next—Pat had never even boiled an egg, and I couldn't cook anything, either. All we could do was navigate the local market to find food. I remember eating a lot of mashed potatoes and sausages for dinner. Our first Christmas together, we cooked the giblets *inside* the turkey *inside that nice plastic bag that they came in.*

Rona, who had a new husband named Graeme, was told about our cooking adventures and couldn't stop laughing as we begged her to please feed us dinner the next night.

One night after a show in London, we had dinner with a group of friends. One of the guys offhandedly said to me, "Olivia, you are very ambitious." Right on the spot, I burst into tears. Back then, "ambitious" was a dirty word to call someone, especially a woman.

"I'm not ambitious!" I cried.

I was really hurt, because I associated ambition with clawing your way to the top—as if you would do anything or sleep with someone to make it big in the world of show business. That was the insinuation behind the word. Right or wrong, that was my impression when I was that young, and someone saying it to my face really stung. Only later would I realize that it's a compliment to be called ambitious and certainly nothing to be ashamed of. Early on, however, I would see how certain men didn't feel comfortable with the idea of a woman being in charge of her own destiny or striving for something big.

One of my friends helped me read between the lines: "A lot of men don't feel comfortable with women being in charge or knowing what they want in life and working toward it."

My fortitude was actually a blessing I would need down the line, although I preferred the word "strong."

I know I got that strength from Mum and watching what she went through surviving divorce and moving to another country to help her daughter fly. She was feminist before the word came into fashion, and she was so strong, smart, and selfless. And that was something to be admired.

She taught me that you don't know how strong you are until you're really tested.

Over the next couple of years, Pat and I hit the road whenever the agent booked us gigs, and we even returned to Australia, where she remet her husband-to-be, the amazingly talented songwriter and producer John Farrar. We had all been friends for years. Of course, later he would write and produce some of my biggest hits and become a trusted friend for life alongside Pat.

From our first meeting, John Farrar remembers, "I was playing in this band called the Strangers and we were on a TV show. Liv and I met on the set. I remember thinking, 'She's a very cute little girl.' Then I watched as everybody in the studio fell in love with her almost immediately.

"I knew she had a lovely sound that was different and unique."

When I turned twenty-one, Bruce and I got engaged, which created a stir, since he was separated at the time but not quite divorced. He followed us to Australia when Pat and I went back to do a TV special, but this provoked a scandal when Bruce declared his love for me openly. I was abruptly fired from the TV show because of my boyfriend's "entanglements." I was mortified and felt so badly for Pat.

The bad news continued to roll in. After performing for the troops once more, we came back to England on a military plane. The immigration officer at the airport noticed that Pat's visa had expired and refused to extend it. He even stamped it void. She was terribly upset because she wouldn't be allowed back into England. I always had an English and Australian passport thanks to my mother, so I could return to England to be with Bruce. Pat was the one who told me to go back to London and be with my fiancé. I felt so guilty that I was allowed to return and she couldn't be with me.

"You're ready to do this on your own," she generously insisted.

I decided to return to London to be with Bruce and pursue a solo career. But my heart was hurting. Pat and I had been joined at the hip for so long I wasn't even sure if I could sing without her.

*

Back in London, I moved in with Bruce, and soon I heard that Pat was to marry John Farrar. I was so excited, and we remembered how long ago I told her, "You should go back to Australia and marry that lovely John Farrar." Meanwhile, I was happily nesting with Bruce and our Irish setters, Geordie and Murphy. There wasn't much time for hanging out in our flat because my fiancé's band, the Shadows, were very famous in Europe, Japan, and England.

Sadly, one member of their group, an incredibly talented bass player named John Rostill, had died. John wrote "Let Me Be There," "If You Love Me, Let Me Know," and "Please Mr. Please," and tragically never lived to see the success of his songs. After his passing, Hank Marvin and Bruce decided to start fresh and create a trio. They were looking for someone, and I suggested John Farrar—Pat's new husband—because he was such an amazing singer, guitarist, and songwriter. It wasn't long before it was settled. They knew of John and his talent and quickly offered him the position.

The next thing I knew, Pat was back in England with John and they moved into the house I shared with Bruce. It felt great to have everyone under the one roof, and it was lovely to have Pat around again. With everyone together, John and Bruce began to produce my first album, which was a happy time but also a guilty one. It must have been very hard for Pat to watch her husband produce me without her. I felt my fair share of pangs, but Pat supported me and John. I've always respected her grace and maturity.

We cut the album at the legendary Abbey Road Studios, where I spent my days with my dog Geordie at my feet. There was a moment when he actually knocked the mic stand during a guitar solo in "If Not for You." We left the sound on the album and it still makes me smile when I hear it.

It also makes me smile when I remember that the Beatles were in the next studio with George Martin recording their new album. I was lucky enough to meet them all, as Bruce was good friends with the most famous band of all time. In fact, he told me that Paul offered him his publishing on a song, but first he would want to give it a listen. Paul pulled his guitar out of his car trunk and played a few bars of the song to Bruce, who turned it down. It had a different working title then, but it was "Yesterday"!

One day, I walked in and found John and Yoko sitting around with their arms and legs entwined, young and in love. It's a beautiful memory. I wouldn't see Yoko again until many years later, when I was on my honeymoon. By then, John was gone. So tragic.

In November 1971, at the age of twenty-three, I released my debut studio album, *If Not for You*. The single of that name was written by Bob Dylan and was a major hit. George Harrison had also done a version of it. London disc jockeys, along with romantics everywhere, embraced it. It was an excellent song for lovers of any age.

Decades later, I would find out that it's my husband John's favorite song.

It was exciting to have an album out, and the next months went by in a blur of getting-to-know-you promotional appearances on television shows across Europe, the United Kingdom, and Australia, along with a stage tour. Perhaps I was too young to handle it all, but I went down a path that I would later regret, which led to Bruce and me breaking off our engagement.

I always had the utmost respect for Bruce, who helped to create my sound, and I will be forever grateful to him. He was a very funny man with an amazing creative sensibility, and he also knew how to nurture me. Bruce came up with the idea of the bass voice for my first country records. He helped me develop my taste in clothing and opened my eyes to different types of music and food. I owe him a great deal.

After our breakup, I went to the South of France on holiday. I was sitting on the white sandy beach in Monte Carlo with my friend Chantal, from Australia, who I was now sharing a flat with in London, when she invited me to meet her fiancé's cousin. Out of the water swam a very tall, very blond, very handsome man who was introduced to me as Lee Kramer. We went out that night as a group, and he leaned over and told me, "You sure look better at night than in the daytime."

Well, he certainly had my attention!

We ended the evening at a club, and I was sure I'd never see him again. The next day, I was going back to England. Who was sitting next to me on the flight? Answer: Lee Kramer. He would tell me many years later that he actually paid someone off to get that seat by my side. I ended up dating Lee for a few years, and he even became my manager.

My career was continuing to do well, including a gig on Eurovision in 1974. I was asked to represent England and sang a different song each week on *The Cliff Richard Show*, with the public voting for their favorite. Ultimately, I came in fourth at Eurovision that year, with those incredibly talented people in ABBA taking it out with their song "Waterloo." (I loved ABBA and we became fast friends.)

It was a great career moment, but the same couldn't be said for my personal life. After a breakup with Lee, it was a shambles. For a short time, Bruce and I got back together, but that didn't work out, either.

Single again, I had a few diversions. One day, Russ Regan, head of the record company UNI, called me on the phone about my song "If Not for You." Russ would encourage me later to move to the United States, and I will be forever grateful. He passed away recently, but not before I was able to thank him for his early words of encouragement.

"Honey, you got a hit," he said. "Your song is number twenty-five on the *Billboard* charts. You gotta get over here!"

That settled it. Next stop: America.

FOUR

I Honestly Love You

The offer to travel to America came at a time when I was settling down in London, despite my recent breakup. I had to say goodbye to a little dream house, my first that I bought with my own money. It was an old English cottage with a garden in the back, and I was so excited about fixing it up. The hardest part was having to rehome my precious dogs, who went to live with a family in the country. Then I had to say goodbye to Mum and move across the world, where I didn't know a single person.

A few tears and hugs later, and I was on that plane.

Singing on television was the best way to get your song into the minds of the public, and one of my first performances was on a very popular show hosted by a legend. It was exciting to sing "If" on *The Dean Martin Show* and later on the same episode to do a medley featuring "Just a Little Lovin'"/"True Love" with the Rat Pack legend, which became my first performance in the United States.

Dean was very sweet to me and even a bit shy. I was so young and fearful, but he immediately put me at ease. He treated me like a peer and even knew a few of my songs. All of a sudden, the fear slipped away and we began to sing together. His kindness got me through the moment, and I smiled as he drank what would probably look like whiskey to the audience. It was really dark iced tea, and he was perfectly sober.

In a blink, I was in another studio a few weeks later singing for Andy Williams on his television program. He was also incredibly supportive, as was Bob Hope, another one of my American idols. Later in my life, when Chloe was born, Bob Hope kindly sent her a baby gift!

I couldn't believe I was singing with these legends, lovely men who I'd always admired.

I started my American journey in New York, but my heart soon belonged to California. It was so different from Manhattan, where I had been so shocked by the way people in the shops were so abrupt. "Whadda you want?" they would ask. I burst into tears the first time someone said that to me. I guess I still had some adapting to do.

Eventually I moved to Los Angeles, which reminded me of Australia, with its beautiful weather and endless sand, surf, and beaches. I'll never forget my first drive down the Pacific Coast Highway, my hair doing a little dance out the window. In my little green Volkswagen Bug (my first car in the States), I flipped around the radio dial. Oh my gosh! I was on the radio in America! The thrill shot right through me.

When I first arrived, I stayed at the Hilton in Universal City.

As it turned out, one of the biggest movie stars in the business was staying in the hotel. One day, I went downstairs to the coffee shop and was paged on the intercom system. *Who knew that I was here?*

It was him—he was looking for that blond Aussie girl he saw wandering through the hotel lobby. Tall, dark, and oh-so-handsome, the movie star came over to my table and introduced himself.

"Hi, I'm—"

That much I knew!

Basically, he said, in so many words, that he had affairs with most of the girl singers in town and I was next on his list. My reaction? I was terrified! I wasn't going to be the next *anything*! I don't remember exactly what I said to send him on his way, but I laughed (with him) and mentioned that I was very work-focused (true, and safe!). Inside, my mind was roaring: *You are not going to be that girl!* Then it came to me. There was only one thing to say to him.

"I have a boyfriend," I stammered. Not exactly true, but it did the job in the moment.

He was a Hollywood bad-boy legend with a long list of girl-friends. Not too long after our coffee shop encounter, he ended up dating a friend of mine, actress Susan George. By then I was staying with her and my sister Rona at the Beverly Wilshire. He called up one night when Susan wasn't there and asked me out again. It was easier this time, and I firmly said, "You can't do that! You're dating my friend!"

But he could and did ask. He was my first major movie star encounter, after all!

His name?

I'll never tell.

My decision to move to America can also be credited to Australian singing legend Helen Reddy. One evening I was in Florida and went to see my fellow Aussie in concert. I knew Helen's sister, Toni Lamond, quite well, and she brought me backstage to meet Helen and her husband, Jeff, a wild, fun, and crazy guy. After what was a spectacular show, I walked into her dressing room, where Helen was so warm and charming. She knew the music business and was so helpful to a new songbird finding her wings in the United States.

"Look, darling," she said to me. "If you want to make it in America, you must live here. You have to be available to do things when they ask you. You need to be here, so you must move."

Helen planted a seed in me. This trip to America wasn't just a visit; I was actually relocating. It proved to be a good call.

After my first big hit, "If Not for You," debuted on the American charts at number twenty-five in 1971, I had an even bigger hit in 1974 with the song "If You Love Me, Let Me Know," written by John Rostill and produced by Bruce Welch and John Farrar.

America was letting me know that the welcome mat was out. I made the big move.

Still unsure of where to settle, I stayed at the Sunset Marquis in West Hollywood, a place a lot of people in the music industry used as their home base. My new home wasn't much more than one of those little boxy rooms with a miniscule kitchenette. I remember lying in my bed the first night at the Sunset Marquis and hearing gunshots coming from the streets. *Oh my! Can I go home now?* Everything terrible I'd heard about America seemed to be true: it was the Wild, Wild West. I lay there wondering if I'd made the right decision.

The morning I arrived at the hotel, I ran into Glenn Frey, from the Eagles, who also considered the hotel his Los Angeles "home." He had that great long rocker hair and carried his guitar case like it was the most important thing in his world—and it probably was. Glenn introduced himself, and we talked about our touring lives for a few minutes.

The next day, I received a dozen red roses with a note that read: *Welcome to America. Glenn Frey.* It was so touching to me that someone really famous from a band I loved would go out of his way to make me feel that I was indeed welcome in this new and sometimes scary place. His lovely gesture would never be forgotten, although I didn't have a chance to thank him. I never really saw him again.

Were there more homesickness pangs to come? Of course. There were times when I felt the walls were closing in and thought, *What am I doing here?* But they passed quickly as my career took the next step, and soon Lee followed me to America and we made up. I was back with my boyfriend, and he was acting as my manager again.

My life on the road was about to launch as I embarked on my first major American tour, starting in the heartland of Minneapolis, Minnesota. There was just one problem: I didn't have a band. Thankfully, John Farrar came over to play lead guitar and be my musical director, and my agency arranged some musicians for me.

That first band didn't gel, and they couldn't play my music. By the end of our first eight-hour rehearsal, they hadn't learned it at all.

To put it mildly, it was a disaster of epic proportions.

"Livvy, this isn't working," John warned me.

"We have to get some good musicians," I replied in a worried voice. I couldn't blow this—it would be the first time an American audience would hear my entire set, not just a few songs on different TV shows.

John jumped on the phone. We found a band called This Oneness, and a few hours later, the room was flooded with new faces strumming guitars and playing keyboard and the drums. We rehearsed all night long before getting on the bus at the crack of dawn (where we practiced more), as we set our sights on that first Minnesota date.

Our backstage was a locker room. John came over to me before we went on and sat on one of those low benches, and I waited for him to give me one of those heartwarming "we can do it" speeches. But he didn't.

"Liv, I'm terrified," he confided. "I've never played in America." This was being said by one of the most brilliant musicians on the planet and the most talented one I would ever know.

"We're going to be okay . . . I think," I said in a shaking voice.

"We're going to be okay?" he asked with twelve more question marks.

"Yes," I said, although I wasn't really sure.

For once, I ended up comforting him!

"Olivia is the one who usually gets really nervous before the show. On this first night, she had to calm me down," John Farrar remembers. John is someone who always wants everything to be perfect, and we share that trait.

I was still a bundle of nerves and wondered if the lyrics in my head would be able to actually leave my mouth in song form. This was in the days before musicians had autocue to remind us of the lyrics. I was so frantic that I would forget a line or mess one up that I ran the words of the songs in my head the entire day. In the bus.

In the bathroom. In the quiet moments when I tried to calm my terror. *Would it be enough?*

Something happens in the moment when prep time is over and I take that first step onto the stage. It's the same now as it was on those first nights in England, Australia, and America.

The faces smile up at me.

Hands reach out.

The first note floats up in the air.

I sing.

I'm home.

It ended up being more than enough. The boys in the new band, Dale and Bob Strength, were very sweet, supportive, and talented, thank goodness. We toured on a Greyhound bus with a bathroom that didn't work. If you sat down on the seats too hard, dust clouds would float up to the ceiling. But my band didn't mind. They had a hippie spirit that made it so much fun to be on the road with them. I always remember them with fondness and gratitude because they helped me out on such short notice.

After the first tour was over, Lee and I were enjoying trying again and ended up living in Malibu together in a pretty little house on the beach. It truly was a California dream. One of my fondest memories was a day when we weren't touring when Lee came home with an enormous four-year-old Great Dane who'd been found abandoned in an apartment. Poor baby! His owner had been killed in an accident and no one knew the dog was there alone and starving to death. It was love at first sight, and I named him Zargon. Later, I'd name my music company Zargon Productions! He was my first rescue dog in America. I always rescued animals as a child in Australia, and now I had a home where I could do it again.

It wasn't long before the house filled with even more love. Rona and her son Emerson, then three, moved to LA from London. When I wasn't working, I puttered around the streets in my little VW. (My long-time Aussie girlfriend Coral still has that Bug and has painted it pink!) I'm a homebody type, and it felt so good to set up a real base in America, filled with the people and animals I loved.

As for the culture shock, well, there was only one problem with my new life on the beach. I've always loved going to the movies, and that same summer a terrifying classic-to-be named *Jaws* came out, and it had a profound effect on someone who lived next to the ocean. I vowed never to go swimming again! Even the Great Dane wasn't allowed in the water!

It was a beautiful time in my life, and I loved the tranquility of living outside Los Angeles, away from all the traffic and hustle. I've never liked living in a big city. A country girl at heart, I relished walking my enormous dog along the beach, stopping and talking to other dog lovers and petting their animals. Zargon, who was now thriving and was the friendly type, was so sweet to everyone on two legs, but not so much those on four.

Once—luckily only once—he dragged another poor dog into the ocean and I had to jump into the water to break it up.

Jaws or not, I would do anything to protect all the dogs.

After a concert one night in Jackson, Mississippi, a fan came backstage and gave me the most wonderful present: a gorgeous Irish setter puppy. One nuzzle and I lost my heart.

"This is one of the best gifts I've ever received," I told the overjoyed man. I just had one request: "I'm on the road. Could you please hold on to him for another month or so?"

Six weeks later, I was at LAX waiting nervously. All of a sudden, there came a crate, and inside was this gorgeous auburn-haired pup that was so well behaved. My love affair with Irish setters was entering a new chapter! I had named him Jackson, after his hometown.

My Jackson loved being on the road with me and would hang out backstage before each performance. As he curled up behind my legs, we would go over the set list together. He even inspired a song called "Slow Down, Jackson." A talented songwriting couple, Michael Brourman and Karen Gottlieb, wrote it knowing about my furry baby, and I loved it. I was so touched that I recorded it.

By 1973, my songs, including a cover of John Denver's "Take Me Home, Country Roads," were climbing the charts. Artie Mogull, vice president of artists and repertoire at MCA Records, shipped the single to country stations everywhere, and it received overwhelmingly positive airplay and was a regular listener request. Artie suggested a more country-orientated pop album as my follow-up, which became *Let Me Be There* and included the song of the same name, a big hit that debuted on the country charts and then crossed over onto the pop ones.

I had been playing pretty small gigs, but they were growing from five-hundred-seat halls to ones that held more than one thousand people. As my fan base expanded, one of my shows was at an enormous place, the Astrodome in Houston, where the annual rodeo was in full swing. It was so huge that I had to be driven by cart to a stage set up in the middle of the arena. An added benefit of performing here was that I could smell the horses, and that reignited my childhood love of everything equine. There was only one disappointment that night. My boyfriend and manager, Lee, didn't come to the show with me, and I was really angry with him, since this was one of the biggest venues of my entire career.

I prepared to give him a little attitude afterward backstage. Well, maybe more than a little. . . .

"What did you think of the show?" I asked.

"I didn't see it," he said.

I was getting ready for a small quarrel when he grabbed my hand and said, "Come with me."

"Where are we going?"

"You'll see what I was doing," he replied. I wasn't sure why he was leading me to a barn out the back where they kept the horses for the rodeo.

"I bought him for you," he said, opening a stall door. The most beautiful palomino quarter horse, named Judge, stood looking at me with his wise dark-brown eyes. I couldn't even speak. It was the best present I could ever receive, and Lee was instantly forgiven.

We shipped Judge to our home in Malibu, and he was an amazing horse. Straightaway he became my hobby and my passion, and my baby. If I wasn't working or on the road, you could always find me with my horse or the dogs.

Judge and I would ride at sunset down the beach in Malibu, sand kicked into the gentle breeze and the smell of the sea all around us. I loved that my boy was such an affectionate horse and would often turn to nudge me lovingly with his nose.

Don't get me wrong, I couldn't wait to perform again, but

those early-evening rides in the hills and down the beach defined pure joy.

One day in 1974, John Farrar and I were at my house going through a pile of songs sent to him as options for my next record.

"We were sifting through boxes and boxes of tapes and cassettes sent to me. Remember, this was in the days before CDs," he says now. "We had a system, which was sitting there and basically playing them all."

He put a record on the turntable, and immediately the lyrics broke my heart. The song was written by the talented Jeff Barry and a future legend, Australian composer Peter Allen, whose life would later be the fodder for the hit musical *The Boy from Oz*.

My heart stopped when I heard the lyrics: "I love you . . . I honestly love you." It was so simple, with a meaning that was deeper than the ocean. Those words made me stop and think because they touched me. I could certainly relate, and I knew that everyone would be able to make those words fit their own personal story of love and perhaps even loss. Just putting the word "honestly" into the mix made it even more poignant.

No lies.

No denying it.

I honestly love you.

"I have to record that song," I told John, who was nodding furiously. He booked time at a little recording studio in London, a place where magic happened for me and many other artists.

A few days later, on a cold January day, I walked up rickety wooden stairs and took a few steps into a room where there was only a small recording booth above and the studio below. I had to stand still (so they couldn't hear the noise of my feet above them) and sing. It was no frills. Just some sound equipment and a great song.

I did only three takes of "I Honestly Love You," with a brilliant pianist friend named Alan Hawkshaw, who played that unforgettable introduction that most piano players still have a hard time getting right. It was one of those shimmering moments, and we ended up using the first take.

I sang it from my heart. I'm not a power singer but more of an interpretive one. Part of that song sounds like it's almost a whisper, which seemed right because it was about the most tender and sensitive emotions in life.

John Farrar said something to me that day that I'll never forget. He told me he used to listen to music on his crystal radio and that it was very intimate. "Imagine that you're singing to that one young person, me as a boy, who is listening on their crystal set," he said.

It made singing very intimate to me.

Over the years, I was so proud to hear from fans how they loved this song and what it meant to their lives. I would hear about the love between people, parents and children, and people and animals. The song was timeless in its appeal and limitless in how it could spark the imagination or take you back in time to that one unrequited love. I would sing it years later to one of my true loves, my mother, when she was dying.

It was one of those songs where you just *knew*. If only you could bottle that kind of phenomenon, then every song would soar and become a classic.

Of course, not everyone agreed that we had a hit on our hands. The record company actually wanted to release a different song as my next single, but, with the help of my friend Artie Mogull, we insisted that "I Honestly Love You" was the one.

What a great call!

We released the single first in Australia in early 1974 and it quickly became a worldwide pop hit. It was my first number one single in the United States after launching there in late April that year.

I was very proud that the song was certified gold and surprised it reached number six on the country charts, since it's not really a country song. Years later, I would rerecord a new version of it, produced by David Foster, on my album *Back with a Heart*, with Babyface on background vocals.

The Seventeenth Annual Grammy Awards took place on March 1, 1975, at the Uris Theatre (now the Gershwin Theatre), in New York City. Andy Williams was the host. The award for Record of the Year was presented by none other than John Lennon and Paul Simon. John took the stage and said, "Hello, I'm John. I used to play with my partner, Paul!" Paul said, "I'm Paul. I used to play with my partner, Art!"

The nominees were: Elton John, for "Don't Let the Sun Go Down on Me"; Roberta Flack, for "Feel Like Making Love"; Joni Mitchell, for "Help Me"; Maria Muldaur, for "Midnight at the Oasis"; and me, for "I Honestly Love You."

These were all songs and artists I absolutely loved and adored. I couldn't believe that I was in the same category as these incredible artists! What a privilege.

And the winner was . . . "I Honestly Love You"!

Art Garfunkel accepted the award for me because I was on tour. I also won the Grammy that year for Best Pop Vocal Performance, Female, which was especially sweet. When I look at those

Grammys now in my office at home, I still can't believe it, and I wish I could have been there to accept them in person.

All of a sudden, the phone was ringing off the hook. Every magazine and TV show, it seemed, suddenly wanted to interview me.

My response? "Wait . . . They want to talk to me—the girl from Oz?"

FIVE

Have You Never Been Mellow

By 1974, Pat and John had moved to Los Angeles, and I was thrilled to have my dear friends so close. One day, John called me to say he had written a song for me called "Have You Never Been Mellow." It was a gorgeous song, and it became the title of my new album, released on MCA in the United States in January 1975.

> *Have you never been mellow?*
> *Have you never tried to find a comfort from inside you?*
> *Have you never been happy just to hear your song?*
> *Have you never let someone else be strong?*

"Mellow" shot to number one on the charts, becoming another single to be certified gold. The album also went gold and sold more than one million copies. The album would also include one of my favorites, the sweetly pleading "Please Mr. Please," another John Rostill song.

The Country Music Association (CMA) named me Female Vocalist of the Year in 1974, and the honor sparked a bit of an uproar and controversy. I was a newcomer on the country scene, and the old-timers wondered what I was doing winning the award. I didn't really understand the separation of country and other music, since I believe that music is music and just naturally crosses over. Some CMA members resented it so much, they split from the organization in protest and formed their own chapter. I felt terrible about it but not bad enough to return that award!

A few country artists, including the incredible Dolly Parton and Loretta Lynn, stood up for me. I've always been very grateful for their support. Later, I would record Dolly's "Jolene," and we had dinner. She's such a delight and just gorgeous.

Life became a bit of a whirlwind at this point. I was juggling my time between studio and the road, and I was also given my own ABC TV special, an hour-long show that aired in November 1976, featuring many of my hits.

Soon after, I had to jump on a plane to the United Kingdom to star in Big Top Show at Windsor Castle. I worked with Elton John, and he was a hoot—very funny, warm, and kind—just delightful. I even invited him to be on my US television show, *Hollywood Nights*, with Tina Turner, Andy Gibb, Cliff Richard, Toni Tennille and the late, great Karen Carpenter, who became one of my dearest friends.

I still miss Karen a lot to this day. She and I became friends immediately. I was drawn to her terrific sense of humor and, of course, her extraordinary talent. She was quirky and fun, and we really enjoyed each other's company.

Karen's lush voice was truly astonishing and reached the depths of my heart. We talked about what she wanted for her life and what I wanted from mine. No topic was off-limits.

She got married, and it sadly ended fourteen months later. That's when the anorexia really hit her hard. She became so thin it was frightening, but she still mustered the guts to divorce her husband, break out on her own, and move to New York for treatment. I was so proud of strong and determined Karen.

I truly believed that she was on the road to recovery. She had the most gorgeous town house she was putting the finishing touches on. She adored anything Disney, so her house was full of all whimsical things and beautifully done.

The last time I saw her, we were both staying at the Drake Hotel in New York and she looked so much better. She had gained some weight and was bouncing back, shopping, laughing, and doing all the things she used to do. It was one of those moments where you sigh with relief, and I truly believed that the crisis had passed.

I was in Los Angeles, listening to my car radio on the way to a restaurant for a lunch meeting with Pat, when I heard that Karen had died. It was as if the sky fell to earth. My stomach hit the ground. This couldn't be possible. I had a date to see her *the very next day*.

Devastated, I arrived at the restaurant and cried all the way through our lunch. Pat tried to comfort me, but I was inconsolable. Karen was so young and full of hope and promise.

Karen Carpenter's death was a great loss, not only to her friends and family but also to everyone graced with her gorgeous voice. We will never know what she could have done artistically, which was sad for everyone around the globe. She was bursting with talent and creativity, but that was only part of it. She was also a kind and authentic human being.

I've always wanted to respect Karen's privacy, and I know that her struggle was a hard one. Perhaps there can be a positive from such a terrible tragedy: her death marked the beginning of raising awareness about anorexia and body image. Little did I know that, later in my life, I'd be confronted with this insidious illness with my own daughter.

Karen shined a bright light on anorexia, which allowed so many others to heal, including my own Chloe. Karen never got a chance to tell her story, but I'm so proud of my daughter, who is working on telling her own.

We have Karen to thank for all the lives that have been saved after women and men found treatment and acceptance from their families and society.

One thing remains: I still miss my friend.

By the late seventies, I was facing my own stresses and needed to make a few important business changes. It was time to renegotiate my contract, and this quickly escalated into a lawsuit that became a famous case of MCA versus me. My longtime lawyer, John Mason, sent them a letter saying that my contract was now terminated for several reasons, including their failure to adequately promote and advertise my music.

My contract had been for an initial two-year term with three one-year options to follow, equaling five years—and it was now seven years. MCA argued they could extend again past the five-year period, claiming I owed them additional albums. They even countersued and filed an injunction against my signing with another label.

It was my life, my career, and my music at stake.

The influential and powerful Lew Wasserman was the head of the label at the time and he scheduled a meeting to speak with John Mason about these issues. When John told me about this, I said, "Is there any chance I could meet with Lew Wasserman before we are in litigation?" My lawyer tried to convince me that this was not the way you handled disputes. The artist and CEO don't argue it out—that's why we have attorneys. But it was important to me to have my own voice when it came to my career.

The fateful meeting was scheduled. "All Olivia's idea," John Mason says now. "Making it even more interesting, Lew said that unless we agreed to his terms, he didn't want to see Olivia face-to-face." We didn't agree. For some reason, Lew decided to let that go, and soon John and I were in an elevator heading to the top floor of MCA to face Lew, who had decades of experience dealing with artists and winning. My mood in one word? Terrified!

I was in my midtwenties, suing this huge corporation and having to face a man who scared the hell out of me. Looking back now, I realize that it was a pretty gutsy move, especially as a woman. Most women were told to just let the men deal with the legal aspects of being in show business.

This Aussie wouldn't hear of it.

Lew had home-court advantage. His massive desk was placed higher than anything else in the room because it (and he) were set on an actual platform above the rest of us, so he would have the power and could gaze down at us. "It was like a king looking down from his throne," John Mason recalls. "What I remember most was this heavy and dark antique furniture making the room look even more formal."

Intimidating? It was beyond. I was the ant and he was the ant-eater, or maybe I was the meat and he was the lion. There was no if, ands, or buts about it: I was making money for him, and he didn't want to let me out of my contract. He said that I owed him additional albums and would never release me until he got them.

"He was generally nice to Olivia," John remembers. "He was never angry or threatening, but it was pretty clear that he was in control and wanted those albums."

I'll never forget his huge black-framed glasses, which made his eyes look really big.

I walked out of the room crying because I was so mortified about the meeting.

"I gave Olivia a lot of credit for having so much strength," John says. "She's not an aggressive person, or litigious. But I learned one thing about Olivia on that day. She doesn't back down. She doesn't want trouble, but she's not afraid of it.

"The next day, they filed a lawsuit," John adds. In the end, we went to court, losing the first case but pushing on until the California Courts of Appeal changed the verdict and we won. "The case was groundbreaking for all artists," John says. "Olivia was able to keep all her masters and own her next album and every single one since we won that suit."

That was my first nasty experience in the business, and I decided I'd let John handle it all in the future.

He was right that I wouldn't back down, though. I'm proud that my case changed how record companies craft recording contracts. Instead of basing them upon the number of years, it would now be about the number of albums required from an artist.

The lesson was: you can't go around a problem. You have to go through it.

And sometimes you have to go a little . . . crazy.

Once, when I was on tour with Paul Williams, we traveled on a private jet to each gig. One crazy night, Paul and I (with my nice-girl image) got into the worst whipped-cream fight at thirty-five thousand feet and we made a gigantic mess. I'm sorry we did it, but there are times when you just lose it! Later I heard that someone asked, "Who was on that plane? Led Zeppelin?"

"No," they were told. "Olivia Newton-John."

Embarrassing!

One of the interesting parts of fame is that you get to meet so many actors and musicians who you admire and look up to. I met many stars over the years, including Clint Eastwood when I did a photo shoot on his ranch in Carmel, California. He came to my trailer with his little daughter on his hip, which was quite endearing. Clint made my day because he was so delightful.

Another big star who was kind to me was Jack Nicholson. I met him when I was filming a special in Aspen with John Denver. I'd see him at a lot of parties, and he always gave me a smile and a quick chat.

I spent a day with Dustin Hoffman when I auditioned for *Tootsie*. He was really funny and suggested we just walk around one of the neighborhoods in Malibu. We talked about movies and life and finally found ourselves walking up a long driveway by mistake. Imagine the homeowner who looked up, saw us, and actually did say, "Can I help you . . . two?"

"Oh, we're looking for our lost dog," Dustin riffed.

I was also up for the Richard Gere World War II movie *Yanks* but didn't get that role, either. Richard was lovely to me, and it was nice to meet him.

Perhaps one of my biggest star encounters happened at the Cannes Film Festival when I was just in my twenties. I stayed at a beautiful white hotel in that scenic city on the water. One day I was sitting in the tower, where they served a lovely afternoon service. I sat looking at the glistening water as the cool breezes floated over a steaming cup of English breakfast tea. The tea was served on a beautiful silver tray and accompanied by tiny sandwiches and cookies that were delicious.

I spooned sugar into my cup at the exact moment, in the South of France, the iconic film star Gloria Swanson swooped up those stairs. There she stood in full makeup with a bright silk scarf around her hair and wearing a long, flowing robe with bangles on her wrist. She was absolutely gorgeous, and looking right at me . . . and the tray filled with treats.

"Darling," Ms. Swanson said as she approached. "Don't eat sugar. It's poison." It's amazing that she was aware of the health risks of sugar back then, and I should have listened to her. Now, it's forty years later and I'm finally on a no-sugar diet. I'm a slower learner!

And then there was Elvis.

I was really excited to be invited to see the King at the Hilton in Las Vegas. It was a celebrity-packed row, with Tim Rice and Andrew Lloyd Webber sitting next to me on either side. During the show, Elvis shocked me and sang my song "Let Me Be There." It blew me away to hear him say my name, because I was such a big fan. After the show, I went backstage to meet him and got another big surprise. Doris Day was there, too—I've always adored her.

Doris was warm and welcoming, but sadly I never met Elvis up close and personal. His road manager said there was an emergency and Elvis had to leave the building.

Literally!

I did hear later that Elvis told others that he was the one who told me to record "I Honestly Love You." Not true. We never spoke! But I'm still so knocked out that he said my name.

I met some of my comedy icons when I hosted *Saturday Night Live* in 1982. I was the first host who would also sing that night. I'll never forget doing a sketch called "Olivia Newton-John Goes to the John," where a fan encounters me in the bathroom. (Shades of real life since it has happened to me several times!) I had met Gilda Radner in the past and now Eddie Murphy. They were nice to me, and it was a rush to go live from New York City.

One of my most eye-opening celebrity encounters happened in an elevator in Japan when I was on tour and ran into Cat Stevens. I glanced over at this very handsome man with long, dark hair and a beard, wearing a gorgeous velvet shirt and beautifully tailored pants. We said hello and he graciously invited me to his show that night.

I couldn't believe the Cat who walked out on stage in torn jeans and a white, grungy T-shirt—so different from the elegantly dressed man in real life.

That's show business.

I've even been fortunate enough to meet several US presidents. I was invited to the White House when Ronald Reagan was president and George H. W. Bush was vice president. I was privileged to take my mother and sister as my guests, because usually you're allowed only one person. It was an amazing experience made even better because we were together. I went to the White House again many years later when George H. W. Bush was president and I was invited to sing at the annual Christmas program. I had Rona with me this time. It was very exciting to line up before the show to meet the president and first lady.

"Oh, so good to see you again," he said to me. I had met him once before, during my Reagan visit, but I was shocked that he remembered, since it had been a long time ago.

It was soon time to shake hands with First Lady Barbara Bush.

"I can't believe your husband remembered me," I said.

"Well, you're so ugly, dear," she replied with a smile.

I loved her from that moment!

The president and first lady were whisked away, and it wasn't long before the Secret Service approached us. "The president has invited you and your family to come to the White House for a drink after the show," he said. We were thrilled, and even more so when President Bush greeted us in the lobby of the White House with the stunning black-and-white-checked floors and breathtaking Christmas tree. He had a drink in hand, carefully wrapped in a white napkin. (We'll never know his drink of choice!) He escorted us personally from his private elevator to the residence, where he gave us a tour. It was an unforgettable evening.

A few years later, Rona and I were in the Qantas lounge in Los Angeles waiting for a trip back home to Australia when a man in a dark blue suit with a small pin in his lapel approached us. "President Bush is in the back of the room and he'd like you to join him," he said. We did and had a lovely chat with the former president, who was on our flight. He and Rona had several laughs together.

"Come on board with me. I'll get you on the plane early,"

he said, which was wonderful. We were escorted onto the plane, where we all prepared for the long, fifteen-hour flight. About halfway through the evening, the same man in the blue suit was back. He said to my sister, "President Bush asked if you'd like to sit with him."

"No, thank you," said my sister.

"What are you doing?" I whispered to her.

But she insisted. "I just want to sleep."

The next morning, we made sure to say goodbye to him. He turned to Rona and said, "I can't believe you turned down the chance to sleep with the president."

Rona lived off that story for years!

Over the years, I was lucky enough to meet four presidents, including Ronald Reagan, both President Bushes, and Bill Clinton.

Being in show business is a go-go-go lifestyle, but there were moments when I allowed myself to relax and really get away from it all. I remember the first time I vacationed in Hawaii: Rona and I joined a large group of "lunatics," including Sammy Davis Jr., Totie Fields, Carol Burnett, Steve Lawrence, Eydie Gormé, Helen Reddy, and her husband and manager, Jeff Wald. I was new to their group and asked what to wear during our first dinner out together.

The always helpful Jeff told me, "It's dressy, Liv."

Check.

I showed up in a beautiful, flowing white dress—everyone else was in shorts and T-shirts. I wore heels; they were in flip-flops! I apologized, yet the next night I actually listened again when Jeff told me to dress casually. Of course, everyone was dressed up. Finally, I got the joke. By the third night, I was ready to tackle this head-on and showed up wearing three layers: a nice dress over shorts over cutoff jeans. *Ha!* Jeff and Helen couldn't stop laughing.

The next time I came to Hawaii, Helen and I upped the ante and wore grass skirts with coconut bras and sang "My Little Grass Shack" to a delighted and adorable George Burns when he arrived in the driveway of our hotel. Thank God there wasn't YouTube in those days!

Not that I would have cared. I was, and am, always ready to be part of a good laugh.

And little did I know, the best fun of my life was about to happen.

SIX

You're the One That I Want

Chicago, 1971. Composers and writers Jim Jacobs and Warren Casey wrote a play about youth culture, girls, and greasers, and set it in 1959 at fictional Rydell High School. You might have heard of this place. It was based on the real William Howard Taft School in the Windy City, but it felt like it could have been set in Anywhere, USA.

The story hit every nerve because almost everyone had lived it. The plot revolved around ten working-class teenagers as they experienced their senior year in high school and were forced to deal with peer pressure, sex, values, love, dancing, and the perennial question: "What comes next?" Followed by the heart-stopping and gut-wrenching: "Will we ever see each other again?"

A wop ba-ba lu-bop, a wop bam boom! That play was called *Grease.*

With a knockout rock-and-roll score, the play debuted in Chicago at the small Kingston Mines nightclub, where it was dubbed a bit raunchy, raw, aggressive, and even a tad vulgar. It was all of the above—and that was the idea. One journalist wrote: "I expect that this thing called *Grease* will close in four days and we will never hear about it again."

But it didn't close, and, although future productions were tamed a bit, there were still mentions of some very real and poignant issues of the day (or any time period), including teenage pregnancy, bullying, gangs, and that desperate need to fit in and find the one you really wanted. It also featured timeless topics of love, friendship, rebellion, sexual coming-of-age, and the thin line between the last days of adolescence and emerging adulthood.

No one thought it would ever be made into a movie—despite the fact that the play not only lived on but also left Chicago and received raves on Broadway and then in London's West End.

That, they said, was supposed to be *that*.

Cut to 1977 in Hollywood, when the biggest movies of the day were *Star Wars*, *Close Encounters of the Third Kind*, and *Annie Hall*. Movie musicals weren't exactly burning up the silver screen like they did in the fifties and sixties, and many considered the art form old-fashioned, something your parents saw when they were teenagers.

I, on the other hand, always loved movie musicals. *The Sound of Music* was one of my favorites.

One quick aside: I was fortunate enough to spend many Sunday evenings in Malibu with Julie Andrews and Blake Edwards for movie nights. These were always beautifully catered family gatherings and a who's who of wonderful actors and actresses. Their daughter Jennifer became a friend and even played my then-husband Matt's wife in *That's Life!*, a movie that Blake directed and starring Jack Lemmon and Julie.

When I was pregnant with Chloe, I'd go to their house to swim because they had a lovely big pool. Julie was always the most fun, charming, and welcoming woman. I loved her and her beautiful voice. I also adored her performance as Mary Poppins. I even took a five-year-old Chloe to meet Julie. I said, "This is Mary Poppins." Chloe looked up at her quizzically, to which Julie said, "That was many years ago, darling." Now, I use the same line with young children when they look at me that way. Thanks, Julie, for that classy lesson.

Now, back to *Grease*.

At this same time, on the small screen, a wonderful young actor from New Jersey was becoming a household name with a sitcom called *Welcome Back, Kotter*. During his summer hiatus from the TV show, he put a lovable, IQ-challenged young man named Vinnie Barbarino on hold and donned a now-iconic white suit. He had audiences cheering and wanting to be him as he boogied his way across the floor at the 2001 Odyssey Club in Brooklyn. The music said it all: "You should be dancing."

When I first met John Travolta, *Saturday Night Fever* had been filmed but wasn't released yet, so I had no idea what was in store for him. But it wouldn't take much more than a few minutes at my house with him to realize I was in the presence of someone who was destined for major stardom and would be one of the greats of our time.

He was a triple threat—acting, dancing, and singing—plus all that charisma and incredible sexy movie-star looks. His sexiness was innocent, but the truth was those gorgeous baby-blue eyes had so much behind them, including great pain. Tragically, he had just lost his beloved girlfriend, actress Diana Hyland, to breast cancer. He remained sweet, open, very sincere, and vulnerable.

Hollywood knew something was brewing for him, and the race was on to figure out who would be lucky enough to work with Travolta next. He signed a three-picture deal with Robert Stigwood, a then forty-two-year-old Australian impresario who loved to mix movies with music.

The first movie in John's deal was actually based on a play that was close to his heart. You see, John auditioned for Danny for the original stage play *Grease* at age sixteen and didn't get the lead, which only made him hungry to prove everyone wrong. Perseverance paid off, as he auditioned again and again for many of the roles. Eventually, he was cast in a road company production of *Grease* in the role of Doody, one of the T-Birds. What I knew about John was, when he wanted something, he would stay completely focused. That's what he always was—and remains. Focus plus talent.

Stigwood was planning to bring back the movie musical and partnered with producer Allan Carr, who optioned *Grease* in 1975. Everyone in Hollywood knew that this was a movie project that had seen its fair share of starts and stops. The rights to the film had been sold three or four times before Carr got his hands on them. At one point, *Grease* was even going to become an animated feature, but that was scratched, too.

Carr and Stigwood made an unstoppable team, though. Both were 100 percent on board, and they were given a $6 million budget from Paramount. All systems were go, so it was time to find Sandy and Danny.

John Travolta was the easy first choice for handsome, rugged, too-cool-for-school Danny Zuko. But I was so busy touring the world that *Grease* wasn't even on my radar.

In 1976, fate intervened.

Helen Reddy invited me to a dinner party at her house in Los Angeles, and I planned on having a lovely night catching up with my good friend and her husband, Jeff. It turned out that Helen had invited an eclectic mix of guests for supper, and, over "pass the butter," I met Allan Carr. He was a charming man—a showman with a big personality—who was small in stature, wickedly funny, told great stories, and kindly said that he was a big fan and loved my music.

"I Honestly Love You" had been number one on the charts, as had "Have You Never Been Mellow," and my new album, *Don't Stop Believin'*, was doing well on the charts. We talked about the songs and my touring life. It was a wonderful meal, and Helen and Jeff were amazing hosts. After the plates were cleared, Allan and I continued to chat about nothing in particular. He hadn't even brought up his next project.

Yet.

Somewhere between coffee and brandy, he began to talk about this little musical that was his newest obsession, in fact he'd optioned the film rights, and maybe I had seen the play on my travels—and, by the way, it had the most wonderful songs and was a great role for someone who might want to act, sing, and jettison their career to the next level. He said this was going to be big. Not just United States big, but a worldwide phenomenon.

"I can't wait to see it," I said sincerely.

"You know, we haven't cast the female lead," Allan said in a casual voice. "You would make a wonderful Sandy."

Over coffee at Helen's house, Allan even talked to me about

John Travolta playing Danny and how everyone was so excited for him to do this role he was obviously born to play. My first thought: *He is so cute on his television series. He's a great and funny actor.* Allan mentioned he was a few years younger than me, but it was no big deal. I was always good at math (ha!) and ran the numbers. *I'm twenty-eight, and John's twenty-three.* I could not play a high school student at age twenty-eight!

Why are we having this discussion?

Between sips, I had a few more fleeting thoughts. *Could I play a high school student? Could I look like I was seventeen?*

No! No! No!

Age wasn't the only issue. Most people don't know this, but this wasn't my first brush with the movies. In fact, I made a few doozies. When I was fifteen, I made a movie musical called *Funny Things Happen Down Under*, which I filmed with Ian Turpie. It was a family movie musical about a barn used by a group of children for singing practice. When the barn is in danger of being sold, the children dye sheep strange colors and market all that funky wool to save the barn. They even had a sheepshearing contest to raise money. It's best remembered today for being my first film, and I did love the experience of filming it. It was great to work with the kids and especially the animals that also appeared in it.

Oh, and there was music in it!

Later, I did another movie musical. In 1970, I starred in a British musical film called *Toomorrow*, about a group of students who pay their way through college by performing in a pop band of that name. Then we are taken up into the sky by aliens while singing . . . I'll stop now because you get the idea!

The project was the brainchild of Canadian theater and film producer Harry Saltzman, who produced the James Bond movies, and Don Kirshner, an American music publisher, rock music producer, and talent manager for Carole King, Neil Diamond, and Paul Simon, among many other songwriters. He also put together successful pop groups including the Monkees, Kansas, and the Archies.

The idea was to put a pop group together and do a series of movies with the musicians. The four of us were Ben Thomas, a handsome American cowboy singer; Vic Cooper, an English Tommy Steele–type, musical-comedy star, and Cockney boy; and Karl Chambers, a tall, gorgeous, lanky drummer from Philadelphia. And then there was me, the Aussie girl next door.

My audition involved meeting director Val Guest, who was wearing a white shirt with a cravat and a suede jacket. He had a mini mustache and a little cigar dangling from his lips—the stereotype of what you'd think a director should look like. We discussed the script and he said, "There is one part of the movie where you will get into a time machine and go back to being a little girl. We will regress in time."

It sounded so exciting until he said, "And then all your clothes will whip off and you will be in your bra and panties."

My heart dropped and I realized I couldn't do this movie if naked time travel was a part of it.

"I can't do that," I said firmly. "I don't want to be in my underwear."

In the end, they changed the script and it was never mentioned again. It was a good lesson in saying no.

On the weekends during the shoot, we were invited to Harry Saltzman's mansion in the countryside outside of London. I had never seen opulence like this expanse of land where horses roamed and a huge swimming pool where movie stars tanned. Often on these Sunday afternoons, actors Roger Moore (in his pre-Bond days) and Michael Caine would stop by with their lovely wives. They were delightful and down-to-earth, and made me feel very comfortable.

We also went to Don's house for a party, where we met a jingle singer named Jamie Carr who was hilarious and cracked us up. By us, I mean Rona and me, as she was with me (again) as a chaperone. Jamie would take Rona and me out and call us "the whore" and "the virgin," never explaining which one of us was getting what moniker.

The perks of working with Don was that he was quite generous. He sent me an expensive bottle of Bal à Versailles perfume and a beautiful yellow suitcase with a black stripe down the middle. I never had a new suitcase or fancy perfume. I was blown away by his generosity.

In the end, though, *Toomorrow* was a disaster, and I wasn't sure if I would ever act again. There were some positives, including my lifelong friendship with actress Susan George, who interestingly enough was set to play the role before me but her agent wouldn't let her do it because it wasn't serious enough. (Lucky for her!) I'm so proud that she set up a foundation called Lasting Life in 2016, after she lost her wonderful husband, Simon MacCorkindale, in 2010. We also share a passion for horses, and she raises the most beautiful, award-winning Arabian horses ever at Georgian Arabians, the name of her farm.

As for acting, my thought: *Why risk it?* I didn't want to make another mistake that would last forever on celluloid. I reasoned: *Maybe this just isn't my thing.*

"My music is going well," I told Allan Carr. "I'm not interested in making another movie. And I'm twenty-eight and too old for Sandy. And I can't do an American accent."

"I love your music. And you're not too old. You look so young," he said.

His mind kept moving fast. He would talk to the writers and change the *Grease* script to make Sandy an Australian transfer student spending her senior year in America at Rydell.

Wow, they were really trying to make this work for me! But I was still hesitant.

"I'm anxious about making *any* movie," I tried to explain.

He didn't want to hear any of it.

"Sandy could be a great role for you," Allan cajoled. "A legendary role."

Helen's husband, Jeff, would also try to convince me that this was a good role for me.

I agreed that I would at least see the play before I made any final decision. I was on my way to London, and Richard Gere had the lead role onstage as Danny Zuko at that time. He was beyond wonderful in it.

Something about *Grease* began to nag at me.

It's so much fun. The songs are wonderful. Sandy is a great character. The tone is making me nostalgic for high school—well, not really. But still. And with Sandy's switchover, it would give me the opportunity to play two different types of girls. Could I even pull that off?

And then I decided: I would pass.

I would say no. That made the most sense. I would work on

new songs and go back out on the road. Sandy was someone else's role. It was right to walk away. No regrets.

And then Danny Zuko himself walked up my front steps.

I was back from London and living at a beautiful ranch in Malibu that I had purchased as my new home. A few times while driving around Los Angeles, I had seen someone navigating the roads in a sleek butterscotch-yellow convertible Mercedes. John Travolta was actually very cute behind the wheel. "Striking" is a word that perfectly described him—and it does to this day.

Allan kept phoning both me and my representatives about the role of Sandy, and I floated back to undecided again. Somehow a decision was made that John Travolta would come talk to me at my home.

Little did I know that John had his eye on me in those days from my music. As he told me years later, "I fell in love with you, Olivia, the first time I saw you on an album cover. You were wearing a blue shirt. It was love at first sight from a picture. I had this image in my mind that Olivia Newton-John was everybody's ideal girlfriend—the kind of girl who would invade your dreams."

Wow!

"I was asked who would be my perfect leading lady in *Grease*, and there was only one human being on this planet I could see as Sandy," John said. "That person was Olivia Newton-John. I told the producers, 'I promise you that Danny Zuko's Sandy is Olivia, and no one else should play it.'"

*

I'll never forget that day. My eye caught a flash of yellow, and I saw John Travolta drive through my ranch gates. I went outside to be greeted by those piercing blue eyes and the warmest smile on the planet.

In person, John Travolta radiates pure joy and love. He is one of the most genuine and sweet people on earth, and he really cares for other human beings on a deep level. That day, John greeted me with a big hug like we were already lifelong friends. There were no expectations or promises. We were just two people who were lucky enough to spend a gorgeous sunny afternoon enjoying each other's company.

We took a walk around the ranch so I could show him my horses, and immediately we just liked each other. And with every passing moment, he was calming my fears about what we could do together with the film version of *Grease*.

I'll let John tell it:

"I went to her house and I loved Olivia. I thought, *We're off and running*. I thought she'd hop on board, but then she explained that she had considerations. We were both in our twenties, and she was worried about playing a high school girl. I assured her that we wouldn't be fooling anyone with the casting. No one in the cast would be acting their actual age, and I reminded her that this is done all the time in Hollywood."

In the end, we agreed that an actual screen test would be a good way to make me feel comfortable.

How could you say no to John Travolta?

When Danny Zuko pulled out of my driveway that day, it did feel good to know that soon we would know if it was going to work—or not.

I insisted that I wouldn't do the screen test without John because I wanted to test our chemistry. (Even though I failed chemistry at school!) *What if John doesn't like the way I act? What if we don't connect?*

I knew I'd be performing with some wonderful actors and actresses who would be playing the Pink Ladies and T-Birds, all coveted roles.

"You will be great," John insisted, and he was so passionate about it that something deep inside of me began to actually believe it.

John made a quick call to Allan and soon I was speaking with Randal Kleiser, the director who would be making his theatrical feature-film debut with *Grease*. John already knew Randal, as he'd directed him in a beautiful and moving TV movie called *The Boy in the Plastic Bubble*. I told Randal and legendary choreographer Pat Birch, who also wanted me on board, that I still couldn't say yes or no to *Grease*, but I would do that screen test with John.

A week later, I was on the Paramount lot in Los Angeles, where a driver dropped me off near one of the large, warehouse-style soundstages. I steeled my nerves because this wasn't my world.

And then it happened.

John Travolta came out to greet me.

Our eyes met.

When we walked inside the room together, it was magic, and everyone saw it. Knew it.

They couldn't deny this kind of chemistry. We were right next to each other. Up close and personal.

Sandy and Danny standing there in the flesh. The best part? We hadn't even read one line.

There were so many scenes we could have read for my screen test, but we settled on the pivotal drive-in-movie scene and filmed it in the actual car, a 1948 cherry-red Ford Deluxe convertible, that would be used in the movie. The first step was the makeup trailer, where the pros did my hair and makeup to prove that I could be seventeen again.

Even I couldn't believe what a high ponytail, a ribbon, and a little bit of petal-pink blush could do. I wanted to call Mum and ask for permission to stay out late that night with my friends!

John was doing a little transforming, too, with the help of the *Grease* team, who slicked back his black hair and tossed him the perfect leather jacket. We climbed into the car, slid next to each other, and he said the line: "Sandy, would you wear my ring?"

I replied, "Danny, I don't know what to say. This means so much to me because I know now that you respect me."

Two seconds later, he jumped at me and went in for a little grope. As a shocked Sandy, I jumped out of the car and threw the ring at him.

"You can take this piece of tin!" I cried, walking away.

To which John wailed in that pleading voice, "Sandy, you just can't walk out of a drive-in!"

Everyone laughed because the chemistry was palpable. "As much as I loved her before we did the test, I was madly in love with how she was as Sandy," John said. "Olivia fit *Grease* like a glove."

I couldn't deny the on-screen spark we were creating. Randal and Pat were already calling our pairing "electric." What I liked the most about the whole Danny/Sandy vibe that day was that, as characters, they were equals. She might have looked pure and innocent, but she followed her heart and her head while staying true-blue to her choices. He could dish it out, but so could she. Yes, she would put on that hot costume at the end, but he would also change for her and wear a letter sweater to capture her heart. The motivation to be together went both ways.

Little did I know then that my future great friend, actress Didi Conn, also would screen-test that week, but not for the sweet, beauty-school dropout Frenchy. Originally, there was some talk that she might make a good Rizzo—but as we all know, she was so obviously Frenchy. I can't even imagine the movie without Didi in that role, or without Stockard Channing tormenting me as Riz!

It wasn't long before the rest of the cast was filled out. The Pink Ladies would also include Dinah Manoff as Marty and Jamie Donnelly as Jan. Danny's T-Birds would consist of Jeff Conaway as Kenickie, Barry Pearl as Doody, Michael Tucci as Sonny, and Kelly Ward as Putzie. The funny thing was that Jeff had actually played Danny Zuko onstage.

There was just one name to add to that list.

Olivia Newton-John as Sandy.

"Yes," I finally said. "I'll do it."

Those four words changed my life.

Shooting took place during the summer of 1977. In a blink, I had my call sheet for the first day. The twist was the first day on the set was unlike any other film I would ever do.

There would be no rehearsal time. No table read with the cast. We actually had a sock hop! This was Allan Carr's idea, and it was a great one. He wanted us to feel bonded like lifelong high school friends, and to that end we were required to have some fun. That entire first day was spent doing all these dances in giant circles, joking with one another, laughing, and even playing a few tricks. It was a brilliant way to create an instant vibe of familiarity.

And then to work. John and I shot the opening beach scene where Sandy and Danny have their big goodbye amid all that surf and sand. We shot at Malibu's gorgeous Leo Carrillo State Park, which was just a quick minute from my house.

It was a brilliant summer day as John and I frolicked on the shore and then raced each other into the foamy ocean, where the waves threatened all that fifties' hair and makeup. It didn't matter, because we were in the moment, flirting, kissing, and establishing what would later become one of the most beloved couples in movie history.

And then it was back to actual high school. The interiors of *Grease* were filmed at Huntington Park High School— unfortunately during a summer heat wave with a broken-down air-conditioning system and a horrible smell in the hallways. Sandy's dewy glow wasn't just the result of that first flush of love or makeup but was also created partly by sweltering interior temperatures that shot past the hundred-degree mark. I'm still shocked that half the movie student body didn't pass out.

The truth was, the heat didn't matter, because we were having so much fun. On set, I was Sandy and not Liv, because all of us referred to one another by our characters' names. To stay in the past, we even sang a lot of fifties songs during the breaks. In so many ways, it made me nostalgic for the high school experience I never actually had in my own life when I was going to school in Australia. It was so loose and fun at Rydell, while I wore uniforms at my real Australian high school. Forget about running into your crush in the hallways. At my school, the boys and girls had to use separate entrances and stairs, so we would never even meet or glance at each other. Our hormones were under wraps; at Rydell, they were celebrated.

Quite often, poor Randal had to tell all of us to just settle down because we were becoming too rowdy. But when the cameras stopped rolling, the party rocked on. Hormones were abundant, even though most of us had left high school behind many years ago.

Jeff Conaway was the first one to greet me when I arrived on set, and he was very kind and sweet. As a wonderful side story, he met Rona when she came to visit me on the set, and they fell in love.

Maybe I should have been the chaperone this time around!

(I planned a beautiful engagement party at my house to take place on the July Fourth weekend. I had a dance floor put over my swimming pool and 150 people were invited. Two days before the party, they had a big fight because Jeff wanted her to sign a prenup. She didn't believe in it although she would never have asked for a dime. So they broke off the engagement. I had my assistant, Dana, call and say we were still having the party. A few people didn't get the message and turned up with engagement gifts. It was a who's who of guests. Six months later, they made up and we went to Vegas. They were married after we saw Frank Sinatra that night.)

Jeff believed in total authenticity when it came to his character. A few times he could be seen sucking the neck of accomplished stage actress Stockard Channing. Why? Well, they weren't dating, but Jeff insisted that when Riz got "a hickey from Kenickie" he had to give it to her himself.

No stunt hickeys for him!

I wasn't very experienced in the acting world, but I had so much support from the cast. Didi in particular was so loving, and she took me aside to go over our lines together before shooting. It felt as natural as Sandy's relationship with Frenchy. Life imitating art.

"Just be yourself, Liv," she told me, and it was good advice. Soon I felt I *was* Sandy—she felt real to me.

John was equally protective of me, and he proved it during the big bonfire scene where Rizzo pulls Sandy through the crowd and then shoves her into Danny Zuko's face. Remember, Danny's absolutely shocked to see Sandy because she's supposed to be back at school in Australia. At first, Danny lovingly yells, "Sandy!" One glance at his boys, however, and he gets embarrassed and begins to act cool in front of the T-Birds. Sandy is devastated when her summer crush is nothing more than a jerk.

I did the first take, only to have John walk right in front of the camera during my close-up.

"Sorry, I messed up," John apologized to Randal.

Gently, John took me by the arm to one side of the parking lot. "Liv, I did that on purpose because I don't want them to use that take," he whispered. "I know you can do better."

I had great love and support from him—and the feeling was mutual. I would be forever grateful for his concern.

Now, let's set the record straight. Did I ever date John Travolta?

On the set of *Grease*, John would tell me, "Liv, it's every guy's dream to have you as their girlfriend."

"I don't know about *every* guy," I teased.

Yes, we really liked each other and there was an attraction, but we would never date because we were both involved with other people at the time and both of us have a loyalty streak that runs deep. Later, our busy lives meant we went our separate ways. The truth is, it never went beyond friendship with John, despite the fact that the fans wanted (badly) for us to become a couple in real life.

I asked John Travolta about it the other day and this is what he remembered:

"At the time, we were both involved with other people and we were respectful toward the people we were with, so . . . that was that," he said.

"Never the twain met in *that* way," he said with a smile. Then he reminded me, "It almost happened between us a few other times, but it didn't. Sometimes life just offers you the wrong timing. We had to leave it as dear friends."

In the end, we left the making out to Sandy and Danny, but the deep feeling of sisterly love I have for John continues to this day.

And since we're on the topic, let me just say it wasn't tough having to kiss John Travolta—professionally speaking. In fact, it wasn't tough at all, although having to do it in front of the crew was a new thing for me. Most of us don't kiss someone in front of thirty people! When it came to our lip-locks, there was the lighting guy on one side and a microphone in my face on the other. I was trying to keep the right angle and stay in character. It wasn't particularly romantic.

On-screen, however, it was the type of chemistry that you can't fake. You either have it or you don't.

We had it—thank goodness.

Every day on the *Grease* set, Allan would tell us, "I've seen the dailies and they're amazing." You never know if a producer is just being a cheerleader. I had the hardest time watching the rushes of what we filmed that day—I have always hated to watch myself and still find it nearly impossible.

Now, I can actually watch the movie, but back then . . . Forget it!

I guess when you're young, you're so insecure about every imperfection. Now, I look back and think, "You were perfect! Look at that skin tone. Look at that baby face!" But on the *Grease* set, Sandy Olsson herself was her own worst critic. Luckily, there was no time to dwell on it because we were working twelve-hour days.

On the weekends, all thoughts of rushes and dailies were put away. Allan threw massive cast parties at his gorgeous house in Beverly Hills to celebrate and keep up the energy levels.

Here are a few Sandy particulars, starting with her all-American pure looks. I had a great team, including the legendary Albert Wolsky, who created the costume design for *Grease* and then countless other films, including *All That Jazz* and *Bugsy*. During the early fittings, I must have tried on hundreds of poodle skirts and spun around so many times I should still be dizzy. Famed hairdresser Arthur Johns, my personal stylist at the time, did the famous Sandy fifties' flipped do and the curly look at the end. Yes, that was all my own hair. My makeup artist Connie Ortega was equally as wonderful and would give me honey masks in the morning before putting on my makeup to create that pure, good-girl, dewy look. I was grateful to my mother that I did look very young for my age—a Sandy bonus. (I look at my daughter at age thirty-two now and she's absolutely perfect. What was I worried about in those days?)

It wasn't enough for Sandy to just look the part, though. I had to learn to really move. I'd been promised that I wouldn't have to join any of the dancing scenes, but one day on set, I could see Pat Birch watching me intently as I was having some fun and dancing around. Later, she remarked, "Olivia, you can actually move. You're a natural."

All of a sudden, I found myself in a choreography class.

The original plan was that Sandy would not dance with Danny during the *American Bandstand* dance-off scene. Plans were rapidly changing, and soon I would be hand-jiving like the rest. Before we did one twist on camera, there were three weeks of dance rehearsals with Pat at the helm. Each day, she had us warm up, stretch, and then memorize the choreography. It was really playful, plus great exercise. And the fact that my dance partner was John had me over the moon.

He recalls, "I loved dancing with Olivia. It was really beyond your average dancing. It wasn't novelty dancing for the movie, but somewhere between novelty and Broadway choreography. I told Olivia, 'With a little encouragement, you can do it. You can go the distance.' And to Pat I said, 'Why not try Olivia for the dance scenes? The fans will love it.'

"I was thrilled to find that Olivia is an amazing dancer," John says. "She tried it, and it was perfect. What happened is on film forever. It's part of movie history."

It wasn't long before it was time to shoot the hand-jive scene—this wasn't just a big night shoot but an entire week of filming in a different high school gym located in downtown Los Angeles. The popular American rock-and-roll group Sha Na Na took the stage each day, and that infectious music blasted from the speakers. There hadn't been a big musical scene like this one done for a long time, and you could feel the excitement in the air—and unfortunately you could smell the sweat. It was stifling hot in that gym as well, and we couldn't run the air-conditioning because it would interfere with the sound recordings.

Each night for that week, we would hand-jive for hours, and it was electric. John threw me into the air—we practiced it about a million times—and then tossed me between his legs. I can still feel it now—his hands on my waist and the rush of air sweeping through my hair and over the ripples of that spaghetti-strap white chiffon dress. In that moment, well as I would find out, everybody wanted to be that girl.

Once we had that scene in the can, it was off to shoot the drive-in scene, which was filmed at the real Burbank Pickwick Drive-In, an old-fashioned make-out spot for movie lovers where, sadly, a shopping center now stands. I'll never forget John reaching over to grab me in the car. Of course, I was nervous, but that worked because Sandy wasn't exactly calm, given that she was trapped in a car in Make-Out Central. All I could do was imagine what it was like to be seventeen again with my first boyfriend!

By the way, all the sexual innuendo in *Grease* was what made it fun for adults while it sailed over the heads of the kids. I loved the part where Danny Zuko is left all alone at the drive-in. He sings a sad song and watches the screen, where the hot dog jumps into the bun.

I would never be able to look at hot dogs—or buns—in quite the same way again!

Grease is a musical filled with wonderful songs, but halfway through shooting, Randal thought that we needed a few fresh tunes that would help define the movie experience. I brought in my old mate John Farrar, who quickly wrote "You're the One That I Want." I remember John coming to the set really early in the morning and telling me he had been up all night working on something new. He played me the song just once, singing all the parts, and in that moment, I knew it was a hit.

John Farrar recalls, "Randal wasn't particularly enamored with 'You're the One That I Want' at first. Olivia really liked it, and so did the cast. But the director was shaking his head."

Randal quickly changed his mind, though, which was fortunate. The song went on to become one of the bestselling singles of all time, with more than fifteen million copies sold worldwide. How did John come up with the joyous, infectious "Oooo oooo oooo" part?

"I needed something between some of the lines and added 'Ooooo oooo oooo.' It just fit," he said.

John would also write another major number for *Grease*: "Hopelessly Devoted to You." After the movie wrapped, we needed one more song, so John wrote it and then Randal and I went back to the set with a skeleton crew to record Sandy's moment of heartbreak as she stares into that blue plastic kiddie pool.

"Hopelessly" ended up climbing both the country and pop music charts, reaching number three on the Billboard Hot 100 List. It even earned an Oscar nomination for Best Original Song. I was honored to sing it at the Academy Awards—despite the fact I'd eaten some bad clam chowder a few weeks before at a very fancy restaurant in England and had a raging fever of 102 degrees. I was feeling terrible, but I was determined not to miss that amazing experience.

In fact, I had hepatitis, the infectious one you get from bad seafood, and since this was the Oscars, I had to kiss a lot of people.

Then I had to call them later on and tell them to get tested! Even my doctor said, "Dearie, why did you have to kiss so many people?"

Alas, we lost to "Last Dance," but that was fine. I love Donna Summer.

Meanwhile, Louis St. Louis and Screamin' Scott Simon gave us another song, named "Sandy." Who could forget when John crooned, "Sandy, my darlin', you hurt me real bad"? Louis wrote that song in about fifteen minutes. It didn't hurt that his first girl-friend's name really was Sandy.

In this business, it doesn't happen all the time, but when magic is in the air, you can feel it.

"Look at Me, I'm Sandra Dee," written by Jim Jacobs and Warren Casey, was in the original stage play and a highlight of the second act. We filmed that scene at a private residence in East Hollywood with all the Pink Ladies present to make fun of poor, unsuspecting Sandy, who just wants to find a few friends.

I hadn't done too many girly sleepovers when I was young and wanted to really experience what it felt like to have a group of girls gang up on me. There I stood in my virginal long white nightgown (buttoned oh so far up) and said in my I-can't-believe-it, crushed voice, "You making fun of me, Riz?"

I felt devastated for Sandy, especially when that bullying Riz just brushed it off and replied, "Some people are just so touchy." Just looking at wonderful Stockard, the ringleader of my angst, with her smirk and Sandy wig, I felt deeply uncomfortable in real life. I was so in character that it was really affecting me, and I wanted to burst into tears.

It turns out, so did someone else! "I felt so protective of Olivia and Sandy that it was tough for me to be mean to her during this number," remembers Didi Conn. "It was my job to be mean to her! But I just hated that she was being bullied." As for Frenchy's big ear-piercing moment, audiences saw her take Sandy's virgin pin to do the job. "I couldn't use a real pin on her ears, but I did tweak her hard enough with my nail that it gave Olivia a real startle for the cameras," Didi said.

After we shot the sleepover, it was time for the big finale. Little did we know that a pair of sleek, skintight black pants would set off a worldwide tremor that would last for—oh, about four decades.

SEVEN

Grease Is the Word

You could call this a tale of two Sandys. You see, I never thought of my role in *Grease* as playing only one character. Even back when I did the screen test, I knew that I was reading Sandy #1—as I liked to call her. After weeks of filming, she came easily to me because most of us have Sandy #1 in us. But we also have a bit of Sandy #2! Number two smoked, wore black leather and high heels, and wrapped her legs around a boy as he danced her through the grounds of the high school. Sandy #2 was deliciously wild, and there was a great buildup of excitement inside me to finally bring her to life.

The first step was the costume department. It was decided that Sandy #1 would have to ditch the poodle skirts and prim high collars and wear all black, leaving nothing to the imagination. Albert Wolsky didn't disappoint. He found these body-hugging, high-waist, skintight, black sharkskin pants (even better than leather!)

that were actually from the 1950s. They were so old, and there was just one pair, so there was no room for error. One rip and—disaster.

When I tried on those pants for the first time, the zipper was broken and Albert didn't want to rip them trying to put in a new one or remove the old one. Instead, I'd be sewn into them each morning!

My first thought after hearing this complex fashion fix: *What if I need to pee? What am I going to do?*

One of the most memorable moments of my entire career was the first time I stepped out of the wardrobe trailer in full Sandy #2 mode to show Randal. When I say we went full-out, it's an understatement. I had the sexy, curly hair (thank you, Arthur Johns), thick black eyeliner, and mascara galore. My lips were slathered in bad-girl red lipstick, my top was squeezed tight, and my legs and bee-hind were poured into those pants! *Tell me about it, stud*, indeed! The final touch was red peep-toe sky-high heels from my own closet. Yes, I suggested the shoes, knowing I could move in them because I wore them in my real life. Don't ask me how I used to wear these shoes, but I did!

Unfortunately, I gave them away for a charity auction a few years after the movie, never knowing how special they would become—or how much money they would have brought in for my hospital!

On that night when Sandy #2 was debuted, there were gasps, catcalls, and a lot of whistling.

My first thought after that reaction: *What have I been doing wrong all these months? All these years!*

John was actually filming the song "Sandy" during the moment I left my trailer and strutted my way across set. There he was sitting on that swing set and feigning a broken heart, when I slunk past. I remember he stopped singing, midnote, as his head jerked up and his eyes popped.

"Tell me more! Tell me more!" he stood up and shouted. We laughed so hard because it was exactly the reaction I wanted.

John Travolta remembers, "I couldn't believe it. It was just so right to see her with that Marilyn Monroe hairdo, holding the cigarette, and in those sky-high heels. It was just too good to believe. It was so perfect. And I knew the audience would have the exact same reaction that I was having—a heart palpitation."

It felt empowering as pure adrenaline and the idea of claiming my own sexiness rushed through my body. It wasn't antifeminist—it was my choice in that moment. All the men on the crew began to do double and triple takes as they turned around to stare at me with jaws that headed south. I think a sandwich or two hit the floor.

I heard a grip whisper, "Who's the new broad? She certainly puts the sizzle in *Grease*."

"It's just me," I said, and smiled.

That night wasn't about acting. It was about acting out. Later, I would hear that all the girls on the set immediately wanted that outfit, and all their guys were willing to buy it for them—immediately! If only I had thought to make copies of those pants and sell them, I could have made a fortune.

In that moment, I memorized the feeling. I knew exactly what jolt Sandy would experience and the emotions that would race through her when she stepped out of the crowd as this new version of herself.

This was a light bulb moment for me personally, too, because I was more of a hippie-bohemian type when it came to my personal dressing style, and this was va-va-va-boom! Later, people would say it was a terrible message to give young girls, as in we were telling them to sex it up to get their man. But it was about choice. Wear those pants, or a dress down to the floor. Empowerment comes from calling your own shots and being who you want to be.

That outfit would pull the shy Olivia Newton-John out of her comfort zone in other ways, and it even gave me the courage later on to release the song "Physical." That last scene in *Grease* instantly changed my image. It wasn't long before I would release an album with a cover shot by Helmut Newton, the famous German fashion photographer and close friend of my father.

On my album cover for *Soul Kiss*, I looked very sexy and sultry, with absolutely nothing on my back—a look Helmut created. I also held a riding crop. Me—really!

One thing was clear: Sandra Dee was no more!

The actual filming of "You're the One That I Want" presented a few challenges. I couldn't really eat or drink that day on the outdoor set located on the grounds of John Marshall High School in Los Angeles. I limited myself to a few sips of water and no food, and joked that I was getting dehydrated and Sandy #2 might pass out. At lunch, they actually had to unstitch me to eat and then restitch me after a bathroom trip. It was a painstaking process, but there was no other choice, and it was definitely worth it.

That exhilarating feeling was multiplying when the cameras rolled and we began singing that great song, which was so reminiscent of the fifties.

You better shape up
'Cause I need a man
And my heart is set on you!

It was a rocky number with a bit of yodeling that was really catchy, and it had a wonderful hook.

You're the one that I want
Oo-oo-oo, honey
The one that I want
Oo-oo-oo
The one I need. Oh yes, indeed

Oh, that John Farrar. He's so brilliant.

"There is a look on my face as Danny sees Sandy for the first time dressed this way. It's pure lustful shock," says John Travolta. "I wish I could say I planned that look, but it was so organic that day on the set. I just took one look at Olivia and it was written on my face. She was the one we all wanted!

"In that moment, she was everything mixed into one," he adds. "She was every fifties' sex symbol all at once. Pow! Yet she was an original who you had never seen before. The quintessential package. Was she Marilyn? Liz? Or Ava? She was all of these things we wanted to see, but even more.

"I got this buzz just from looking at her," he says.

As for the dance, which culminated in me leaping up and wrapping my legs around John's waist, he said, "We improvised with her wrapping her legs around me. Pat wanted to find steps that were natural to us and we did with this jump. I knew that we had to end the song with something big or that number would be anticlimactic. You always have to put a button on a big number. Lifting her in my arms and her wrapping her legs around me was a button to that song.

"I said, 'Why don't I lift you up in one joyous swoop?'"

I was game for anything and raced toward him. Suddenly, I was in the air. John was strong and caught me as my legs wrapped around him. We were off, racing across the high school field for the last number, "We Go Together."

"You're the One That I Want" was released as a single in April 1978, before the film even opened. Within weeks, it would be number one on the pop charts. Every time I turned on a radio, there were songs from the movie playing.

One last thing about that moment: I wasn't an expert smoker. Remember how I said I tried it as a girl and hated it, and then again to develop a sultry voice (couldn't do it, choke, choke, choke). It was Pat Birch who told me to take just one puff and then purposely toss the cigarette onto the ground, putting it out with my stiletto as John comes toward me. I was awkward about it, actually no acting needed, which showed that the newly confident Sandy still had a bit of the good-girl underneath.

Sandy #1 was lurking, which was why she didn't know what to do with that cig. People say it is so sweet and charming to see both Sandys struggling to come together as one.

A little thing that translated into a big moment.

We wrapped *Grease* in the autumn of 1977 and had the long wait until June 16, 1978, which was our official release date. As I ushered in the new year, I was invited to see what was called the "unsweetened" first-cut version of the movie. This meant I'd be watching it without all the finished music or many of the special effects. These screenings are usually top secret, and ours was conducted on a gray January day on the Paramount lot where it all began.

John Travolta was there, along with Allan Carr, John Farrar, and a bevy of Paramount executives who were nervously hoping (and praying) that this would be a big hit. I could see the worried look in their eyes as they silently wondered, *Did we indeed reinvent the movie musical?* Would Paramount be seen as risk-takers or fools?

Again, all that made *Grease* wasn't all there that day.

The animated opening sequence was a work in progress, and Randal was still editing the "Hopelessly Devoted to You" scene. Despite these gaps, the general consensus was that *Grease* was "a fun movie," but there was still a general anxiety about how audiences would respond to such a clean movie set in the 1950s. It was 1978 and the world was in a different place. Would those fifties' ideals seem dated and silly?

We would have to wait a few months to find out.

My life as a recording artist meant a busy start to that New Year. I was actually back in the studio working on a new album when I got word that the *Grease* premiere would take place on June 2 at Mann's Chinese Theatre on Hollywood Boulevard, which would actually be closed down for the event. All of a sudden, it seemed quite real—and quite big.

June arrived in a flash, and suddenly John and I were rolling down Hollywood Boulevard in the actual "Greased Lightning" car, a 1948 Ford Deluxe convertible. No one had seen the finished movie yet, but the word on the street was positive.

As we got closer to the theater, we got an inkling of what was to come and began to smile at each other nervously. It was quickly becoming clear that *Grease* wasn't some fifties-throwback movie.

It was an event the likes of which Hollywood hadn't seen in quite a long time, for a musical or any other movie. Later, it would be described as a premiere that was as big as the one for *Gone with the Wind*.

The roar of the crowd was deafening. It was as if we'd arrived at an Oscars ceremony or a major rock concert.

"It was nothing short of phenomenal," John Travolta reminds me. "It was exactly what the Beatles went through when they arrived in the US. I was ready, but even I couldn't believe it. It was something I had to witness with my own eyes. But I knew this was historical."

Hollywood Boulevard was a complete madhouse.

I never expected the kind of pandemonium surrounding me, or the thousands of fans who lined up on each side of the street, almost causing a full-scale riot. There I was in my gorgeous little pink poufy prom dress made by my dear Aussie friend, costume designer Fleur Thiemeyer, who also designed for Rod Stewart, Poison, Pat Benatar, and KC and the Sunshine Band, to name a few.

That night, I allowed both Sandy #1 and #2 to attend by mixing bangs with longer, curly hair. John looked every bit Danny Zuko in black pants, a black tee, and a greaser-type leather jacket with large silver zippers that caught the swirling spotlight shooting between us and the night sky.

It wasn't long before things got really out of control. We pulled up in front of Mann's to walk the red carpet, only to have kids begin to climb and then jump down off the barricades. Even before we stepped out, they were climbing all over the car, and when they couldn't get inside they started rocking it back and forth while the rest of the crowd pushed harder trying to get to us. People were screaming loudly and clapping wildly while security discouraged them from actually getting in the car with us! We were tossed around and jostled back and forth, but it wasn't too scary. It was exhilarating!

"They *really* want to see this movie," I whispered to John, and we burst out laughing.

Finally, we made our way inside the theater, and the excitement inside was every bit as raucous as what was going on outdoors. The cheers felt like a big ocean wave. *Saturday Night Fever* had now been out for six months and John wasn't just a huge movie star. He was an icon.

Before the movie started, actresses dressed like Rydell High School cheerleaders, complete with pom-poms and skirts, ran from the back of the house, down toward the screen to do an opening cheer. That was all we needed. The already frantic pitch of the venue was turned up about a hundred notches to almost deafening. The entire audience began to cheer with the girls as they stood, arms overhead, going wild. And these fans hadn't even seen a frame of the movie yet!

And then the lights dimmed.

The opening credits began to roll.

John and I appeared as our cartoon characters, and the audience continued to explode into laughter and joyous applause. It was so hilarious, so perfect. They loved it! The cartoon was a last-minute addition, and it changed everything. It set the mood and allowed audiences to feel comfortable leaving behind today as they took the trip back to yesterday. It was a brilliant move on Randal's part.

By the end of that animated sequence, the line between 1978 and the fifties began to blur and then disappear. We were time-traveling back—and everyone was along for the ride.

John and I sat with Randal, Allan, and the rest of the cast, and the relief from our section was palpable. By the time we got to Sandy #2, the crowd was gasping, cheering, wolf-whistling, and then singing along to songs that they already knew from the early radio releases—another genius idea.

From that moment on, *Grease* would take on a life of its own in cultural history.

Both *Saturday Night Fever* and *Grease* weren't really supposed to be big box-office hits. At least that's what the experts said.

I prefer to quote screenwriter William Goldman, who once famously said, "Nobody knows anything."

After the premiere came the red-hot, invite-only after-party on the Paramount lot. It was amazing, although I don't remember too much of it because I was meeting someone new about every second. Isn't it strange how big life events like that now seem like a blur? I do remember that I shed my poufy prom dress and changed into Sandy #2 by wearing a skintight pink shirt and purple spandex pants, shades of the sharkskin ones in the finale. We danced all night long. Finally, the girl who went to work at age fifteen went to the high school prom!

It wasn't long before John and I were off to London for the European premiere in the legendary Leicester Square. This time around, we left the "Greased Lightning" car at home and arrived in a big black limo. I expected a far calmer experience but was 1,000 percent wrong. Once again, the fans were beyond excited, gathered in large masses, and many actually broke down barriers set up by those nice London officers. Again, they climbed on the roof of our car while trying to slide through the windows to "meet" us. Exciting, yes, but it was also scary this time around because we weren't expecting the frenzy.

John Travolta remembers, "Honestly, I didn't think we would make it. The limo started to cave in from the top. The fans were about to come in through the roof because they were pounding and jumping to break through to meet us. Everyone underestimated the impact of the movie. There weren't enough police around, so the crowds just took over."

A little shaken and rattled, we somehow managed to walk the red carpet and wave to all our London fans.

Fleur made me another pink number for this event. We would work together for many years to come, collaborating on all my stage costumes as she traveled the world with me on tour. I really admire her talent and great knowledge of color. Sandy #1 and #2 were both grateful for her eye.

Within a month, *Grease* became the highest-grossing movie musical of all time, and it remained that way until 2017, when a movie called *Beauty and the Beast* stole the crown. (*Grease* is still at number two, followed by *The Greatest Showman*, *Chicago*, and *La La Land*.) *Grease* was shot for only $6 million and would eventually gross more than $400 million worldwide, smashing box-office records. The soundtrack spent three months at number one, while the song "You're the One That I Want" sold more than fifteen million copies.

And it lifted my career into the stratosphere, while John became an iconic movie superstar.

Pretty much everyone in the summer of 1978, from little kids to grandparents, saw *Grease* at least once, and sometimes two, three, or four times. (When I perform now, I always ask who in my audience has seen *Grease* and just about every hand goes up. Blows my mind!) There really was something in it for everyone. Despite those early nerves, the executives were thrilled because no Paramount picture ever grossed $100 million so quickly, with the soundtrack eventually selling one hundred million copies.

I'm often asked why *Grease* hit such a nerve with audiences around the world, and the easy answer to me is that it transports people back to a happier time when the world seemed nicer and choices were simple. Everyone can relate to someone in the cast— either they were that person or they knew that person, thanks to clever writing by Jim and Warren. I believe that the film says so much about the beauty of first love and the importance of lasting friendships that carry you through both good times and bad.

I'll always be Sandy to a lot of people, and that's fine with me. John says that he feels like we were part of history and he wouldn't trade *Grease* for anything. I must say that I agree. *Grease* did so much for us on so many different levels.

Even now, eight-year-olds come up to me after one of my concerts and call me Sandy, or (my favorite), "Look, it's Sandy Newton-John!"

The twenty-two-year-old pants were voted the third most iconic movie outfit of all time, and they sit in my closet now. I've never tried them on since—well, maybe once this year just to see—and I'm not telling! I'm so thrilled I hung on to them. For a few years, I even wore the jacket in my show, but then I'd leave it backstage after the number. One day my amazing publicist Michael Caprio said to me, "Is this the original jacket from the movie? Are you crazy? This will be worth a lot one day." So I retired the outfit. This year, I'll auction the pants and jacket off and donate the proceeds to my Olivia Newton-John Cancer Wellness & Research Centre in Melbourne.

John and I were approached several times to do *Grease 2*, which was released in 1982, but I don't think the material ever got to a script stage that we thought could work. As I look back, I'm glad we didn't do it. You can't capture greased lightning in a bottle twice, and it was best that we left it alone.

I do have a funny vision for *Grease 3* in my head, where Danny and Sandy meet up in an old people's home and we still have all the moves.

We can do the hand jive from our wheelchairs!

Oo-oo-ooo, honey!

EIGHT

Suddenly

The wheels are in motion.

There were those in my inner circle who told me that my post-*Grease* life would be very different—and they were 100 percent on the mark. That point was driven home when I began to tour again and found myself in France, where the movie was a huge hit. I had a night off before my show and wanted to blow off some steam. Why not go to one of those fabulous Paris clubs and dance?

I just wanted to blend in on the dance floor like any other Parisienne out on the town for the night. Armando Cosio, my hair and makeup artist, put a long black wig on my head, and I wore something very un-Sandy-like, a bohemian white outfit, while Lee put on a suit. This was just about as un-Sandy and un-Danny as we could be. An hour later, after this well-thought-out preparation, we arrived at a French discotheque—and in one second, I heard a chorus of "*Bonsoir, Olivia! Bonsoir, Lee! Je t'aime* Grease!"

Comment dites-vous "impossible to hide"? Even for one night!

My new motto: why not just embrace it? I pulled off the wig and had a great time.

A few months later in 1978, I released my tenth album, *Totally Hot*, with a sexy cover showing me in all leather leaning on a wall, in homage to Sandy's transformation in *Grease*. Songs such as "Deeper Than the Night" and "A Little More Love" raced up the charts, and the album immediately hit the top ten in the United States. It went platinum as the *Grease* soundtrack also rocketed to platinum.

It was thrilling but exhausting, plus I was a little bit lonely. Despite that fun time in Paris, Lee and I didn't see a future for our relationship. After we broke up, I really needed time to reconnect with myself, family, and friends, in the cherished haven of my ranch-style home in Malibu. It sat on three acres bordered by wild, hilly countryside, and it was my secluded paradise.

The main living space was large and open, and there were a few bedrooms and an office. The master suite was the entire second level and had the most stunning pitched wood ceilings, as well as a fireplace and a gorgeous balcony to sit out on at night. The land was covered in fruit trees and meandering pathways, and there was also a pool, a tennis court, and a barn. *Could I have horses—many horses?* I couldn't wait to spend time there, unwind, and just take a moment to breathe.

Spending time with my animals is always the perfect way for me to find my center again. After gifting me with Judge, Lee gave me a new baby, a sleek pitch-black Tennessee walker from Aspen, Colorado.

We met this horse when I was filming a TV special with John Denver, and I was taken with his beauty. However, this poor horse was a stallion and a little too much for me to handle. On the advice of a vet, I had him gelded. He was not happy, and on my first ride with him after his gelding, he bolted on a steep hill. I had one foot in the stirrup for balance at the time when he took off. I couldn't get my other leg over, so I fell off. Shaken, I was quite badly hurt and had neck and back issues that laid me up for a long time. It really wasn't his fault, though; the poor boy was probably in pain.

Soon I rescued three other horses. One of them was a racehorse named Straight Pipes. I also had Alex, a big chestnut quarter horse. And when I bought the house in Malibu, a sweet old boy named George had come with the property.

"Do you want to keep him?" the real estate agent asked.

Did I want to keep him? The more creatures on four legs, the better! I even stopped counting the cats that would be moving with me.

There were also two wonderful coyote-cross pups that ended up staying after my horse caretaker found them by the side of the road one day. I named them Paco and Quita. I also rescued several other dogs from pet shops where the poor babies were stuck in too-small cages and could barely turn around in their sad, cramped conditions. In a blink, they were roaming my property, running free, and giving me grateful licks.

Then a girlfriend from England called, wondering if I could take in her beloved English setter. Sure! What was one more? *Nine dogs, including the coyote pups; six horses; a bunch of cats . . .*

It was heaven—and it was mine.

My dream house was a wonderful sanctuary for me, but soon I would be leaving it to go on tour. I savored those last days, waking up in the morning to the wild birds that came calling, and riding

up into the hills on my beloved horse with my pack of dogs following me. On my ride, I passed my huge veggie garden where I grew
corn, tomatoes, potatoes, and various other things I ate to maintain a healthy lifestyle, even before that was on everyone's mind.
My exercise was riding, dance class, tennis, hot yoga, and hiking
those hills.

The house cost about $365,000 for three acres and the build-
ings. That seemed like an incredibly large amount of money to me
at that time, but now it sounds so ridiculous when you hear about
real estate prices in the same area. Recently, that same house was
sold for $10 million! Years after I sold it, I went back to look at it
when it came on the market again. Yes, I felt a few pangs of nostal-
gia, but I believe in moving forward in life—and never back.

Memories are what you carry with you forever. That's why
moving forward is the healthiest and most enriching path because
you bring the past moments along but still forge brave, new territory. Think of it this way: the earth is constantly changing. We are
part of her—Gaia—so we should also change. It's just not realistic
to think that anything will stay the same, because we don't control
anything. I believe it's such a gift to embrace change.

You step in the river and you go with the flow.

Another thing I loved about that house was the privacy it offered
me as my career hit new heights. I loved my fans, but a part of me
needed some "just me" time.

A few so-called fans didn't agree—and wanted to get a bit too
personal.

I had my first stalker at this time, and it was just so odd. This
was in the days before the internet, and Mr. Stalker kept sending

me weird and threatening letters by mail. I didn't read them. My security people did, and it was a bit upsetting. The fact that he knew where I lived freaked me out, so I had 24/7 security at the house run by the master, Gavin de Becker.

Mr. Stalker would not be deterred on his quest to meet Sandy, though. Luckily, the police finally caught this person on a traffic misdemeanor while I was on the road (thank goodness!). The creepiest part was that the police found a list of people he wanted to kill, and my name was on it. He had already killed his entire family. Scary, scary stuff!

On my security team's advice, I took a vacation to Hawaii. While I was catching some rays on the beach, another stalker climbed the fence surrounding my Malibu home and broke in. Gavin's men were on the case and found this stranger relaxing in my bed. How she got in there remains a mystery. I was just glad that I wasn't in that bed when she slipped inside the house.

Despite the minor downsides of celebrity, I continued touring, while struggling to find my next movie. After *Grease* was released, Allan Carr spoke to me about a film he was producing called *Can't Stop the Music*.

"You would be perfect for it," he said for the second, third, and fourth time.

I loved Allan and will always be grateful to him, but this time I didn't agree. The script just didn't seem right for me, and I had to decline. The film, starring the Village People, would eventually find its female star in Valerie Perrine. Allan was a bit peeved for a bit and didn't talk to me for years, but he eventually got over it and we remained good friends until his passing in 1999.

Reporters kept asking me when I would do my next film, but I still didn't have a movie project in the works.

Then, in 1979, I got a call from my agent, who said that there was another project featuring fantastic music in which I could play a muse. It was called *Xanadu* and the script was surreal and different, exploring new territory. The name "Xanadu" was a direct reference to the summer capital of Kublai Khan's Yuan empire and was prominent in the poem "Kubla Khan" by Samuel Taylor Coleridge. ("In Xanadu did Kubla Khan / A stately pleasure-dome decree.")

The movie musical took a leap from the source material. It would address the roller-disco craze that first swept Venice Beach in California and then the rest of the country. In fact, there were several competing roller-disco projects in the works, and the producers were determined that *Xanadu* would be the first one out the gate.

I wasn't given a script but rather a twenty-page outline, and it did sound fresh, entertaining, and intriguing. I also liked that *Xanadu* would take audiences into a mesmerizing fantasy world, and I appreciated that there was no violence in it. More than anything, I identified with the message about dreams coming true.

My muse character, Kira, was on a mission to help a man named Sonny Malone (who was cast later and played by actor Michael Beck) fulfill his dreams in a place that was an actualization of his wishes. An older man, named Danny McGuire (also uncast at the time I got the offer) would help them along the way. A bit of movie trivia: I suggested Aussie actor Mel Gibson for the role of Sonny. I had met Mel a few times and he was always very charming to me. He had also just made the movie *Mad Max*, and I could see that he was going to be a huge star. The producers didn't see it that way and turned the idea down. Can you believe it? However, Michael Beck, who'd just finished a movie called *The Warriors*, was a great choice.

Xanadu blended an old-fashioned musical with larger-than-life, otherworldly elements, and included massive, way-ahead-of-their-time dance numbers, tightrope walkers, and even jugglers. This was all thanks to choreographer Kenny Ortega and his vision.

I was told that the group ELO had agreed to do the music, and immediately I asked if John Farrar could write my songs. Director Robert Greenwald quickly agreed, and John ended up writing some of my favorite songs of all time for *Xanadu*, including "Magic" and the ballad "Suddenly," along with "Dancin'," "Suspended in Time," and "Whenever You're Away from Me." I sang "Suddenly" with my dear friend and mentor Sir Cliff Richard. After Cliff had been so wonderful to me early in my career by introducing me to English audiences, I had the opportunity to return the favor, which was wonderful.

One night, Robert went to the home of the great Gene Kelly to offer him the role of Danny. I loved that Gene Kelly, legend, committed to the movie through a handshake deal at his front door. Gene also mentioned that he had a few conditions. For starters, he refused to sing or "touch one toe," which meant that the legendary man of movement was refusing to dance in the movie.

Robert figured that he could change Gene's mind down the track and they shook hands. Then I got the call that I would be costarring in a film with one of my favorite dancers of all time.

It wasn't long before Gene wanted to meet with the film's choreographer, the supremely talented Kenny Ortega, who was just at the beginning of what would be a long, celebrated career, which included going on to work with Michael Jackson. Something happened in that meeting that had Kelly and Kenny not only dancing in the room but starting to choreograph some numbers for *Xanadu*.

Gene reconsidered. Yes, he would touch toes after all.

Xanadu was filmed on the Venice boardwalk (the muse mural), in Palisades Park in Santa Monica (where Kira first kisses Sonny), and at Malibu Pier (when Sonny falls into the water), plus the Hollywood Bowl (where Kira and Sonny drink champagne). Gene filmed his dancing scene at the real Fiorucci store in Beverly Hills, where the rich and famous bought their suits and found their personal style.

On the soundstage at Hollywood General Studios, I worked with both Kenny and his cochoreographer, Jerry Trent, on the big dance scenes. The set was filled with exuberant young dancers, excited actors, and a crew that believed we were creating something special. The daily energy was amped way up, which made it a really thrilling atmosphere.

I met *the* Gene Kelly for the first time at a dance studio in Los Angeles, where we were set to rehearse our tap-dancing number. Yes, there would be a dancing duet for me with the man who did *Singin' in the Rain*! I tried hard not to let my nerves get the best of me. When they told me that Gene was going to be in the movie, they sent me for tap-dancing lessons for three months before we shot the movie. I had to learn the dance in three weeks while looking like an experienced pro. Gulp!

Now I was doing it—and with Gene Kelly! It turned out that he was a lovely man—warm, sweet, and very disciplined. I loved his work ethic: Gene made it clear that he wanted to rehearse constantly, as in daily, before cameras rolled. And he was going to direct that segment for the two of us. Everyone simply nodded and said, "Yes, Mr. Kelly. Whatever you want, Mr. Kelly."

Much too soon, it was time for cameras to roll. There I was, dressed up as a 1940s military person, walking into the studio scared to death.

That first day, I pulled out my tap shoes and Gene took me through some very basic steps, which was kind of him. Others could have just thrust me right into the choreography without the basics. That was the thing about Gene: it wasn't about him looking like the best dancer. He wanted the entire dance to be the best dance ever, which meant everyone would look his or her best.

At age sixty-seven, he probably knew it would be the last time he danced on-screen. Lucky me to be his partner.

We rehearsed every single day from that moment on, and he was always so nice to me. He would welcome me with positivity and remind me that movement is one of our most precious gifts as human beings. Later, I would find those words to be so true when I dealt with mobility issues while fighting cancer.

One of the other dancers who auditioned for the role of Sonny was Matt Lattanzi, but he was too young. Matt was tall, dark, and handsome, and Gene jokingly called him "Valentino." "He really does look like a young Valentino," Gene told me with a wink. And he knew the real Valentino!

Despite how nice and friendly Gene was, I still found dancing with him to be totally intimidating. Luckily, Kenny was always there, and I made sure that he kept us in sync.

Gene had a list of rules for the day when we finally filmed the tap-dance scene. He would only do it if we shot on a closed soundstage. There could only be Gene, me, the camera operator, sound, and lights, and Kenny. No one else could be present, including the film's director.

I showed up the day of our number a little nervous, but it was wonderful to hear the music and start dancing with this icon. And it was a total relief that no one could see my trembling knees before Gene yelled, "Action." I was in a straight skirt and small heels, but the problem was we hadn't rehearsed in the costumes. Luckily, it took only a few minutes to get used to them. Gene choreographed the dance to make me look like I had been tapping my entire life.

Gene taught me lessons that went beyond dancing. One day on the *Xanadu* set, he said that there had to be a raison d'être for everything you did, on the dance floor and in life. (Kenny misheard him and joked, "What did Gene just say about be Raisin Bran? What does cereal have to do with it?")

Gene meant that there has to be an important reason or purpose for someone or something to exist. "We always need a reason for being. A reason at the core," Gene explained. "Something that excites you. Motivates you. Thrills you. That gives you purpose to do the work in the first place." I already understood that purpose is one of the most important things in life.

Just being around Gene Kelly was beyond thrilling. I'll never forget the moment I was able to introduce my father to him. Dad was a stickler for hard work and professionalism, so meeting the great actor-dancer was a treat for him.

Gene would also dance his way through a scene at Fiorucci, where he skated around the famed clothing store on roller skates. I couldn't believe that he did all of his own skating for the movie. But why not? He said that he loved both ice- and roller-skating since he was a boy growing up in Pittsburgh.

When you watch the movie, he might be sixty-seven, but that happy look on his face when he's roller-skating makes him look like a boy. (I find it hard to believe, but I'm now older than Gene was when we made the movie!)

My experience of roller-skating could be summed up in one word: *pain*.

Michael Beck and I were filming the duet scene for the song "Suddenly" written by John Farrar. (I sang the song on the album with Cliff Richard, while we skated to it in the film.) We were roller-skating and singing on a concrete floor when I took a bad step, fell backward really hard, and landed smack on my bum. It hurt so badly that I saw stars—and I don't mean Gene Kelly. There I was on the floor moaning in excruciating pain but insisting that in a few minutes we could continue filming the scene. Instead, I was rushed to the emergency room. It would be all over TMZ now, but in those days thankfully it was a quiet visit to the ER and a private diagnosis of a cracked tailbone. *This can't be happening to me.* We still had so much filming to complete—and the show gave us no choice but to go on.

The doctors at Cedars-Sinai Medical Center iced my behind and gave me elephant-size painkillers while suggesting I take a few weeks—*weeks!*—off to rest. I told them that was an impossibility because I was in the middle of filming a movie and then limped back to the car with my rear end killing me.

And, of course, the movie did go on.

It was embarrassing, but from that moment on, I sat on an inflatable doughnut-like ice-filled cushion between takes to rest my tailbone. Oh, how my bum ached after the dance sequences! But somehow and someway, I did them. My lifelong work ethic kicked in. This broken muse just shut up, gritted her teeth, and hoped that the magic of Xanadu would help her get through those moments between "action" and "cut." It turns out that my backside would be in pain for a long, long time after shooting—a little souvenir from the set.

And my tailbone incident happened unfortunately before we shot my actual roller-skating scenes. There was only one thing to do.

"No, I don't want a stunt double. Audiences will be able to tell," I told the director.

I got a little help pulling up my leg warmers, put a big smile on my face to hide the agony I was feeling, and was swept up in that moment of living in Xanadu as I rolled along.

We filmed for three months, took time off for Christmas, and then did reshoots until March 1980, including adding the gorgeous "Don't Walk Away" animation scene created by Disney's master artist Don Bluth. I loved that the little bird figure representing me in the cartoon part had on tiny leg warmers—the same color as the ones I wore in the movie.

Prior to our summer release, the singles of *Xanadu* were released on the radio, similar to Paramount's plan with *Grease*. It was a great move because I had number one hits in England, Europe, America, and Australia with the title track "Xanadu" and "Magic."

Side one of the soundtrack album featured my songs with John Farrar, and side two featured the songs of ELO. I did duets with Cliff Richard, the Tubes, and even Gene Kelly for it. The album went number one all over the world.

The film opened on August 8, 1980. The reviews weren't exactly stellar, which hurt. Roger Ebert gave it two stars, calling it "mushy and limp." Ouch! He did go on to say that there were still reasons to see the movie, including Gene and me, plus the soundtrack. One piece of ink that particularly stung was a headline in a newspaper that read: *Xana-don't!* But it's funny to me now.

I believe that movies find their audience, and this one was created with so much talent, love, and creativity, along with the desire to take risks and make a film that was utterly original. Over time, audiences embraced *Xanadu*, making it the cult hit that it is now. It's constantly on cable TV, and fans write that they watch it while dancing across their living rooms.

Even now, when I mention the movie, eyes light up. "It's a classic," I hear, and that makes me proud. People constantly talk to me about the making of the movie, and there are midnight showings and sing-alongs in the United States and Europe.

I still get letters from people who wonder if Xanadu exists because they want to move there! Or they write to tell me that they've seen the movie eight, nine, or ten times.

I think it all goes back to those amazing songs that I continue to sing in my shows and which get some of the biggest applause. I have to confess that "Magic" remains one of my all-time favorite songs, and I love how the words apply to my life. Thank you, John Farrar.

> *You have to believe we are magic*
> *Don't let your aim ever stray*
> *And if all your hopes survive*
> *Destiny will arrive*
> *I'll bring all your dreams alive*
> *For you*

The songs of the film *Xanadu* were not the only gift it gave me. Remember the young "Valentino" I met on the set? Matt Lattanzi was ten years younger than me but smart, sweet, and very handsome. I liked that Matt was very down-to-earth thanks to his upbringing in Portland, Oregon, where his dad, Charles, worked as a maintenance foreman and his mother, Jeanette, was a stay-at-home mom. We became good friends and soon we were having long talks in my trailer about movies, music, life, and our shared love of the environment.

He was a breath of fresh air who would soon become a very important part of my life.

NINE

Physical

Just before *Xanadu* premiered, I was shocked to discover that the prime minister of Australia had nominated me to receive an Order of the British Empire (OBE) from the queen.

I was excited when I heard about the nomination. I guess they chose me because I put Australia on the map by making the most popular high schooler on the planet, Sandy, an Aussie. Deep down, I could hardly believe it. I remembered that little girl coming over on the big boat from England, and now I was about to receive something so incredibly prestigious—from the queen of England.

The ceremony took place at Buckingham Palace with both of my beaming parents and my sister in attendance. It was a wonderful excuse to gather the family together. I remember standing there in my little white suit with my red hat and red gloves, next to a group of elegant gray-haired men in morning suits. We were all there to receive different kinds of awards, and some of the men were even being knighted. It was so impressive.

I stood behind the roped-off area while Queen Elizabeth II, looking so majestic in a perfect pink cashmere twinset and pearls (no crown), handed me my award and said a formal "Congratulations, dear!" It was such a regal moment with the beefeaters standing on both sides of the queen. She may have said more, but my heart was beating so loudly I couldn't hear anything.

I did a well-practiced curtsy and accepted the award, then searched for an exit sign and found a much-needed toilet at the bottom of a long stairwell. After "powdering my nose," I managed to actually fall up the stairs of the royal loo. Not many people can say that! I didn't hurt myself, but it remains an embarrassing and funny memory of a beautiful day.

Looking back, most of my success I owe to fellow Aussie and Commonwealth friends who produced me, wrote for me, or managed me over the years. The list of names is long—Peter Gormley, John Farrar, Roger Davies, Stevie Kipner, Peter Allen, Peter Hebbes, Fleur Thiemeyer, plus support systems including Lizzie Kipner and, of course, Pat. We have lovingly been referred to as the Aussie Mafia.

This brings me to another Aussie collaboration, called "Physical."

In 1981, Aussie songwriter Steve Kipner and British musician Terry Shaddick wrote a very catchy song called "Physical" for Tina Turner. Tina thought the lyrics were a bit sexy for her and suggested to Roger Davies, her manager and my friend, that they offer it to me. (Thanks, Tina!)

At the same time, Lee Kramer was managing a bodybuilder named Frank Zane who was Mr. World. Lee had heard the song

"Physical" in its early stages and thought it would be perfect for an upcoming Silver Surfer movie, based on the comic, that he had optioned for Frank to star in. Lee told me about the song and then casually asked, "Maybe you could sing it?"

I took a listen to a rough demo the songwriters had created and said, "Yeah, it's a really good song. It's very catchy."

I agreed to do it and went into the studio in LA, where my trusted John Farrar produced it for me. I loved what we did, but then had a panic attack about it. This song was raw and edgy. Maybe it was too raunchy? The lyrics had me singing: "There's nothing left to talk about unless it's horizontally!" In another moment, I'm crooning, "You gotta know that you're bringin' out the animal in me."

Stop, stop, stop! I was having a Sandy #1 moment!

All of a sudden, I didn't want to "hear my body talk." I didn't want to get physical!

I was flying back to America from a trip to London with my new manager, Roger Davies, when I began to freak out. "Maybe we shouldn't put it out," I fretted to Roger. "It's just too suggestive."

"Olivia was concerned that she would lose her wholesome girl-next-door image," Roger recalls. "I said, 'Don't worry, you can blame me.'"

It was too late to take it back anyway. The record company released it and "Physical" began climbing the charts.

Maybe if we redefined the idea of getting physical, it would take on a whole new meaning. That was my last-minute-panic suggestion.

"Let's make it about exercise . . . that's it! We can take the focus off the other part . . . Sort of like a double entendre," I suggested. "We can do this in a video."

"I persuaded Olivia into financing a full-length video of the entire *Physical* album with all thirteen songs," Roger remembers. "At the time, pop videos had only just begun, and Olivia became a pioneer of the genre with her introduction of plotlines into music videos."

We hired English director Brian Grant after I decided to take this big financial risk. Grant loved the concept of me working out at a gym doing actual aerobics (all the rage back in the day) while I sang the song to some rather big guys who really didn't want to exercise in the first place.

The final shot of the video is two guys walking out arm in arm. I never thought twice about this gay subplot. I've always had gay friends and family members. Love is love is love. I'm so proud of Australia's decision in 2017 to finally recognize gay marriage.

Of course, my look in the video was key. And it turned out to be perfect timing. As we got ready for the shoot, I was set to attend the Grammys. Armando Cosio met me at my hotel before the awards to decide what to do with my long hair. Armando was extremely talented, really funny, and adorable, plus I trusted him.

"Tell me about your outfit for the Grammys, Liv," he said, trying to find some hair inspiration. I was going to hit the red carpet in red jodhpurs and purple boots.

"What if we chop off your hair?" he asked, holding his breath and expecting a quick "no way." Long hair was still the most popular style.

"Okay," I said.

I've always been pretty adventurous, and it felt so liberating to let all that hair fall to the floor as a new, sleek look began to materialize. There is nothing like a little shearing to make you feel free!

I believe when you cut off your hair, you've shed the past, and a new look is always a great way to move forward.

That it was!

When it came to the "Physical" video, I asked my friend Fleur to design a look for it. She had been cutting up T-shirts for rock-and-roll artists for a long time, so on the set, she grabbed her pinking shears and chopped away. What was left was a blue cut-up shirt that she would tie over a white tank top and pink tights. She added a basic white headband. It was such a fun outfit that I joked, "I should start a clothing store."

Well, I did, but not until later!

The video was an instant hit. It taught me to not be so critical of myself and my choices. Now when I look back, I have to ask: *What the heck was I so worried about in the first place?*

It wasn't long before women at gyms across the country were dressed exactly like I was in that video. That haircut also became all the rage, and stores were selling out of headbands, while scissors everywhere were slashing old T-shirts. It turned out to be amusing and fun to think of myself as a trendsetter and to shake the world up a bit.

Let me hear your body talk indeed.

Fortunately, we sold *Let's Get Physical* to run as a prime-time TV special, which debuted on February 8, 1982. It was watched by 35 percent of the US viewing audience, and it picked up a Best Art Direction Emmy nomination. Meanwhile, "Physical" won a Grammy for Video of the Year in 1982. We never looked back. The single "Physical" went on to become number one for ten weeks in America while the video earned me a Grammy Award and global recognition.

There was some flak along the way, too. In Utah, I found my song banned from the local radio stations, which was a career first for me!

By the way, we shot the *Physical* album cover on the beach in Hawaii with the wonderful, world-renowned photographer Herb Ritts, who became my good friend. He was such a lovely gentleman and sadly died in 2002. I will never forget him creating an iconic photo of me in a red tank top with a white headband, head tilted back, and wet from a dip in the ocean.

"Physical" would become my biggest hit, and Billboard would eventually list it as number one in its Top 50 Sexiest Songs of All Time, number one in its Top 100 Songs of the 1980s, and number six in its All-Time Top 100. Pretty amazing!

Seems like the things in life that I was most afraid of ended up working for me. This was raunchy and out of my comfort zone, but it did take my career to another level. To think I was so worried about this song at that time seems funny. Compared to what's on the radio today, it sounds like a lullaby, don't you think?

The big lesson is I learned to face my fear—and do it anyway.

By 1983, I was ready to take a break from touring, which takes so much discipline and is both exhilarating and exhausting. I've always found that if I keep changing beds every night, I hardly sleep at all. My routine on the road was I'd work out for an hour before going onstage, or even enjoy a game of tennis to unwind. I have always been careful to eat all the right foods and get enough rest to counter the stresses of road life.

All the travel and wear and tear was worth the wonderful feeling of singing onstage. It was never about the applause. I just love to sing. I was always realistic that the next night they would be standing, cheering, and flicking their lighters for someone else.

Mum would come out on tour with me several times a year, and she turned out to be quite outgoing on the road. She was an excellent photographer, and when she became good friends with Los Angeles Mayor Tom Bradley, she took several great shots of him.

Mum made great friends across the world. She was like a real-life Auntie Mame! Mum always loved people and nature—two traits I inherited from her. She also taught me to not take things for granted, a lesson that I would rely on time and time again in the future.

After *Xanadu* was a bit of a flop, I wasn't offered many more movie roles. But there was one exception. More than anything, film producers were constantly trying to find ways to reunite John Travolta and me in a movie and recapture some of that *Grease* chemistry. We wanted to do something together, but there just wasn't a lot of good "somethings" around.

We were finally handed a script by director/writer John Herzfeld called *Two of a Kind*. Originally, we passed, but then we reconsidered. John and I agreed that what was on paper needed work, but it was kind of cute. In the end, we said yes simply to work together again.

The plot revolved around God having just about enough of

human attitude, so he plans to destroy the planet. A quartet of bleeding-heart angels ask for a deal: if they can find two truly good souls, Earth will survive. Unfortunately, the angels stake the future of the species on a thieving bank teller, Debbie (me), and Zack (John), an inventor/con artist.

I loved reuniting with John, but I also enjoyed that in this role I would be able to show a range of emotions including rage, anger, hysteria, and tears. Prior to filming, I worked with an incredible acting coach named Warren Robertson in New York.

There was a scene in the film where I had to do a major break-down. I could hear in my head how I wanted to do it, but somewhere between my brain and my lips were inhibitions, and I knew that I had to get through those.

Warren helped unlock the door between my head and my mouth. That's the only way to describe it. I always remember Warren telling me, "No one knows what you're thinking to get to the emotional place you need to go. It's not written on your forehead."

On set, I was still having a little trouble getting into the scene when John Travolta appeared. Right before my close-up, he came up and said something out of character and sort of mean to me. It really shook me. When I did the actual scene, I was able to cry and be hysterical. When the director yelled cut, John smiled. He'd done it on purpose. He just wanted to help me get to that place of emotion. Again, John helped me with my acting like he did in Grease.

He had just finished filming Staying Alive, the sequel to Saturday Night Fever, and was in incredible physical shape. He had his own personal trainer, Dan Isaacson, so I started working out with John and Dan. Every day before rehearsals, we did a dance class and hit the free weights in the gym. The three of us had so much fun together and got on really well. We've remained friends for life.

The film premiered in December 1983 and proved to be a box-office disappointment, but luckily the soundtrack had some great music in it, including the song "Twist of Fate," written by Peter Beckett and Steve Kipner and produced by David Foster.

I guess *Grease* was a hard act to follow.

Soon after, I would branch out with another former partner. My dear friend and ex–singing partner Pat Farrar, who had been married to John for quite a while by then, wanted a new challenge. I had just returned from Australia and said, "Oh, Pat, what I wouldn't give for a milkshake and an Aussie meat pie! Don't you miss 'em?"

This wasn't the first time I'd felt like this. When I was on the road with my Aussie manager Roger Davies and his then wife Nanette, we would talk about home a lot and the things we missed, particularly the special chocolates, cookies, and other treats from our childhoods.

One day I began thinking it might be fun to open a little place where all the Australians could hang out. The English had Tudor House in Santa Monica, but there really wasn't an Aussie place. On my birthday that year, I had a little party, and Pat and John were there. That was the first time I told her about the idea. She shared that she had been thinking about opening a boutique where she would sell clothes. Both wide-eyed and bushy-tailed, we decided to combine those dreams. It felt good to be a duo again.

Then Pat and I were on our way to Australia together to do our favorite thing—shop! We brought several empty suitcases because this was a business trip. We had decided to open a store called Koala Blue. Part of it would be a real Australian milk bar, with newspapers and fast food, milkshakes and lollies, and in the rest of the store, we'd sell all manner of things Australian. My sudden homesickness would be cured!

It was true that we knew nothing about the retail business, but once again Pat and I decided to conquer the world with hard work, a sense of humor, and our Aussie can-do spirit. What else did we need? We arrived in Sydney and walked through the Rocks, where we found Ken Done's store. We were really taken with his cartoon-like koalas. Quite innocently, we went inside and asked him to design a logo for us. He created it in scarlet, sunshine yellow, emerald green, royal blue, and hot pink.

We found a great location on Melrose Avenue in Los Angeles, which was a funky, upcoming area where we could afford the rent. We even managed to get a license to serve Aussie beer and wine right away. That was unheard of, and I don't know why the city let us have it, but they did and we were stunned. Pat and I were always a great team.

As for the meat pies, an Aussie favorite, unfortunately we couldn't get a license to bring them in from Australia. We heard about a Texas company that was making the real thing, so we flew out there for a pie tasting. It wasn't quite as a good as a wine tasting, but it was still fun. By the way, they were delicious.

In early 1983, at the grand opening at 7366 Melrose Avenue, Dame Edna Everage didn't smash a bottle of champagne but instead broke a bottle of Vegemite against the wall. This is a very salty Aussie staple that you have to grow up with to love. At least the Australian yachting team, who came to our opening, appreciated the joke. I encouraged our American guests to "try the Vegemite. You've got to try it. At least once!"

I just love it with avocado on toast. Maybe I'll start a whole new trend here!

Reporters asked me about the name, so I explained that we thought about a million different ones. I came up with the most Australian thing I could think of: Koala. When we were driving around Sydney Harbour with that gorgeous azure sky, Pat came up with Blue. It was a shared-duo thing yet again. There we had it: Koala Blue. I always loved acronyms, and amusingly, I realized that the letters of koala might also stand for Korner of Australia in Los Angeles.

We printed up some T-shirts to give away at the opening with our Koala Blue logo on them. We had some left over and, not knowing what else to do with them, we put them up for sale in the store. We were sold out within two hours, so we made more shirts and found we couldn't keep them in stock. We added sweatshirts to the line, and they flew off the shelves before we could blink.

What we found in the coming months was that the people were not just hungry for meat pies and milkshakes but also for Australian fashion and anything with Koala Blue on it. That's when we expanded into a full-on retail clothing business, which was thrilling. Pat and I couldn't contain our excitement at our new venture. We got to shop globally four times a year for "business reasons" and took full advantage of it! We even hired our own designer, Linda, who helped us put our ideas into production.

No matter how busy I was touring or recording, I never ever missed a KB shopping trip. Pat and I loved designing those semi-fitted sweatshirts, flowing rayon skirts with lace petticoats underneath, and oversize sweaters that were so chic and comfortable. We purchased fun aluminum earrings that were hand-painted in Australia and other goodies. Pat and I had similar tastes, so it was easy for us to agree on the look. Often, we'd show up at work with the same outfit on!

I lived in Koala Blue clothes during those years because they were the kind of comfortable, go-to fashions that felt and looked good. I would get out of bed, toss on a Koala Blue shirt over jeans, and start the day.

It wasn't long before we expanded into books, jewelry, children's clothing, and artwork. Even the candles were imported. To keep the "down under" vibe going strong, the store featured a video screen playing all the Aussie bands and, of course, Australian football—Aussie rules!

Our milk bar was perfect for when I had a yen to go back home. It was a seven-seater where we sold milkshakes, plus Aussie snacks like lamingtons (vanilla sponge cake frosted with chocolate and sprinkled with coconut—give me some now!), Violet Crumbles, Tim Tams (our favorite cookies), and Caramello Koalas.

Eventually, we expanded into a number of exotic locations across the world, including Japan, Canada, Australia, Singapore, Hong Kong, and Hawaii. We went to nearly all the openings, where we'd serve Australian bubbly. At one point, we even had our own KB wine.

We were a big hit for quite a few years, and I enjoyed having the stores as a new creative outlet. As for the business part, we left it up to the CEOs and business managers to deal with the bottom line. By 1990, there were thirteen corporate-owned stores, financed by me and Pat (our first mistake), and forty-nine licensed stores around the world.

By 1991, sadly, our Koala Blue company had to file for bankruptcy after eight years of being in business. Sales had started to falter due to rough economic times. We'd also expanded too fast, and when the recession hit, we got badly hurt. I felt terrible for the investors who'd lost a lot of money, as we did.

We were partners and would go through this together. When we went through legal trouble in 1992, the powerhouse lawyer representing us, Marshall Grossman, suggested we each get our own lawyer. He was shocked when we looked at him and said, "No matter what happens, we're in this together. Fifty-fifty." We were a duo—even when things went wrong. Unfortunately, we did the one thing you're never supposed to do in business, which was invest our own money.

It was a sad ending to a lovely dream.

TEN

Warm and Tender

*You're the dream that I knew you'd be
And I love you completely, my Chloe.*

In the early eighties, with my career going strong, I was ready to make another major change in my life. Matt and I began to see each other more seriously during the last months of shooting *Xanadu*.

It was a romantic time, and also one that made me laugh when he would stay with me at my hotel. In the morning, the hair and makeup artist from the film would arrive early and Matt would hide in the cupboard with a blanket and pillow, so he could get a few extra winks of sleep without anyone (except his girlfriend—me!) knowing he was there. The minute we would hear the knock on the door, he would grab his pillow and go hide.

No one knew that we had our first kiss at Will Rogers State Historic Park while taking a hike during production. Enough of my life was out in the world for public consumption.

I was keeping this for myself.

Living in our own little world was not only fun but also a smart choice. We wanted to keep it private because the last thing I needed was splashy headlines about my personal life. Only my most inner circle were aware that I was crazy about Matt, who loved to be in nature and enjoyed the same simple pleasures I did.

Some of the nicest memories I have of those times were driving into the wilderness and either camping out or sleeping in a van. So much for craving a posh lifestyle! Give me a moon, stars, and a tent! We'd go for long walks and hikes up into the mountains and sleep by a beautiful, tranquil lake. In the mornings, we'd catch fresh fish for breakfast before hiking up a rocky path to places unknown. It was so peaceful, which was the exact opposite of my busy life on tour. We even went to Napa Valley with my dad, and Matt drove us around to all the gorgeous vineyards for lazy days of wine tastings and delicious food.

Eventually Matt moved into my Malibu house with the horses, dogs, and cats, who all adored him. He was natural and refreshing. Matt liked to drive and took me on splendidly long road trips. These were all things I'd missed because I'd started working at such a young age. I've always thought that Matt was helping me live the childhood that I never experienced.

I loved how Matt came from a big family of nine siblings. My parents lived in different cities, and I grew up in part as an only child after my brother and sister moved away. His big, friendly family with all their laughter and energy around me felt like a warm blanket. When I was with Matt's family, I was just his girlfriend— nothing more or less. I did the dishes and helped his mom stir the spaghetti sauce. There was none of the big-star stuff.

One of Matt's sisters, Brenda, then sixteen, latched on to me like I was a big sister. I adored her and took her under my wing.

There was no talk of Hollywood or rock stars or "who do you know?" There was simply great food, and quite a lot of it, always on the stove, in the oven, and on the table—plus lots of fun and laughter. Matt's mom was Polish, and his dad was Italian, and both loved to spend time in the kitchen creating something delicious. The holidays we spent with them were exactly what I craved.

Matt and I traveled a lot, and I enjoyed seeing the world with him. I can't remember him formally proposing or even calling my dad in Australia to ask for my hand. All of a sudden, we were simply making wedding plans, despite the fact that the magazines screamed that there was an age gap between us. What age gap? Who cared?

Matt and I had been together for five years and we were at the point of: get married now or forget it. Relationships need to move forward, and this was our next step. I decided to take the plunge, despite my fears of marriage.

I was terrified to marry Matt, but this had nothing to do with him as a person. I was petrified of marriage because I was so afraid of divorce, since I'd suffered emotionally from my parents' breakup. I'd also watched Rona go through two divorces that were not pretty, and that took my fear level into the red.

When the time came, though, to my amazement, I said those vows with no trepidation. On December 15, 1984, we were married at my ranch with seventy close friends, my mom, dad, sister, and brother, plus Matt's entire family in attendance. It rained that day, but that didn't dampen our joy—not even for a minute. My beautiful dog Jackson was my ring bearer, and we tied the ring to his collar. Jackson was always attached to me like glue—including at the altar.

We honeymooned in Paris, where Matt bought me a beautiful pearl and diamond engagement ring. We had never done things in the supposed right order—but it worked for us.

I was pregnant and found out while we were planning the wedding. I lost the baby. I had a few miscarriages during my marriage, and each time my heart was broken.

In 1985, I suspected I might be pregnant again. I had been craving avocados for days. Racing off to the store, I couldn't wait to get home and take one of those over-the-counter pregnancy tests. I was thirty-seven at the time, peeing on a stick, and the news was great. I was going to have a baby!

What made it even sweeter was the fact that my dear girlfriend Nancy and her new husband, Jim, married within a few months of us, soon also found out that they were pregnant. I had told her to "hurry up," so we could do this together. We were due at the same time and even went to the same obstetrician. "We're having twins," Nancy and I would joke. It was so much fun to go through our pregnancies with each other.

We went through her morning sickness (I was fine and didn't throw up once), bought all the books of what to expect while we were expecting, and planned our future nurseries while waddling around our homes. Nancy would call me with graphic descriptions of her bathroom bouts, and I would say, "I'm sorry, love. I was a bit out of sorts this morning, had a spot of tea, and it settled down."

One evening we took Nancy and Jim to a party at Sandy Gallin's house in Beverly Hills. Sandy was one of the most powerful managers in the entertainment industry and was even part of the team that booked the Beatles for their first appearance on *The Ed Sullivan Show*. He worked with Elizabeth Taylor, Cher, Dolly Parton, Whoopi Goldberg, and Michael Jackson. Sandy was the person who helped me fall in love with orchids because beautiful ones were all over his house.

His parties were major events, and at this one we were treated to a psychic's revelation about the upcoming births of our children. The psychic told me, "Your child is a teacher. She is going to come into the world to help you learn. The baby will change your life and is an old soul."

I couldn't wait to meet my special gift.

I absolutely loved being pregnant and took a break from my touring life to enjoy this charmed time. All I wanted to do was to experience it while hanging out at home. My third-trimester days were spent on my comfy floral couch in my favorite pale-blue oversize KB T-shirt knotted over my right hip and matching long skirts. I loved the tiny bulge protruding from my tummy that slowly turned into a large round bump. Matt and I were so excited about impending parenthood.

We decided to remodel the Malibu ranch house. I wanted to add a couple of rooms for the baby and made sure they would be ready for my due date. I wanted this done, but I was also superstitious about it and didn't want to do too much before he or she was born. For the longest time, I didn't even buy any maternity clothes. I didn't want to know if I was having a boy or a girl. I wouldn't tempt fate.

We did go over a few names: Chloe for a girl; Jesse for a boy. Chloé perfume was my favorite at the time, as was the clothing line.

I was still nervous because of the past miscarriages, but I pushed past that mentally and adopted a positive outlook. *This time it would be fine.* With the passing of each week, I was getting more excited, but I remained practical, too. I had ultrasounds to put my mind at ease; even though deep down in my heart I knew everything was fine, at my age, I still needed a little medical peace of mind. When I had my amniocentesis, my fears were calmed when I found out that the baby was healthy (thank God).

"Do you want to know if it's a girl or a boy?" Dr. Edward Liu, my hilarious ob-gyn, asked. (He is still in my life, and we joke that we've been "together" longer than I've been with any other man I've known.)

I didn't want to know, and neither did Matt. We craved the surprise.

At thirty-eight, I was considered an older mother, so I was being closely monitored. I even gave up my vigorous workout regimen. In those days, they called pregnant women over thirty-five "elderly multigravidas," which sounded just awful. I didn't dwell on that not-so-subtle ageism and just listened to Dr. Liu's advice. My exercise consisted of gentle walks and swims. I ate right, stayed mellow, and took up gardening and knitting. I even tried the pottery wheel until I couldn't get close enough to it with my belly. Somewhere I still have an orange handmade sweater and a blue, pink, and yellow baby blanket that I knitted myself.

Physical? Forget it! My feet were up on the couch. The rockstar siren image from my *Soul Kiss* album cover, the one shot by Helmut Newton? Who was that woman? I was just a pregnant lady with swollen ankles and a big tummy.

I began to ease past my fears and even began planning to attend a Lamaze class. My real dream was to birth my baby underwater with the dolphins. I actually made inquiries to see if that was possible, but I was talked out of it because of my age. Rona had been

through a few natural deliveries and it just took a quick call from
her to calm me down when it came to my options.

Meanwhile, my mum was over the moon! She sent little
smocked dresses like the ones she made for me as a little girl, plus
crib blankies and other baby goodies from Australia. Her advice to
me was to get exercise, stay calm, and rub olive oil on my stomach
daily to avoid stretch marks. Mum already had plans to come visit
after I had the baby to help out.

Matt and I also talked about the future and where we would
raise the baby. We thought that Australia might be a better place to
raise a family because the air is so clean, the food is pure, and there
would be fewer security issues. At the time, I thought we would
quickly have a second child. "A boy and a girl," we vowed.

This was also an important time of reevaluation for me. My
music was still going well, but I was really focused on what was
important in my life and wouldn't allow my career to control my
personal happiness.

Every night, I would sleep with my hands on my stomach and
feel the baby kick.

This was what mattered.

Just before Christmas in 1985, I felt several sharp, stabbing pains
racing through my midsection. It was much too early for the baby,
who was due in March, so Matt raced me in to see my ob-gyn. It
was one of those heart-stopping moments where you're holding
your breath for the news. Dr. Liu informed me that it was possible
that I could be having late-term miscarriage.

In that moment, I didn't panic.

Miscarriage? *I wouldn't hear of it.*

"What can we do?" I asked. The answer was that I would be put on complete bed rest, which meant a few steps around the house a day and showering, but that was it for me for the next eight to ten weeks. Hopefully, it wouldn't be that long until I gave birth.

That wasn't meant to be.

A few weeks after the New Year in 1986, I was taking a shower and, while soaping up, my water broke. It was a beautiful sunny day, and I remember washing off and then going downstairs to calmly tell Matt that he was about to become a father. He held it together pretty well, although I know he was crazy nervous on our drive from Malibu to Cedars-Sinai hospital.

It was still too soon for the baby to come into the world.

But someone didn't want to wait any longer.

I still wanted to have a natural birth, but I wasn't dilating. I was in labor for seventeen hours. It was such slow progress that the doctors were forced to give me a drug called Pitocin, a synthetic form of a hormone that your body processes naturally during labor. It sped up the contractions and also helped me to relax, because seventeen hours was a long time for both me and the baby to be in this kind of stress.

As labor progressed, I was exhausted, cranky as hell (every mother knows exactly what I mean), and facing a dreaded epidural, while Matt was completely hyper and filming away with a video camera. By this time, I wasn't shy. If you told me I'd be lying there with my legs wide open, lights on me, a spotlight on my crotch, and someone with a video camera shooting my every move . . . Well, by then, nothing embarrasses you anymore. The pain wipes away the shyness.

As we were about to hit hour eighteen, I accepted the offer

of an epidural because the pain was pretty intense. I went numb immediately, and that part was heaven.

I had heard horror stories about epidurals, and I hadn't wanted one. In fact, it terrified me more than childbirth. It would turn out that my fears were warranted in this case because the needle hit my spinal cord.

Funny how life works.

I believe sometimes fear is an invitation. If you spend a lot of energy fearing something, no matter how hard you try to avoid it there are times when you end up having to deal with it—at least that's been true in my life.

I know this is going to sound crazy, but at the last minute, after seventeen hours of labor, I had one simple request.

"Matt, can you find my lipstick?" I asked.

"What?" he said in an amazed voice.

I had to put on my favorite coral lipstick because I wanted the baby to see me looking nice when she came out! It's amazing the things that become important in times of extreme chaos.

Or maybe I was delirious from all the pain, which was now gone, thanks to that shot.

The love of my life came into this world a few weeks prematurely on January 17, 1986. She made her debut at 5:17 in the morning, and it is no surprise that seventeen is now my lucky number.

After a quick exam, the doctor put Chloe in my arms for the first time. She was the most beautiful angel, newborn pink and perfect, with bright blue eyes and fair hair. Thank God, she was perfectly healthy even though she was early. I remember staring into those pure, innocent eyes for the first time and starting to laugh.

I was overwhelmed, bursting with love and smiling like crazy because my baby brought me so much joy. Chloe was also so funny from moment one. Her little facial expressions made me giggle. They say you are what you are when you're born. I could see this beautiful, funny child as she slept in my arms.

This was life on a setting known as perfection.

When the epidural wore off, I had the headache of the century and was shivering and shaking. The epidural had actually punctured my spinal column and I was leaking fluid. My regular internist, Dr. Giorgi, a practical, wonderful female version of Lieutenant Columbo, stepped in and ordered a spinal patch. This meant they were planning to take blood out of my arm and inject it into my spine to cause a blood clot to stop the leakage. All of a sudden, I felt like a plumbing disaster instead of a new mother.

This "glitch" was actually quite major. I had to endure a second epidural, which unfortunately didn't work. I was terribly afraid, and I couldn't sit up for about a month afterward.

The miracle of Chloe's arrival into my life made everything else insignificant by comparison. Babies have a way of wiping every slate clean. But I couldn't deny the pain.

The headaches were so bad that I had to mainly stay in bed for the first few months of Chloe's life because getting up and down was excruciating. I was lucky enough to have a nanny to help and bring my baby to me for breastfeeding. I did that for a long time, and that skin-to-skin contact with my child was an experience that can't even be put into words.

I had the best times with my beautiful new daughter. Chloe was a natural actress from the day she was born. She would make funny faces to get attention (not entirely unlike her mother), and eventually would love to sing as much as I did. All I wanted to do was watch her grow and develop, and it was the most joyful and magical time. The love that I had for my child was a love I had never experienced before in my life.

It was overwhelming that I had this tiny human being to take care of and protect. I knew every choice I made and everything I did would affect her for life. I could always be found hovering over her crib to make sure she was breathing.

I wish you could bottle the feeling of a dark night in a sweet-smelling nursery, watching your happy and safe child sleep.

This was why I was born.

Sadly, there was a bit of anxiety mixed in with my joy. The headaches went on for five long years and were pretty severe at times. I would sleep in dark rooms until they went away.

It took my body a long time to heal itself.

Six weeks after I gave birth to Chloe, on March 3, 1986, Nancy and Jim Chuda, my dear, dear friends, had their daughter, a beautiful fair-haired baby girl they named Colette. I was so honored when I was asked to be her godmother. It was as if we each had two daughters, and we knew the girls would grow up as sisters and best friends. From that moment on, we did everything together and went everywhere as one big, happy family.

The joyous cries of those baby girls filled every space.

As for getting back to work, I was getting there—slowly. When Nancy and I were still pregnant, we collaborated on a screenplay called *The Perfect Specimen*. We were actually way ahead of our time with this idea. We were talking about Matt, how perfect he was for fathering a child, and we wrote a whole story in which a woman can't find the right man to father her baby, so she goes to a sperm bank to find "the perfect specimen." When she gets pregnant, the hunt begins to find the anonymous donor.

I remember Nancy and I taking our babies into Universal Studios and sitting on the floor with them for a pitch meeting with one of the most powerful female executives in the movie business at the time, Dawn Steel, who sadly later died of breast cancer.

During the meeting, Chloe had fallen asleep on my right breast and it grew swollen with milk to the point where it looked like a bowling ball. I had a privacy blanket over me, and, luckily, we left before I had milk running down my shirt.

The studio optioned it from us, but sadly it was eventually dropped when John Hughes made a similar film called *She's Having a Baby*.

We didn't much care. We were raising our daughters side by side in the haven of Malibu. That far outweighed the time we would have spent on some tumultuous movie set fighting with script doctors over lines.

It was a playful, joyous time for my family, and it wasn't a bit surprising to anyone that the next album I did was for my daughter.

It turned out Chloe was not a good sleeper, and I spent many a night trying to soothe her. I searched for the right music to lull her to sleep, and I couldn't find it. There was one easy solution that could turn into a family legacy. I recorded *Warm and Tender*, an album of children's lullabies, in Melbourne live with the beautiful and world-renowned Victorian Philharmonic Orchestra. It was produced by my bestie John Farrar, with orchestrations by Graeme Lyall. These were classic, timeless songs, and I wrote the title track with John, "Warm and Tender," for Chloe.

For the most part, I put my career on hold to really experience life as a wife and mother. Matt was a wonderful father, and soon we went on family car trips. He even took us camping when Chloe got a bit older. Our greatest love was having family adventures—even if there were a few not-so-great moments.

In Wyoming with Nancy, Jim, and Colette, we were going to explore the wilderness, and even stayed with a friend who owned a hunting lodge. By now, the girls were two years old, toddling about and talking, and they were smarter than anyone knew. Both grew up loving animals, so they were a bit freaked out to see the deer and other big animal heads on the walls of that lodge, which was a sadly common thing.

Chloe kept trying to go behind each wall to see where the rest of the animal was. She was determined that each animal could be freed to go live a happy life in the mountains.

Poor Nancy and I had to explain to the girls that the animal bodies . . . um . . . weren't there anymore. We couldn't very well say that some mean people shot them and stuffed them. Talk about giving your two-year-olds nightmares!

Try telling even the simple version to a hysterical two-year-old who couldn't deal with the fact that anyone would take the heads off such beautiful creatures. The girls were so upset that I thought we might have to find another place to stay for the trip. Using some newly acquired motherly ingenuity, Nancy and I ran around putting large bath towels over the animal heads so they would be "out of sight" and thus "out of mind."

We had so many mommy adventures back in the day. When the girls were about two and a half, all of us flew to my farm in Australia for a live filming of a Christmas program where I would sing "Waltzing Matilda." Chloe and Colette loved the great outdoors and had so much room to run in the fields on the farm. We were always worried about those dreaded brown snakes biting two trusting little babies, so we kept an eagle eye on the girls as all of us frolicked in the sun and our plastic swimming pool. Poor baby Colette did get stung by a jellyfish during one of our swims at the beach and had to be rushed to an ER. She never cried even once; she was so brave.

These were such happy times for me. I loved that the girls were so grubby by the end of the day that we would dunk them together in the tub and then transfer their clothes straight into the washing machine. The truth was, I loved doing the washing and hanging it outside on the Hills Hoist, where it would dry, making it smell so delicious from the flowers and fresh Aussie winds.

My other great joy was fueling the girls with organic and delicious food. At the farmhouse, I was always at the stove cooking up Chloe's favorite dish, tofu rice. I'd make Vegemite soldiers with toast. All of us would sit on the terrace, eat, and watch the cows wander in the pasture down below.

We did try a trip without the kids once, with Sarah, our nanny, staying with the girls while we took a couples' trip with Nancy and Jim to Alaska, where we stayed at Yes Bay Lodge. There were many warnings about bears, but we still took our hikes in the woods, where I did an impromptu a cappella concert and sang my heart out to an audience of trees. Someone told me that singing was a way to keep bears away—the opposite of my usual goal of drawing fans in! This time, I really didn't want to participate in a meet and greet.

I remember watching in horror as Matt stood under a tree way too close to a mama bear's cubs. "Matt!" I yelled. "You are much too close. Get out of there."

I sang even louder.

*

In 1988 I had the honor of performing for HRH Princess Diana in the Australian bicentennial concert in Sydney with Cliff Richard. I remember the princess being very beautiful and charming. Unfortunately, I can't remember what she said to me. At the time, she was nowhere near the legend she would become before her untimely death, but I was grateful to meet her. She was very special, and I could feel the kindness in her eyes.

I was almost entirely focused on Chloe, though, and no matter what I was doing, whether it was singing for royalty or promoting an album, all I could think of was getting back to her.

Back at home, I decided I wanted the *Warm and Tender* album cover to feature me with Chloe and Colette in each of my arms. The principal photography took place on our lot for a new house overlooking the Pacific, with both girls dressed in white. Colette wore a tiny brooch from her grandmother while Chloe wore my locket. Both girls were comfortable with cameras, but for some reason Chloe was fussy that afternoon and wouldn't kiss her mom. There was no time to spare as the sun dipped low over the ocean.

Like any younger "sibling," Colette would go one better. As the sky turned the most gorgeous color of purple-pink she stroked the back of my blond hair and then smacked a big kiss on her godmother's lips. (She was so proud of herself!)

I used the photograph of Colette kissing me for the album cover. Little did I know how significant that picture would turn out to be.

ELEVEN

The Flower That Shattered the Stone

In the hearts of the children, a pure love still grows. . . .
Like the flower that shattered the stone.

In 1990, we were on holiday in Colorado Springs with Nancy, Jim, and Colette. The girls were four and running around in their little knitted gloves and warm ski suits. Suddenly Colette stopped and complained of a bad tummy ache. We wouldn't see her play anymore for a couple of days after Nancy tucked her into bed. A worried Nancy told me that, unlike a twenty-four-hour flu, this just wasn't passing. Her baby was still in pain and it seemed to be getting worse.

She went home to her pediatrician, who did tests, and I remember thinking, *It won't be bad. She just needs a little medicine.*

The doctor pulled Nancy and Jim aside and told them every parent's worst nightmare. He thought that Colette might have a serious kidney tumor. Tests followed, and soon the results were in. I was one of the first to learn that she had a very rare form of kidney cancer called Wilms' tumor, usually only found in children under the age of five and people over forty.

All I could do was to be there for Nancy, Jim, and our beautiful Colette.

It was almost unimaginable to watch this formerly healthy little girl, who ran like the wind and explored the world with such curiosity, slow down and become sicker and sicker. It wasn't long before she began suffering terrible pain, and then she had to deal with the side effects of chemotherapy, including nausea, lack of energy, and the loss of her baby-fine hair.

It was heartbreaking for all of us, and even more tragic because her father, Jim, had just lost his eighteen-year-old son, Andy, a handsome and delightful young man, a few months prior in a surfing accident. Nancy had also recently lost her brother, John.

I had another miscarriage and wasn't sure if I would ever carry another child to term. This was devastating—I so wanted Chloe to have a sibling. So while we were dealing with all this tragedy, Matt and I decided to adopt a child from Romania. The idea struck me after I wandered into an antiques shop one day and met a wonderful woman who had seen the heartrending pictures of Romanian orphans on TV. When she spotted a particular little boy, she turned to her husband and said out of the blue, "That's my son." She went off to Romania to find that actual child, which she eventually did, and brought him back as her son. Not long after the adoption papers were filed, she returned to adopt his sister.

This story was so inspiring, and I knew that there were an overwhelming number of orphaned babies there. Could one of them be our son or daughter?

As our darling Colette grew weaker, my heart broke at how Chloe would protect her best friend. Once, when Colette was feeling stronger, we took the girls to Disney World in Florida. By this time Colette was bald and in a wheelchair a lot of the time. All the kids passing her would stare, and some would point. Chloe was so protective of her "sister" and just couldn't stand it. She even told a few: "Don't stare at my friend. It's not nice!"

The love that the girls had for each other touched my heart. For Colette's last birthday party, we had an Easter egg hunt in a garden with the girls holding hands and enjoying a beautiful spring day. It would be one of their last play sessions together, and Chloe did her best to make sure Colette was having fun.

Not long after this, I had to go to Spain briefly to do a TV show. It was an obligation of mine that I couldn't cancel. On the way back, I was planning to go to Romania to find a sister or brother for Chloe. In fact, my suitcase was filled with clothes and toys for the new child. I think it was my gut instinct that this was something I needed to do.

I never made it to Romania.

Backstage in Spain, an hour before I was supposed to perform, I got a phone call from Matt. I learned that after a courageous time spent on this earth and having suffered more than any child ever should (or any adult, for that matter), our beautiful and darling Colette had died. She was just five years old.

I didn't want to perform.

But I couldn't leave.

How could I sing? But how could I not?

They had flown me all the way to Spain for the show, and I had no choice but to get out there and entertain the people. *The show must go on.* For once, I hated my old adage. I steeled myself as I prepared to fulfill my obligation. In my dressing room, my body told me that there wasn't a signed contract in the world that could handle the next few hours. My hands shook and I couldn't stop crying. How would we live without our Colette? All I wanted to do was get on the next plane, throw my arms around Chloe, and be there for Nancy and Jim.

I allowed my tears to flow—I was utterly heartbroken. My emotions were completely out of control, and I didn't know how in the world I could sing "I Honestly Love You" without falling to my knees and weeping in front of the audience. What if I started to cry and I couldn't breathe or get the words out? *I just lost my second child*, I thought. *What happens if I break down right in the middle of the song?*

There was only one thing to do.

"Colette," I said out loud before taking the stage, "I know you're with me. Please show me you're here so I have the strength to walk out on that stage and sing."

In the next moment, I felt what can best be described as a rush of cool air. It was like a caress, as if something had lovingly brushed up against my face, and it reminded me of that day in Malibu shooting the album cover. It felt like a wing, and it was so very real. It was as if she was telling me that it was okay. To go on.

With a newfound strength, I walked out on that stage and began to sing.

> *Maybe I hang around here a little more than I should*
> *We both know I got somewhere else to go*
> *But I got something to tell you that I never thought I would,*
> *But I believe you really ought to know.*
> *I love you.*
> *I honestly love you.*

I wasn't fine, but I sang well that night for Colette, and I didn't break down onstage because I knew that a little angel was with me. In a strange sort of way, she felt closer than before when she was in the hospital, and she has been with me ever since, along with my parents, my sister, and other close friends who have passed away, like Karen Carpenter and John Denver. I often feel as if they hover around me, especially when I perform. They are two of my spirit guides who I ask to support me before every show, and they keep me strong and focused.

They're gone, but their love never dies.

I'm not sure how any parent gets through the anguish of losing a child. It was hard enough being Colette's godmother. What if the fates were reversed? Each night I could barely stop staring at my Chloe sleeping peacefully in her bed.

Nancy and Jim, who are devout Buddhists, chanted their way through the agony, and poured their pain and grief into starting a foundation. They began to suspect that Colette's illness was a result of environmental toxins and formed the Children's Health Environmental Coalition. I was proud to help them start this worthwhile foundation that is now called Healthy Child Healthy World (www.healthychild.org). It helps educate parents to protect their children and families from harmful environmental toxins.

I became the national spokesperson, and of the many hats I have worn in this life, this one is particularly close to my heart. Their logo still features Colette's silhouette.

One of our first successful fund-raisers included sponsorship from HUD, the Housing Urban Development governmental agency, and we were thrilled to honor Senator Barbara Boxer during our first big fund-raising concert. Erin Brockovich joined our board. We even did a special evening called Friends for the Environment with an all-star cast including Meryl Streep, Goldie Hawn, Cher, Bette Midler, Robin Williams, and Lily Tomlin. Clint Black and Kenny Loggins joined me onstage to sing. There were also several private events. There was a special anthem written for the charity by longtime friend Joe Henry and John Jarvis called "The Flower that Shattered the Stone," which will become the title of my dear friend Nancy's memoir.

In 1997, I traveled to Sundance to meet with Robert Redford, who helped us create a children's health summit. John Travolta's wife, Kelly Preston, worked with us on a video about children's health called *Not Under My Roof,* which became a huge educational tool. Later, I went with Jim, Nancy, and Kelly to Washington, DC, for a congressional gathering in which Hillary Clinton and Senator Boxer spoke of the most important mission on earth: protecting our children.

Children are our future, and they really deserve to live in a world with clean air, water, and food.

After Colette passed, I never went forward with the adoption because my hands were full and my heart took a long time to mend. Instead, I put my energy into this work. I served as the goodwill ambassador for the United Nations Environment Programme. The environment is something so close to my heart, and I was so proud to carry that banner for them. Later, during my recovery from breast cancer, I would write an album called *Gaia,* with the following lyrics:

I am your mother—born of the sun.
I gave you shelter—what have you done?

Your heart's in turmoil—my world's in pain.
I need to turn you back home again.

I felt so closely connected to the earth at that time that I wrote it from Mother Earth's perspective because I felt her pain so deeply.

Nancy and Jim remain two of my dearest and closest friends. How they handled their unrelenting grief while still caring for others earned them my lifelong respect and love. These were two people who always asked, even during that incredibly painful time, "How are you?" They have been such an integral part of my life and happiness. Grief is just proof that you loved.

Long before we had children, Nancy's stepdad, Jerry Breslauer—my business manager for many years—told me, "One day you will meet my daughter Nancy and be best friends."

His words were certainly prophetic.

TWELVE

Don't Ask Why Me

Don't ask why me, why me, why not me?

In 1992, I was doing a breast self-examination at home and I felt a lump, but I didn't panic because I'd had lumps before and had them checked, and it was always fine. My gynecologist diagnosed me with "lumpy breasts," or fibrocystic breasts. I had even had needle biopsies for lumps in the past and luckily they were all benign. But this lump did give me a moment of pause.

I was extremely tired. In fact, I'd said to Rona recently, "My blood feels like water. It's like someone drained all the energy from me."

Maybe it was that I'd just come back from Brazil, where I'd represented the UN at the Earth Summit and recorded a song for the environment. I was truly honored to be there, but it took a lot of energy out of me.

I came back to Los Angeles worn out, and I knew I didn't feel right.

When I found the lump in my right breast, I went to have it

checked. Why did it feel different from the others? It was a little painful to the touch, and I'd felt occasional little sharp pains shoot through my upper chest when I was in Brazil.

But the mammogram revealed nothing. I insisted to my surgeon, Dr. Phillips, that we do a needle biopsy—and we did. It also showed nothing of concern. Given the way I was feeling, though, the doctor and I discussed it, and he felt it was important to do a surgical biopsy. I would have to wait for the results.

Some women might have stopped at that last bit of good news, but I always say that if you feel deep down like something is wrong with you, then you need to trust your gut. You know your body.

Ask for the tests.

It's what saved my life.

While I was waiting for the results, Rona and I received a call saying my father was very ill and we should get there quickly. We jumped on a plane and arrived in Australia to face the fact that my father, who had been diagnosed with liver cancer, was very ill. It had snuck up on him and the entire family. One day, he was reading the paper and sipping his coffee, and the next day, he was in a fetal position, barely able to speak. He deteriorated so fast.

With great pain, I had to tear myself away from my father's sickbed to return to Los Angeles to start rehearsals for my world tour. I told him I'd be back soon and had to leave because I had so many people counting on me. Again, the show must go on. All night long on that plane ride home, I cried and cried.

In my heart, I knew I would never see my father again—and I was right.

"Daddy, I will be back to see you the minute my tour ends," I told him as I kissed him goodbye for what would be the last time. He smiled and said he would look forward to it. I didn't want to leave that room and lingered for a long time. I loved my father so much.

What was wonderful was that my mom got a chance to see him one last time. Something good always comes out of the bad. I truly believe that in my heart and soul. My mother and father were able to say goodbye to each other. He even apologized for hurting her all those years ago.

I came home from Australia right before the July Fourth weekend, planning some of the million things you do before a world tour. There were set lists to create, plus meetings with my manager and my musical director, along with my clothing designer. I spent as much time as possible with Chloe, savoring every minute.

I even forced myself to relax a bit.

When the world ground to a halt for the holiday weekend, we went to the San Juan Islands, joining some friends at their beautiful vacation home. Pat and John were with us.

This was a special place for me, where the snow-capped mountains seemed to touch the sea and the scent of pine trees filled your senses while you witnessed the beauty of the elegant and majestic madrone trees. On one particularly memorable visit, after all this stress, my spirit finally soared again when I experienced a rare and magical thing. It was a convergence of ninety-six orca whales from three different pods. My friend Debbie Bledsoe had received a call from the Whale Watch Society to say the orcas were out. This was a group of friends who couldn't wait to call each other with a sighting. We'd taken off into the bay and turned off the boat's engines in the middle of this beautiful orca convergence.

Don't tell anyone, because you're not supposed to do it, but we wanted to hear them breathing and talking to each other. There were mothers with their babies and elderly whales with worn, beat-up dorsal fins reflecting their battles and victories in their beautiful, silent world of the ocean.

It remains one of the most magical moments of my entire life.

This trip was different—even a bit eerie. We took the boat out and I didn't see one whale. The water felt bleak and the slate-gray sky was empty.

A sadness fell over me.

Later that day, I was beyond wiped out as we sat on the dock, listening to the lapping waves and the rattling of the chains on the boats secured to their anchors. It was supposed to be life-affirming and peaceful, but I couldn't relax. Something was bothering me, and I had to ask Matt a question. He had been paged while we were changing planes in Seattle. Why? He just shrugged it off.

A few minutes later, Matt went inside to take a phone call. When he returned, I could see that something was wrong.

"I'm so sorry to tell you, Liv. Your father has died," he said, hugging me.

It was July 3 in Australia, my brother's birthday, and that made it even harder. But there was no time to deal with the waves of emotions over losing my beloved dad. Later that day, we flew home and I saw that the answering machine was blinking. Matt already knew what it was about, but he didn't tell me. Remember that page at the airport? He held it in because there was enough to deal with concerning my father. The page was from my trusted longtime assistant, Dana, saying that Dr. Phillips had called. He wanted to see me in person on Monday.

I knew right away.

Doctors don't want to see you in person unless it's bad news.

Oh God, I didn't know what to do! Should I fly to Australia immediately to help make arrangements for my father's services, or wait to see my doctor? And what about all those people relying on me for the world tour?

Nothing could be decided until after that Monday morning appointment.

Just as I'd thought, the doctor told me I had breast cancer, and we would need to act quickly. My right breast, including the nipple, would have to be removed, in what's called a modified radical mastectomy. The breast could be reconstructed in the operating room immediately following the mastectomy, and the nipple could be rebuilt later if I chose. I was told that chemotherapy may or may not be necessary.

At first I was in denial and made a lot of jokes to the doctor. Humor is usually my way of coping. From denial, though, I moved to cold fear.

Frightened to the core, all I could do was stay wide awake, thinking of Chloe, who was only six. I was her mom—an unbreakable bond. What would become of her life without me in it? In those dark night hours while the world slept, my mind raced with the most horrible possibilities. It seemed as if daylight would never come. Finally, I went to bed to capture a few hours of needed sleep, but I was too restless, and after staring at the ceiling I went back downstairs with dread in my heart.

As I paced, it felt like my legs were so heavy I could hardly move. My heart sunk low.

The next day, I canceled my tour, one of the hardest things I've ever had to do. In the grand scheme of things, it wasn't. But I was concerned about everyone else now that their jobs had been canceled.

I had to stop. Regroup. Work on changing my mind-set.

This challenge was put in front of me for a reason, and I would rise to it. I set out to find out as much as I could about breast cancer and my options.

Nancy told me, "You are going to set the tone. You have to decide that you're going to be okay—and truly believe it."

I can't stress it enough. Your mind is a powerful tool, and only one person is in control of it: you.

You must believe in the power of you.

Four big words: *I will be fine.* This wasn't said with a wavering voice or with tears. *I **WILL** be fine.* I said it in the strongest possible way, firmly, and with a sureness and conviction that I felt down to my toes.

I *had* to be fine.

I went ahead with the surgery, hoping and praying that chemo could be avoided.

I wanted to remove the cancer and get on with it.

Yes, I was frightened, but I vowed that after my surgery I would open my eyes and take the first step on my road to recovery. My cancer would be something of the past and my body would begin to repair itself.

After surgery I was wheeled back to my room, where I would open my eyes to find my oncologist, Dr. Van Scoy-Mosher, sitting on the edge of my hospital bed. "We got it, Olivia," he said. The breath I had been unconsciously holding was released. "But I think we'll do a six-month course of chemo just to make sure."

Just what I was scared of the most. I would have rather used natural therapies. Pat had another perspective.

"Why wouldn't you do chemo?" she said. "Just to be sure. Do it as a safety thing." And she reminded me what was foremost on my mind when she said, "Liv, you have a little child who needs her mother. You need to do everything to get that last cancer cell out of your body."

"Do it," I said to my doctor.

It didn't help that this happened during what I lovingly call my "Britney Days." Most people face a cancer diagnosis with close friends and family. I was a well-known singer and actress whose every move was followed by the press and the public. Being a celebrity is a trade-off. As good as the perks are (my friends lovingly call me "Passport Face" because I can usually get us anywhere we want to go), you still have the downside. Including having to go through the most intimate and devastating experiences in front of the entire world.

Someone saw me when I went for my first scan. My publicist hated to call me with this news, but one of the papers threatened to run a story saying that I was dying of cancer. This is how they do it. They take a rumor, threaten you with creating a whole drama around it, and then force you to say what's really going on.

I hadn't even told my family yet because they were dealing with the loss of my father. But I made a quick decision to come out, right then, and talk about it before anyone could put fake words in my mouth. I just wanted to be honest about what was happening, so if my family did read about it, then it would at least be the truth and they wouldn't have to believe something even more horrible.

In 1992, breast cancer was not something that people openly discussed like they do now. People whispered the "c-word" and turned away from you as if it were some kind of contagious disease.

I phoned Rona, Mum, and my brother to tell them what was happening. And then I gave my publicist the go-ahead and we announced to the world that I had cancer.

Olivia Newton-John, Australian pop singer and sweetheart, has been diagnosed with breast cancer.

"I draw strength from the millions of women who have faced this challenge successfully," she said Monday.

"This has been detected early because I've had regular examinations, so I encourage other women to do the same. I am making this information public myself to save 'inquiring minds' 95 cents."

Newton-John, 43, shot to fame teaming with John Travolta for the 1978 film Grease. *She has to postpone her Back to Basics Tour, set to start Aug. 6, but she said in her statement, "Doctors expect a full recovery."*

We decided not to tell Chloe anything about my diagnosis for now. She was six and had lost her best friend Colette to cancer. How could a little girl cope with that loss and then her grandfather and now her mom's illness? Chloe only associated cancer with death, and I couldn't do that to my little girl. Not telling her was a decision I later questioned. But back then, I felt that Chloe had enough on her plate, although we did take her to therapy to talk through her losses.

She did spot the strangers who sometimes came to our house to give me medical advice. These people would turn up at our gates yelling, "Don't do chemo. Don't do radiation. Use meditation!" I was amazed at the outpouring, and it was all very well-meaning. But I had to trust my doctors to heal me, while creating my own wellness program to go along with what they prescribed.

"Who are those people at the gate, Mummy?" Chloe would ask me.

"Oh, just photographers, darling," I said.

So I could spare her the worry, I'd set up playdates on the chemo days and she would go and stay with friends. Her dad would take her out the next day or two when Mum wasn't feeling well.

When I showed up for my first chemotherapy session, I was terrified. I actually believed that when they stuck the needle in, I would keel over and die. Fear is a terrible thing. But I survived and even went to a movie right afterward. Nancy's idea, and a good one. Stick to normal things.

As I sipped my anti-nausea drink in the theater that day, I had no idea what I saw on the big screen.

I had seen the horrors of chemo with Colette, and it was her mother who had a frank talk with me about how to deal emotionally with my cancer. I didn't want pity or to be treated like an invalid. "It's all up to you, Liv," Nancy said. "You're going to set the standard for how everyone treats you. If you're positive, everyone else will be positive, too."

Every three weeks, I had another round of chemo, and through it all, laughter was the way I maintained my sanity and balance. I dug deep into my sense of humor even when they were putting the really big needles into my tired veins.

And I used mental imaging to deal with how I felt afterward. This is what really helped me: I would visualize the chemicals as liquid gold going into my body, healing me, drip by drip. I'd see myself as strong, especially during my weakest moments.

> *I've survived so many things*
> *From broken hearts to shattered dreams*
> *In every wall I've found an open door.*
> *I'd miss a step; I'd learn to dance*
> *Come back again with half a chance*
> *Stronger than before. . . .*
>
> *A spark of hope in sorrow's place*
> *Will shine with such amazing grace*
> *Stronger than before.*

I'd be lying if I said I was always positive. I had my moments of tears, fears, and negativity. Sometimes I gave in to that raw feeling of adrenaline-induced terror. I thought of Linda McCartney, who'd died in 1988 of cancer, shocking the world because she seemed healthy and then she was gone. It really brought home how fortunate I was that my strain of cancer wasn't more aggressive. My cancer was estrogen-positive in situ, so it was contained within my breast ducts. This was good news, and I was very aware of how lucky I was because I had lost several friends to breast cancer.

The bottom line is, you have to reach for the good in any situation. I always tried to make the positive voice overrule the negative. The light would push out the dark.

Six months of chemo turned into nine because my blood counts were too low and we had to stop for periods of time. I was doing three different drugs in one push called cyclophosphamide methotrexate and fluorouracil (CMF). I'd go to my oncologist's office and have it administered by his nurse. The second time, Nancy went with me and then we went to another movie. Laughter (and Goldie Hawn) turned out to be the best medicine of all that day.

After each session, I had a weak, shivery feeling like the flu. There were bad headaches, my eyes stung, and I had a terrible burning in my throat as if I'd smoked a ton of cigarettes.

The good news was I didn't lose my hair, maybe because of the ice cap I wore when receiving treatment—it looked like a tea cozy with ice inside, and it was designed to reduce hair loss during chemotherapy. Very cute—and quite helpful!

I won't pretend that it was easy, but I made sure to do everything possible to keep my body thriving. I hired a macrobiotic chef and an acupuncturist who helped with relaxation and pain. I took a course in Transcendental Meditation as a way for me to get out of my head and just live joyously. Herbs, good foods, and vitamins helped to keep my body strong, as did the yoga coach who came to my home several times a week along with a masseur. To help with the nausea, I used homeopathic drops from Germany, and I also used Amazonian herbs (never knowing how important that would be later on in my life).

I went to the wonderful Dr. Soram Khalsa, who is a doctor of medicine and a naturopath who used natural healing and herbs. I did everything I could to heal my body—East meets West.

I did think about the creation of my cancer because I believe that emotions and illness have a correlation. The loss of my father and Colette and the increasing struggles within my marriage were huge stresses for me. Dr. Khalsa even asked me if I was having trouble with a man because some believe cancer in the right breast corresponds to a male figure.

"Do I have trouble with a man? Doesn't everybody?" I joked.

My favorite inspirational woman and author was the marvelous Louise Hay, founder of the publishing company Hay House. She survived very aggressive ovarian cancer—it was dubbed "incurable" when she was diagnosed in 1978. Louise passed away in August 2017 at age ninety of natural causes, crediting one thing for her longevity: a positive mind-set. Louise was my teacher, adviser, counselor, and guide, even though she didn't know me. Her book *You Can Heal Your Life* restored me to the right mind-set each and every night. Her voice pushed away any of my doubts and fears, returning me to positivity. She allowed me to sleep and dream of better days. I was thrilled many years later to thank her for all her love and healing and tell her how she'd affected my life.

After she died, the CEO of Hay House sent me a note saying that Louise hadn't made it known what she wanted done with her ashes. He wondered if I would like a portion of them. I told them that I would be honored, and I flew Louise's ashes to Australia and placed them under a beautiful evergreen tree on the top of the hill at my beloved Gaia, a most sacred space and the perfect place for her as they both share such a healing energy. I love feeling her spirit is there.

I also loved Deepak Chopra and purchased all of his healing books. Evelyn Ostin, the wife of Mo Ostin who ran Warner Bros. Records, originally introduced me to him. She was the one who took me to personally meet Deepak and receive my mantra, plus some lovely advice about healing. Years later, whenever I needed advice, I would go see Deepak, who proved to be a good friend. When Patrick McDermott disappeared (more on that later), I asked for his advice. He told me to repeat the line: "Thy will be done." Not long after I finished my treatments, Matt was offered a TV series in Australia. He was out there for a couple of months before we joined him. My paradise has always been Australia, and I thought it would be wonderful to go down under for a while and have Chloe live a normal life, going to the local school and catching up with her friends. I needed some solitary time, and the farm was a perfect place to meditate, read every spiritual book I could get my hands on, and just relax.

Chloe was enrolled at a charming school called Rous Mill, which was just down the road from our farm. The very first day of school, I took my little girl there and left her happily making new friends. When I picked Chloe up that day, she was crying. "Mummy, Mummy! One of my friends said you have cancer. Is it true, Mummy?" I had managed to keep those publications from her, but obviously the news had hit Australia, and I couldn't keep it from the world.

I held her, told her it was true, but that now I was better and the cancer was gone.

"Why didn't you tell me, Mummy?" asked my wise girl. "I would have taken care of you."

To this day, just thinking about it—and now writing it—breaks my heart.

When I look back, I know that, despite it being an emotionally confusing time for my Chloe, I should have told her. If I could change anything, I would have informed her from the start. I do think this omission impacted Chloe, and possibly even created her trust issues down the road. I think it's better to be honest at all times and just deal with it. What happened that day at school was really a blessing in disguise, because now there was no more hiding.

When you have the truth, you have everything.

We spent the rest of that wintertime in our cozy Aussie home, and it was a lovely period of nesting. I'd wake up at four in the morning, check on my daughter, who was sleeping peacefully, and then go light a fire in the living room. I'd sit in a big, comfortable chair under a blanket and write new songs that were waking me up and had to be written. The funny thing was, writing new music was the last thing on my mind. I wasn't planning to work at all. But the music and lyrics simply wanted to be heard. Inspiration, it turns out, strikes at the most unusual times.

In the middle of the night when the world is quiet, there is a creative cloud, a dream bag we all pull from.

I'd always cared deeply about the planet and the environment, but it escalated dramatically when I was recovering. I was so deeply in tune with nature, and my lyrics sprang out of that amazing connection. Now that I had the time to be alone for extended periods, I found a spiritual part of myself that was always there, which had previously been unexplored.

Being faced with death, I felt profoundly grateful, and experienced a true connection to all of God's creatures.

I wrote an entire album late at night in my house; the songs just came through me. I remember playing some of them for one of my friends, Diana, who told me that her sons, Nick and Stewart, had a band. I hired them, and we recorded the album on a farm in the hinterland of Byron Bay. I could see cows wandering past my window from the recording booth. I had my incredibly creative and dear friends Murray Burns and his partner Colin Bayley produce the album. The indie vibe of it all felt delicious. Even the name was perfect: *The Music Farm*.

Honestly, I had thought that I would retire, that it was the end of my career, but music kept appearing to me, in my head and in my heart, and I knew the songs needed to be heard. It turns out I didn't retreat from my career but rather I went through the fire and reinvented it. I called the album *Gaia* and dedicated it to my father, who'd died of cancer the day I was diagnosed and never complained for a moment. This was for him.

I loved the message of my 1994 *Gaia* album, and it remains close to my heart and the hearts of my fans.

When we found our way back to Malibu, I would often stand on a bluff overlooking the churning Pacific Ocean. In those moments, I would realize what a small piece of the world we really do occupy, and that it's our sacred job to protect Mother Earth. We talk about saving the planet, but it's really about saving ourselves.

Respect me. Respect me.
I need you to protect me.
For it is you, not me.
Whose fate's in jeopardy.

THIRTEEN

No Matter What You Do

I'll send you love. No matter what you say.

Back at home, Matt and I had officially made it through sickness and health, but the closeness you need in a marriage just wasn't there as we reached the ten-year mark together. An illness can be very difficult for couples to manage emotionally, and it drove the wedge between us even deeper. We did all the right things when we noticed the gap and even sought couples' counseling, but it wasn't working.

As I continued to heal, the word was encouraging from my doctors, who said the tumor was gone. I wish my marriage had that same healthy prognosis. By 1996, I had to face the fact that my relationship with Matt had been slowly deteriorating for a long, long time and it wasn't going to get better.

We had been drifting away from each other and weren't the same people who met on set so long ago. Our interests didn't even match up anymore. He liked to fish, scuba dive, and hang out with his friends. I was the one who liked to meditate and read spiritual books. We did meet in the middle, though, as loving, bonded parents of our gorgeous baby girl. That was undeniable.

What consoled me as I struggled with the idea of divorce was that Matt and I had long ago decided that if anything should happen to us as a couple, we would remain close friends—or at least try to—for Chloe. I also had to realize that for a long time we had swept our problems under the rug because we didn't want our little girl to deal with something painful.

Cancer has a way of making you face your worst and wildest fears, though. And I couldn't deny the realization that without cancer, Matt and I would have separated much sooner.

There was no choice but to end our marriage, but I refused to participate in some messy, drawn-out public spectacle. I had watched how others in the public eye had their divorces splashed across the headlines.

Matt and I simply sat down at our kitchen table as friends and worked out the terms. A female judge was our mediator, and, although it was painful, it was much better than sitting in some cold, sterile courtroom and spending hundreds of thousands of dollars on lawyers' fees. It was really important to me and Matt that we make this as easy and as humane as possible for everyone, especially our daughter. I never wanted Chloe to read later on about how her parents dragged personal family business through the mud. Our story was private, and turmoil would not be our family's legacy.

Our divorce decree mandated that Chloe could see both of us as much as she wanted, with me as the primary caretaker. It was so important to me that she maintain a healthy relationship with her father because I would always lament the time lost with my own.

After we signed the final papers, I knew I needed a major change. I couldn't stay in that big Malibu house any longer, and so I moved Chloe and me to a more modest beachside cottage to regroup and plan our future.

Between cancer and divorce, it was a dark time, but I came out knowing that I was more capable and perhaps even tougher than I had imagined.

Sometimes you need to be confronted with difficulties before you can even begin to live up to your true potential.

One of the positive aspects of this challenging time was that my health was returning and my body was feeling stronger every single day. I was cancer-free, grateful, and ready to get on with living.

Initially, you get to the five-year mark and if you haven't had a recurrence then that's a very big deal and a huge relief. You hear most of the time if cancer comes back it's within those first five years. After those 1,826 days, you usually just need to be checked once a year.

Those first years are so very frightening, but I prepared for them well with estrogen-blocking medication, plus herbs, vitamins, supplements, homeopathy, meditation, and yoga. But there were still plenty of scary nights alone in a big bed.

I will never use the word "remission," although I celebrate other men and women who do. Personally, it doesn't work for me, because the word "remission" feels like a question mark. It makes me believe that cancer is still lurking, hiding in the corner, just waiting to come back out. Cancer was a four-letter word to me: "g-o-n-e." I put cancer away, closed the drawer, and kept myself very busy as a newly single mom.

During meditation, I thought about what I learned during this time. I came to find out that:

I could get through anything.

Cancer isn't necessarily a death sentence.

Compassion for others is a healing force.

Gratitude is a medicine.

I was so grateful for each and every day on planet Earth.

I believe that every seven years you shed your skin, and sickness forced me to get rid of mine and renew. In my thirties, I wasn't confronted with my mortality. In fact, I didn't even think about it. But my forties? They were a growing-up time. Now I was committed to my new life and good health.

Chloe didn't need words of reassurance but had to see with her own eyes that Mummy was fine and dandy. I would show my little girl that skies were blue if you decided they were and that you never give up.

She was and is the most splendid part of my life. At six, after a visit to the Big Apple, she wrote a touching and very poignant poem about the trees, asking, *Why aren't there any trees in New York? What have we done to them? How do people breathe?* My girl was always singing—she knew every word to *The Phantom of the Opera.* She would put on little concerts with her friends in our living room and sing all the hit songs of the day, like TLC's "Waterfalls."

She loved *The Little Mermaid* and had a stock of princess dresses that she never wanted to take off. When she turned seven, I didn't have to ask what she would be wearing because I knew it would be white and poufy. For her birthday party, we hired an actor to dress up as Prince Charming. Her bedroom, like most of her friends', was lined with Barbies who lived in a pink DreamHouse.

Chloe always loved animals and even had a pet rat she named Mushka. She couldn't have enough animals around her, which was a trait she got from her mom. She loved Australia like I did because it was a place where she could really experience nature.

Our farm there had an enormous garden, and if she wanted to see bigger plants, we'd go walking in the rain forest next to our home, where we would see the wallabies on the lawn and hear the many wonderful and unique varieties of birds. At the local school, the children would have to wear a hat outside because of the intensity of the sun, but Chloe didn't mind. She felt free in a place where she could do all her sports barefoot. I loved the fact that she had a few years of schooling there and made lifelong friends in both America and Australia. In fact, Chloe can still go from an American to an Australian accent in a second. Brilliant!

I was hoping to spend a few years after my treatment in Australia with Chloe, but then Matt and I split up. Plans changed when I knew she wouldn't see her dad much if we lived so far away. So we moved back to LA, planning to return to Oz every year to reconnect and visit family, friends, and, of course, the animals.

From 1995 to 1998 I didn't record any new albums or songs of my own. I did, however, sing on five tracks written by our mates John Farrar and Tim Rice for my longtime singing partner and friend Cliff Richard's *Heathcliff* soundtrack. We performed a duet called "Had to Be" at the Royal Variety Performance in London in front of the queen.

My dear friend Cliff—now deservedly Sir Cliff Richard—would pull me out of retirement when he asked me to tour with him. Cliff has been a mentor in my life, a man with the most beautiful warm and sexy voice whom I learned so much from about performing. He is always lovely and kind to me and everyone he meets. A true gentleman.

There is no one else I would have come out of retirement for but Cliff, who was so instrumental in my career. I was on his TV series in the sixties and toured with him in Japan as a backup singer with Pat. He said, "You're too young to retire." Then later he said, "I couldn't get you off the stage." I have such immense respect and love for him. Thank you, Sir Cliff!

Aside from these few projects, I decided to take a bit of a break from singing and concentrate on Chloe. But soon I found I couldn't just do nothing. It wasn't in my nature.

And the universe, once again, had different plans for me than I had for myself. Right before Christmas 1996, I felt a strange lump in my throat. X-rays revealed it was not malignant, thank God, but it was some kind of a growth behind my larynx that apparently had been there since I was born.

There would be no throat surgeries for me because that was much too scary; I went the holistic route, getting acupuncture treatments every day for six weeks. When nothing changed, I felt confused—until I realized, during a meditation, that I had been given a gift, the voice that I was born with, and I wasn't using it.

The moment I decided to sing again, the lump disappeared as suddenly as it appeared, and that was the last of it. It confirmed to me what the amazing Louise Hay always said: "You are what you think." The minute my thoughts changed, my body changed. I understood from that day on that I would always sing. It's part of my purpose on this earth, the way that I reach people, and to stop would be like allowing part of me to die.

My life was evolving, and I focused on doing what was in my heart: raising my daughter, supporting breast cancer and environmental causes as much as possible—and singing. This realization helped to inspire my 1998 album, *Back with a Heart*.

I was also surprised with an offer to act again. It was for a film called *Sordid Lives*, written and directed by a highly talented friend of Rona's and mine named Del Shores, who also wrote the stage play on which it was based. I was intrigued by the part he wanted me to play: a lesbian singer named Bitsy Mae. I had seen the play with Rona some time ago and loved it. Back then I said to Del, "If you ever make a movie version, think of me for Bitsy Mae." He didn't forget.

I adored the idea that I'd be wearing tattoos and chomping on a large wad of gum all the time. It was completely against what people would expect of me, and I had a ball. Over the course of two days, at a lake house outside of Toronto, my friend Amy Sky and I wrote five songs for the *Sordid Lives* television series, including the cheeky "You Look Like a Dick to Me." It was written for my abusive on-screen boyfriend Richard.

They say your name is Richard
But you look like a Dick to me.

Enough said.

It was kind of fun because for years there had been rumors that I was a lesbian, even though I had been married or had a boyfriend throughout most of my career.

The rumor mill taught me a lesson: where there's smoke, there isn't always a fire. In fact, there might not even be an ember burning at all.

After playing Bitsy Mae in *Sordid Lives*, I finally got an opportunity to go on the record saying I've always supported gay rights. An article appeared in an issue of *The Advocate*, a widely distributed gay/lesbian magazine, in which Del Shores, who is openly gay, interviewed me.

"Let's talk about the rumor, Olivia," he said.

I answered quite simply. "I'm not a lesbian. Next!" But I also asked him, "How would you like it if I accused you of being heterosexual?"

I think I made my point!

FOURTEEN

Dare to Dream

Just when I thought that my career was going quiet (again), in early 2000 I was invited to sing at the Vatican for the pope. Can you believe it? It was to be an evening concert for people going through difficult times, and I was told that Muhammad Ali would also be there. I was so honored, and decided to take Chloe with me. Her paternal grandparents were staunch Catholics, so this was an incredible moment for her to represent the family and meet the pope. She wasn't particularly excited about going, but that would soon change.

We arrived at the Rome international airport, only to be met on the curb by an Aussie photographer who said, "Love, you know the pope's not going to be there. He's sick." *Wait just a second!* We had flown all the way to Rome to meet the pope and *he wasn't going to be there?* I dismissed this as being impossible, and we drove to our beautiful hillside hotel overlooking the breathtaking city.

We were driven to the hotel by one of the Vatican staff—the

pope's producer, meaning that he produced his records. This was a big surprise to me. The pope had a producer? Who knew the pope made records? Was I back in LA? The producer was complaining in a thick Italian accent, "*I can't believe it! It didn't sell like I thought it would!*" This was the pope we were talking about, and I was having the same conversations I had at a record company!

Time was short, and I had a rehearsal that day, so I dropped Chloe off at the hotel and headed for a cavernous hall with lots of marble and incredibly high ceilings. There were special boxes in the theater where the VIPs would sit. More news: Muhammad Ali wasn't coming, either. It turned out that what I heard at the airport from my Aussie Vatican spy was correct.

The pope had a cold.

He wasn't coming. We flew and the pope had the flu.

I asked my "pope producer" if we could have a private meeting with the pope, expecting nothing to happen, but I had to ask, since we came all that way and it would have been terrible not to meet him.

"Leave it with me," he said.

We ended up staying an extra day, which was wonderful because I was able to take Chloe to see the sights of Rome. We even had a magical tour of the Vatican. Eventually, we received a message with a time—the pope was feeling better and would be able to see us the next morning.

I remember being led through hallways where the walls were covered in beautiful and priceless artworks. Finally, we stopped in a room with a huge, ornate red chair that looked like a throne.

The first thing I saw was his head covered by a small hat and wisps of white hair. His face was ruddy and shiny. His head came through the door first while his body, hunched over, followed. I'm not a Catholic, but I was very honored to meet him. He handed me a box with a beautiful blessed rosary inside and said some words in Italian. Then he took my hands and the hands of my daughter, who was visibly moved and burst into tears.

At the concert, there were people lying on gurneys with IVs in their arms, and people in wheelchairs and the infirm in the seats. It was a humbling experience. No one had told me what to expect, but the concert was for what they called the "Untouchables." It was the Jubilee Celebration for the Sick and Healthcare Workers at the Vatican.

I sang "(Somewhere) Over the Rainbow" for them accompanied by a tall, thin piano player who spoke no English.

Somehow, we got by with a lot of waving of the hands.

Back home, Chloe and I were living in a French-style country cottage in Malibu where I'd wake up early with our Irish setter Scarlett to feed three cats, three dogs, and two cockatiels. I loved that quiet time early in the morning when it was just me and the animals. I'd fix myself a cup of tea and then take breakfast up to Chloe, who was fourteen now and attending a local private school.

I'd drive Chloe to school and her activities, spending my downtime pruning my rosebushes in my gorgeous garden or taking long walks on the beach. If I went into town, I'd take an art or yoga class. Tennis became an obsession of mine, and I hired a private coach because I was hooked on it.

Then, one day, the most wonderful call came in—asking me to perform at the opening ceremony of the 2000 Summer Olympic Games in Sydney. The idea of stepping onto a stage at the 110,000-seat Stadium Australia that September, to perform the new Olympic song "Dare to Dream" with fellow Australian John Farnham, had my heart beating fast.

I was extremely thrilled to be asked to sing for my country in my heart home of Australia. I loved that the Olympics stood for all the qualities that my mum had instilled in me and which I was trying to teach Chloe: strength, determination, and perseverance.

Before I went to the Olympics, I was honored to sing at an LA fund-raiser for President Bill Clinton. This was a small, private dinner in a restaurant where I sang one song and then chatted with the president about our daughters. Bill Clinton was charming and made you feel like you were the only person in the room.

To even things up, I later sang at another fund-raiser for Hillary. I am not a political person, though, and being Australian, I can't even vote. I simply chalked it all up to experience.

Slowly, I began to date again, and now I had a boyfriend named Patrick McDermott, a forty-four-year-old cameraman and gaffer. We met for the first time in Los Angeles while I was shooting a commercial. In fact, it was my mother who pointed him out to me and said, "I'd like to take his photograph. That man has a beautiful face."

Patrick and I found that we had several things in common, including that we were both divorced and cautious about getting involved. He was a thoughtful and considerate person, and funny. He liked to play tennis, hike, and take nature walks. He even helped me prune my roses.

Patrick had his own home in Los Angeles and a four-year-old son who would sometimes come over to hang out with Chloe.

He had a romantic heart and would prepare delicious meals for me that we ate by candlelight on the beach.

My life was blooming again.

As we got closer to the Olympic Games, I was back in contact with John Farnham, who had been a friend of mine for many years. We were both thrilled to be representing our beloved country, and there was a huge build-up to the main event. Chloe and I jetted off to Australia, where I would first record in Melbourne with John. Just in case there were any microphone problems on the big night, we decided to record the song beforehand and were prepared to lip-synch to our own voices as a last resort. Our dream, though, was to sing live, and we headed up to Sydney to have several rehearsals at the actual venue. I'll never forget arriving for the first time at the enormous, empty stadium.

During the few days preceding the opening ceremony, we'd arrive at the venue, and then it was time for immediate lockdown. The security was crazily tight, and this was before the post–9/11 world we live in now. I was thrilled to learn that for the final dress rehearsal the night before the event, we would have a live audience of thirty thousand athletes. It was like a mini-performance in itself, and I was nearly as excited as I would be the next day.

That afternoon, the building crews were laying down carpet and painting it so it would look like the brown earth. As we blocked out our moves onstage, I made John promise to hold my hand as I was coming down the stairs in my high heels. It wasn't about the singing. I felt beyond prepared to perform after so much rehearsal. It was more about my shoes. There. I said it. My shoes! The heels weren't sky-high, but they were tall enough, and I felt insecure about walking across that bumpy, freshly painted, turf-like surface.

It was John's duty to be the Olivia catcher.

"No matter what happens," I implored him, "don't let go of my hand. I can barely walk in these shoes, let alone navigate stairs in them."

"No problem, Livvy," he assured me, grinning in his inimitable fashion. "You can count on me."

That night at the dress rehearsal, fully made up and dressed to the nines in a sparkling silver gown made by Lisa Ho, I grabbed John's hand tightly. I made sure my microphone pack was secure at my back and adjusted my earpiece, so I could lip-synch the words in an emergency. Everything was in perfect order, and as the massive crowd of thirty thousand was allowed to pour into that glorious stadium, I felt ecstatic. John and I sang our way down the stairs (why did I wear those shoes!) and then began to cover the long distance through the crowd to finish our song.

I walked precariously, somewhat secure in John's protective grip—until a pretty girl spoke to him. He became so distracted that he jerked his hand out of mine abruptly while rushing over to say hello. As if on cue, I tripped and fell. When John saw me in a prone position splayed out on the turf, he rushed back to help me. We ended up finishing our song, never missing a beat.

In case I hadn't been humiliated enough, I later heard him telling fans and onlookers in his thick Aussie accent sprinkled with laughter, "I dropped the blonde like a bag of sparkly shit." Later he would tone the story down to "a sack of potatoes." Oh, God love him!

I had to laugh in spite of myself. That was John—an adorable, funny man and one of my favorite singers ever.

It made the night quite memorable. And this was only dress rehearsal!

The night before the opening ceremony, I had been asked to carry the Olympic torch around the Sydney Opera House. I'd asked if Chloe could be with me, and they allowed her to run behind me. I was holding the torch high with the beauty of Sydney Harbour out in front of me, twinkling with stars and city lights. It was magical, ending with me passing the flame to tennis star Pat Rafter.

When it was placed in Sydney Town Hall overnight, burning brightly in anticipation of the next day, I felt so grateful to be a part of a group of lucky people who had represented their countries in this way through the ages.

Finally, the big night arrived, and it was clear and magical. The gates opened for the Opening Ceremony and soon 100,000 people filled every stadium seat, not to mention close to four billion television viewers worldwide. The energy was electric as the greatest athletes in the world were gathered in one place to celebrate this traditional coming together of nations in the country that was my home. My heart began to swell while my nerves were going a mile a minute.

"You're not nervous. You're excited," I repeated over and over to myself, as visions of my fifteen-year-old self trying to form a little rock band crossed my mind. I was suddenly back in my kitchen telling my mom that I wanted to be a singer. And now here I was, representing my country in a gorgeous long dress with those killer silver heels. I clutched John's strong hand so hard that I'm sure I cut off his circulation. This time, he vowed to really not let go—no matter who was distracting him!

I opened my mouth to sing the first few words in perfect synch with the voice in my earpiece and all I could hear was . . . static! This was a performer's nightmare, because if you couldn't hear then you couldn't follow along with the song.

Crikey, I can't hear. The transmission is bad! I thought to myself. Then I glanced at John, singing away, cool as a cucumber. Obviously, the interference in my ears was my problem alone. He was fine, which was demonstrated by his easy and confident demeanor.

I still made my way down those insanely steep stairs with John, who didn't let me fall this time. I was floating as we sang, hand in hand, cutting through the crowd. Although that horrible static was bombarding my eardrums, I could still hear our voices in the stadium itself, but just a little bit—and on a delay. That only added to the chaos. I couldn't time myself to what the audience was hearing because there was a sound delay and my mouth would be moving out of synch with that sound.

This is supposed to be the most amazing moment of my life, I thought. *And I'm screwed because I can't hear!*

Just when I thought it couldn't get any worse, I remembered that the cameraman was about to zoom in for my close-up. All I needed was a billion viewers—give or take a few—watching me sing out of time. It was time to muster all the performance lessons I had under my belt and think on my feet (which were killing me).

I turned my head to the side, a strange thing to do when the camera is zooming into your face. There was no choice, because if my lips were moving out of time, even a speck, the close-up would have been a total disaster. *They won't understand what I'm doing in the director's booth*, I thought. *But they will when I get offstage.*

There was a point when John and I split apart and walked down across the field to sing directly to the athletes. Looking into their young and hopeful eyes, all of the problems of the night seemed to melt away. Many were clicking pictures and reaching out to us. Those hands belonged to dreamers from all over the globe, and the enormity of the moment wasn't lost on me. It's funny how even in a crowd that large, you can look into the eyes of one person, and it feels as intimate as performing in a small room.

We finished our song in that gigantic stadium, and I couldn't even brace myself for the thunderous applause. With a wave and a smile, we walked calmly into the underground parking lot, which were the wings. "I couldn't hear a bloody thing!" I told John as soon as we were out of sight of the audience.

"Neither could I, love," he said as we walked straight up to his manager, Glenn Wheatley, to find out how badly we'd blown it.

"Great job, you two," Glenn said.

"But we couldn't hear a thing," we told him in unison.

"No problem," he insisted. "You were perfect, and the audience loved it."

John and I just stared at each other, amazed. No one knew we'd been winging it. In fact, I didn't even know he was struggling—and vice versa. You can still check out the moment online and it looks as if we're both having the time of our lives.

It was a golden moment.

I understand now that my performance, good, bad, or indifferent, was not the point. I wasn't perfect, and it doesn't matter, I thought to myself as I went back to my dressing room to take off my makeup at the end of a very long day. I had just learned a lesson for the ages, something that would stay with me forever.

There is no such thing as perfection. If you do the best you can, instant to instant, that's the most perfect a human being can ever be. And without these now-hilarious moments, I probably wouldn't have remembered it so clearly.

FIFTEEN

Right Here with You

Don't give up; here I am.
And if you need a helping hand
I'm gonna be right here with you.

The idea for a cancer center in Australia was not on my radar. But one day I got a call from the Austin Hospital in Melbourne and they wanted to talk to me.

I was curious and set up a meeting during my next trip home.

Accompanied by my good friend Sue McIntosh, we drove out to Heidelberg, a suburb in the northeast of Melbourne, to the Austin Hospital and met with their CEO, Jennifer Williams. "We wanted to see if you'd allow us to use your name on a new cancer center," she proposed, explaining to me that it would be located on the grounds of the main hospital.

I had the weirdest feeling as I imagined it in my mind. *My name on a building?* It didn't feel as if I deserved it. I thought that maybe it should be just the Newton-John name, which seemed fitting because my older brother is a doctor and my father was a professor and the former master of Ormond College. I called my brother to ask him about it. "Oh, no, it should be you," he said.

The next stop was a visit to Mum to talk about this amazing offer.

"Mum, they want me to consider putting my name on a new cancer center," I fretted over tea with her.

"Listen, darling," she said in her strong German accent. "In life, if you can help somebody, then you should do it."

It was so simple, but great advice for anyone.

I went back to my favorite hotel in Melbourne, the Lyall, and really thought about it deeply. Part of what bothered me was that this would be a cancer center and I didn't want to have my name dropped before the word "cancer." I needed this to be a cancer *and* wellness center. I could only do it if they included the word "wellness" because including the word "wellness" next to "cancer" would give people hope. You could go from cancer to wellness—yes!

With my friend Sue, I went for a tour of the hospital. The original cancer center was old, dark, and dingy. It first opened in the 1920s and, like every other hospital, they used X-rays to cure cancer (or so they thought). By 1935 it was one of the largest hospitals in Australia. The patients were sitting in those old corridors. That building was dark and sad. Having gone through treatment myself, I understood the need to be in a place of comfort and light. It's difficult enough to go through treatment, but to be in a depressing place makes it so much harder.

I had another meeting with the Austin and I said I would be very honored to put my name on the building if it included a wellness center with acupuncture, massage, meditation, Reiki, Chinese herbs and yoga, among other mind-body treatments. This was crucial to me, although a new concept for a public hospital. They were only used to all the mainstream treatments—surgery, chemotherapy, and radiotherapy.

There would also need to be group therapy for emotional support. That wasn't available to me, but my oncologist gave me the names of two women who had the same treatments that I had embarked on. I was able to discuss it with them and understand what I was going through, which was very helpful.

Most people don't have the funds for nontraditional ways to heal, and I wanted to provide that access. I had to make wellness a condition, otherwise I wouldn't be comfortable moving forward with the project.

During a follow-up trip to Australia, the Austin mentioned that part of the hospital called Zeltner Hall was used years ago for treatment of tuberculosis (TB), or as they called TB patients in those days, "the incurables." I thought, *Gosh, TB was incurable years ago and now that's virtually gone. That's going to happen with cancer!* It gave me a vision. Another sign was that my brother Hugh had once worked at the Austin and had even given lectures at Zeltner Hall.

I also found out the hospital had to make a big decision because adding wellness to the center increased the budget. They said they could maybe convince the government to pay for the architectural build, but afterward the funds to run it would have to come through philanthropy. I knew that one day we could persuade the government to help us with the wellness programs—and I'm still waiting for that day! Patient attitudes are so good at the ONJ Cancer Wellness & Research Centre, and healing is taking place in a dignified, calm, and positive manner.

I'm delighted that now, after seven years, the wellness philosophy has permeated the entire hospital, including offering hand and

feet massages and music therapy in the patients' rooms. We also
have a piano in the lobby where we invite local musicians to play.
A harpist has even come to visit, which was beautiful and soothing.

During Christmas 2016, John Farnham and I sang carols for
the patients and nurses in the lobby—the most memorable audience ever. I kept flashing back to my time at the Vatican with the
audience in wheelchairs and on gurneys and with IVs in their arms.
I'm not sure how I sang with all the emotions racing through me.

This is a lifelong commitment. This is my name, my ethos, my
dream.

The journey to create the ONJ Centre introduced me to some
wonderful people, including CEO Jennifer Williams and director
of fund-raising Peter Dalton, along with a slew of amazing medical
professionals, architects, and campaigners. Of course, the money
needed to fund such an endeavor was staggering. We received
almost $70 million from the government to kick-start the con-
struction, which was generous but not enough.

The Ludwig Institute, a worldwide research institute that would
operate on the grounds, gave us funding in July 2012. My concept
was that everything would be in one building—the research, treatment, and cancer care. This way everyone could collaborate easily
to figure out the best individual plan for each patient.

That same year I went back to Australia to meet with influential politicians who could help, including John Brumby, the trea-
surer of Victoria, who gave us $69 million. (I sang "I Honestly
Love You" to him at the opening of the center and totally made the
poor man go crimson!) I'm very proud to say that he is now the
chairman of the ONJ Cancer Research Institute.

The support that we found took my breath away.

My commitment was to the future patients and, having been one myself, I needed to make sure the details of the place supported the idea of healing on all levels. I personally worked with iconic Aussie architect Daryl Jackson to create the most healing environment possible within this physical structure. What I felt we needed was a place with as much natural light as possible with a courtyard where people could go relax and perhaps even meditate in nature. Daryl and I spent time together discussing colors and design. It was essential to me that the rooms be serene and quiet.

"It's very important to me that someone who walks in these doors can have their treatment and then go outside and feel the sun on his or her back," I said. "If they're stuck in bed, I want them to experience as much natural light streaming into the room as possible and take advantage of the beautiful views of the Dandenong Ranges."

It was also crucial to me that, wherever possible, all the products used in the center would be certified environmentally friendly. Healing in a clean and inspired environment was key.

I was on tour in Tampa, Florida, when the Moffitt Cancer Center invited me to visit their facility. I had just been asked to lend my name to the cancer and wellness center in Melbourne and I was curious to see firsthand what was happening at this highly regarded treatment and research center. I was given a lovely tour, and I was quite taken with the fact that they had a wonderful arts program and an incredible research facility. After a productive and personally fulfilling day there, I was leaving for sound check. That's when I saw a dapper gentleman in a dark suit with silver hair. He walked into the hospital and introduced himself. It was Lee Moffitt himself.

"You're alive?" I blurted out. "I was worried that you had to be dead to have a building named after you!"

The words just fell out of my mouth. Obviously, he was quite alive, and we chatted for a little bit. He was so eloquent and passionate about his hospital, which made me even more excited about the proposed cancer and wellness center in Australia. That night after the concert, I met Lee's wife, Dianne, at a reception.

Lee, Dianne, and I became good friends, and as the years passed, and whenever I needed advice about my center, I would call him. Lee even took the time to come to Australia, meet with our architect, and help us by looking at the plans. The thirtieth anniversary of the Moffitt Cancer Center was in 2016, and it's been named one of the top ten in the United States. Lee is a very special man, and I think so highly of him.

Thank you, Lee, for all that you achieved. It inspired me.

The first step was demolishing the old, ugly building, but we kept Zeltner Hall. I was thrilled to be there and even have a picture of me on a crane. Hard hat on my head, I dug the first hole. Yes!

On June 25, 2012, the first stage of the Olivia Newton-John Cancer Wellness & Research Centre at the Austin Hospital officially opened. It would provide extensive outpatient and radiation oncology services along with the wellness aspects I wanted. It would also offer the Ludwig Institute for Cancer Research expanded research capacity. We would have to wait a year for the second stage of the center to open, which would provide palliative care and cancer inpatient beds. I'm especially proud that the palliative care ward is named after my mother, Irene, as she inspired me to go ahead with this project.

Sharon Hillman, head of fund-raising at that time, had input that was crucial and helped us get the money to keep the project going. She worked with me to organize a Wellness Walk where supporters could help me raise money for the center. I'm so grateful to them for showing up for our first walk, which is now heading into its seventh year.

When we designed the logo for the hospital, we worked with the patients, showing them different colors and symbols. At the opening, I remember having to be at the center at 6:00 a.m. for press. The town car was driving up the hill and my publicist said, "Olivia, look! The ONJ sign is up!" I grabbed his hand and we both got teary.

Then I said, "Michael, that's the best billboard I will ever have."

The moment those doors opened, the center would be one of Melbourne's three leading cancer centers, which is still staggering to me.

I'll never forget the actual opening party. I took Rona, Chloe, and her fiancé, James. All my nieces and nephews who live in Australia were there, along with many lifelong close friends. It was a wonderful, incredible day. It was a major life moment, and I was thrilled to have all of them together celebrating something so close to my heart. I wrote the song "Right Here with You" with Delta Goodrem and Amy Sky and sang it with Delta for this momentous occasion.

I can feel a knowing here between us
Yes, you walk on the path I walk too

It takes just one second, one moment to change your life
But deep down you know you'll survive.

Suddenly your deepest fears are spoken
But you can't let your spirit be broken
It takes just one second to stand up and say it's my life
I won't give up.

Don't give up; here I am
And if you need a helping hand
I'm gonna be right here with you.

There wasn't a dry eye in the center that night.

The one person missing was my mum, who sadly never saw the ONJ Centre because she died in 2003, nine years before it opened in 2012. It took us nearly ten years to raise the money, and I knew Mum would be so proud.

So was my dear friend Pat, who came later for the opening of the Wellness Centre and surprised me with a beautiful portrait she painted of me that now hangs there. Thank you, Pearl (her nickname).

What's so important to me about the work we do at the center is that it's all about supporting the whole person, physically and emotionally, while instilling an important positivity. It has been shown that people who have a positive attitude do a lot better when they're going through cancer treatments. If you believe you will be okay, it gives you more strength. I certainly found that to be true.

Another aspect of the center is teaching the people around

the cancer patient how to best support them. I remembered telling some of my friends the news when I was first diagnosed. They began to cry on the phone (or in person) and I found that very disabling, although I knew their intentions were pure and good. Or they would quote to me stats about survival rates, which made me think about the negative. Not good! It's important to give gentle support and maximum love while encouraging patients to put themselves first.

I make a point of always visiting the patients at the ONJ Centre whenever I'm in Australia. They're so pleased to see me, and the feeling is more than mutual. I want to visit each one and can't spend enough time there. It's my name on that building, and I want to see that everyone is being well cared for. And they are, in a wonderful way. The truth is, I get more out of those visits than they do. You really do get more out of giving than receiving.

On a practical level, I want to hear what's working. I listen to their praise for the staff and how they love the good feeling in the building, including those rays of hopeful natural light that help them feel better. It does my heart good, as well, to know the staff is happy to be there every day because it's such a beautiful place to work.

"Are they taking good care of you?" I asked one of the staff on a recent visit.

"Very good care," she said.

"Olivia, if you're going through cancer, this is the place to be," a patient told me. That makes everything worthwhile.

The patients know that I can relate because I've been there. And looking into the eyes of those people is an important reminder for me of why I took this on. I understand the fear they possess while they go through this journey. If I can offer a kind word, a laugh, or a hug, it makes me feel so good.

Most of all, when I visit them in their beds, I'm showing them a thriver of cancer, which provides a powerful medicine called hope. I've been very fortunate, and I show that it can be done. You can get through this time in your life—and thrive.

I'm *living* proof and I don't take it for granted.

My dream is to see an end to cancer in my lifetime. I believe my incredible scientists and researchers at the ONJ Cancer Research Institute, led by a wonderful medical director and my dear friend Professor Jonathan Cebon, will find that cure and win over cancer. I say "win" for a reason. I don't believe in fighting cancer, because that sets up images of battles and anger. I choose to see my body as winning, which is a much healthier mental picture. Everyone has their own way of finding that victory in their mind.

Suppress it? Ask it to leave? Peace treaty?

However you want to win over it—do it!

My ultimate goal is that one day we will be able to take a giant crane and remove the word "cancer" from the building because the disease will be wiped off the planet. From that moment on, it will just be the Olivia Newton-John Wellness Centre. That would be a dream come true.

And the team at the ONJ was integral when I went through my third and final win over cancer. Even though I was in America at the time, I was in constant contact with Professor Cebon and everyone there.

Thanks for being part of my winning team.

SIXTEEN

Gaia

Respect me. Respect me.
I need you to protect me.
For it is you not me
Whose fate's in jeopardy.

Although my mum sadly didn't live to see the opening of the ONJ Centre, she's always been my inspiration to move forward and help people.

Mum was born during World War One, when food supplies were limited. Due to a severe lack of nutrients, she grew up with serious osteoporosis, which ultimately was the cause of her death. Aside from this, she was always in wonderful health. Even in her eighties, she would run to the car. "Mum, slow down!" I'd yell, but that never stopped her. Each day, she walked in the botanical gardens next to where she lived. No wonder I love nature so much.

One day in 2003, I was in Las Vegas working when Rona called me. "It's probably the end," my sister said. "You should come." I canceled my show (one of only three times I've done that—not bad for a career of fifty years) and jumped on a plane to Australia. Mum was eighty-nine and at home with Rona and Gregg Cave, a man who was like another son to her. He'd been an actor in his younger life and then an art curator, and always a dear friend to my mother.

Mum was fading quickly and in excruciating pain. She could have lived longer but chose to pass on. I was with her for the last week. On the final day, she was surrounded by people she loved including Rona, me, Chloe, Nancy, Jim, and Gregg. She was no longer in pain.

Mum had told me that the moment after her mother, Hedwig, had died, her portrait fell off the wall in her apartment in Melbourne, oceans away from my grandmother passing in Germany. Mum took it as a positive sign from her mother. After my mother died, I went to sit with her hoping for a sign. We had candles all around the room and it was a beautiful atmosphere. In her front hall, we had a table set up with flowers, a lovely photo of Mum and a large candle I brought from America encased in thick glass.

"Mum, give me a sign you're okay and your spirit is okay," I whispered to her as I sat at her bedside. The candles in the room flickered, and I assumed that this was the sign.

At that moment, Rona called out from the other room. I wondered why she was calling me when I was trying to have a peaceful goodbye with Mum.

"Olivia!" Rona cried.

I had no choice but to leave the room and walk into the hallway. That's when I saw it. The glass around that big candle I brought had spontaneously cracked at the center and fallen to the floor. This made me smile. Mum didn't go for the little candles as her sign. She went big.

We felt a sense of peace, and of course, sadness. We missed our mum, but she'd had a good life.

The next few days were a flurry of giving her possessions to people—some of which she had personally pinned little paper tags to with the recipient's name on them. She had been preparing for a long time. We donated other items. Then I rented a car and put some of her paintings and possessions inside to drive to my farm, hundreds of miles away.

I was in mourning, so the drive was a blur. Gregg, Nancy, and Jim were with me, and we talked about Mum the entire way. As we drove through the beautiful, fertile countryside and farmland in Byron Bay that had captured my heart so many years ago, Gregg said, "I should move up here."

"Yes, you should," I said.

It wasn't long before we saw a sign: *Sanctuary for sale*.

Impulsively, we drove up a steep hill to find a stunning, sweeping vista. Tucked away on the left were a number of pink huts. A man came out to greet us who turned out to be a yoga instructor. He explained this land was used for weddings and as a yoga retreat. Looking around, I could see that the place was pretty run-down but naturally beautiful. I was glad that we stopped.

We left, arrived at the farm, and I put my mother's ashes in a special place in the kitchen.

Then we went to bed.

The next morning, I was making tea for me and Gregg and I told him that I'd had a dream.

"I dreamt that we bought that property and we made a place for our friends and family to come. We called it Gaia," I said.

"That's weird," Gregg said. "I dreamt about it, too. Same thing. It was our retreat. But I called it Bella Vista."

"I hate that name," I said, laughing.

We were having a fight over the name of a property we didn't own! And so it began. We started playing with the idea of owning this land and having a place where our friends and family could stay, sort of like a modern commune.

The next week was a blur as I scattered my mother's ashes under my beautiful Moreton Bay fig tree where I want to be scattered one day. Then I went back to America and Gregg returned to Sydney. Sometime later he called me to say he had been thinking about that property, and he wanted to know if I was interested in doing something about it.

Yes, I was interested.

Gregg returned to the property with a banker friend, Warwick Evans. The land had so much promise, so we put an offer in. Unfortunately, someone had put an offer in before us and it was under contract. I told a disappointed Gregg, "If it's meant to be—it will come back to us."

A few months later, the contract fell through!

We formed a partnership of four of us—Warwick, me, Gregg, and his friend Ruth Kalnin—and put in another offer for this beautiful piece of property. I was nervous because it was unknown territory but excited because it was a new adventure. My motto has always been: if you want it, create it.

Gregg sold his business in Sydney and went to live on the property. Here it gets even more interesting. On his first night there, while sleeping in one of those little shacks, he dreamt the whole look of the place, then woke up and actually drew plans for what is there today.

That's how Gaia was born.

We realized that we had a real responsibility with this land. This was a healing place. Gaia started literally as a dream and has grown into a world-class retreat and spa. We have an organic garden where we grow our own fruits and vegetables, and we've brought in incredible chefs and the best healers in the world. I would wait a whole year for our massages there!

I'm so proud of Gregg for devoting his life to making this one of the best spas in the world, where everything is done with loving intention. Everyone who goes there benefits from the beauty and the peace of this special place. Gregg and I talk several times a week about everything that's decided at the retreat.

The ethos of Gaia is surrender.

SEVENTEEN

Let Go, Let God

Let the signs remind you
We are passengers.
Let the signs remind you
To surrender.

My personal life—something I hate discussing with the press—had
bloomed with Patrick McDermott, a cameraman, who was my on-
again, off-again boyfriend for eight years. It might seem strange
that, despite being such a public figure in this day and age, I try to
keep my life private. With the publication of this book, though, I
feel I have an opportunity to talk about this for a moment.

The last time I saw Patrick, he was at my house and we were
deciding to take a break from each other again. The truth is, I
don't really know why I never fully committed to Patrick. When I
met John Easterling, my husband, I knew it was right immediately.
With Patrick and me, there were always questions.

It was June, and Chloe and I were leaving for Australia for a holiday. I had been there about a week when I received a phone call from my assistant, Dana, who asked me if I'd heard from Patrick. I'd received a missed call from him a few days after I arrived in Australia, but when I tried to call back there was no response.

Dana told me that he had gone on a fishing trip on a charter boat off San Pedro in Los Angeles, which was something he loved to do. He was supposed to show up for a family get-together that weekend, but he didn't make it. This was not like him. He didn't pick up his son, either. That set off alarm bells for his ex-wife, Yvette. Me too. He adored his son and wouldn't go on trips with me if it meant he couldn't see his boy.

As time went on and he remained missing, I had such an odd and hollow feeling in my gut. I had been through cancer and divorce, but the idea of someone in my life suddenly being gone without a trace left me with an emptiness I hadn't known before. There were no answers. Only questions.

All I could do was wait for news and take long walks on the beach.

By now, I was incredibly worried and longed for real answers. Dennis Nebrich was the head investigator from the Coast Guard, and he did a wonderful job. As far as we knew, Patrick went on a fishing trip and didn't return. His car was still at the dock. On the charter boat, they found his wallet and keys.

I called my old security friend Gavin de Becker and asked what else I could do. We decided to send a couple of his private investigators to Mexico to certain places Patrick had talked about. I asked Gavin if I should get on TV and do a public plea, but he advised against it. The private investigators placed missing-person posters everywhere in Mexico and made a lot of inquiries in case Patrick had decided to disappear, but nobody had seen him. I also thought he could have gone to Korea, where he was born, but as far as we know that isn't so.

By November 2005, four months after his disappearance, the United States Coast Guard's investigation concluded that Patrick "most likely" drowned.

The media frenzy wouldn't end, though, and there remains endless speculation that he faked his own death. The case even appeared on *America's Most Wanted* and then on *Dateline NBC*. Bogus and manufactured pictures appear every year on the anniversary of his disappearance with articles saying he has been sighted in different places. I find it strange. They're always from a distance, blurry and fuzzy. In this age of cell phones, wouldn't you think that someone would have a really clear picture of him by now and would immediately post it on the internet?

Part of my healing process was building a stone labyrinth as a private memorial to him. My friend, Aussie landscape designer Coral Browning, helped me build it. Patrick loved nature and gardens. I know the labyrinth is something he would have enjoyed.

There is some good that has come from the bad.

The wonderful thing that has come out of this is that his ex-wife, Yvette, and I became close friends. Our main concern has been their son, Chance. Yvette believes that Patrick would never have left his boy. I agree.

I lived in pain for so long over this, but I had to teach myself to live in the now, which is an important life lesson.

The truth is, I'll never really know what happened.

Sometimes you need a new perspective when life turns upside down.

I decided to get out of LA and do a road trip to Vegas to go to a Louise Hay seminar. It had been about a year since Patrick disappeared and I wanted the chance to meet the woman who had helped me so much already. She was my superstar. I wondered if she could help me with this period of my life as well.

I shared the driving with Rona and her daughter Tottie. Along the way we stopped to stretch our legs and get some gas. I was at the wheel when Rona went inside the gas station to pay, and then when she returned we took off. Some twenty-odd minutes later, the people in the car next to us, which was filled with adorable young men, began waving at us. I thought, *How sweet!* and politely waved back. They kept waving and waving—which became pointing. It turns out the gas cap wasn't on and we had been spewing gas all down the highway and they were letting us know!

As Louise taught me, thank God for the little kindnesses in life. We all laughed our heads off while arguing as a family about who filled it and didn't put the cap back on. (It was me—so embarrassed!) Luckily, we had enough fuel to get us to the next gas station. Then, driving into Vegas at night through the desert, we proceeded to get really lost and found ourselves going in circles. When we finally reached our destination, it was straight to the bar at the Wynn resort for three dirty martinis. We'd earned them!

I have to admit that this bar became our hangout after spending all day being so spiritual at the seminar. I needed both kinds of spirit at this point. It was looking inward, followed by dirty martinis and interviewing all the waitresses about their lives.

Life, indeed, goes on. You just have to grasp it.

After five days in Vegas, a very nice police officer pulled us over for speeding on the way home. He recognized me and let us off with just a warning.

Thank you, sir. Another small kindness.

*

It wasn't long before this time in my life would translate into my new CD, *Grace and Gratitude*. It was produced and cowritten by my friend and Canadian singer and songwriter, Amy Sky. Most of the songs were inspired by loss in my life and healing. I've never been a drinker, really, but as I recorded this CD, vodka was my friend. I was still pretty sad, and singing these emotional songs was hard. I have to admit a thimbleful of vodka really helped me. I'm a lightweight!

The music on this CD came from my heart and spirit, and it still gives me pleasure and peace. I loved that we used Eastern influences, including Tibetan and Japanese chants. I was also inspired by my friends Nancy and Jim, who are devout Buddhists. I would pray and chant with them as we said *Nam-myoho-renge-kyo*. It speaks of devotion, determination, and manifesting the good. I also pray with my Christian friends. I respect all belief systems because I believe they all come from the same place: love and forgiveness.

My grandfather Max Born had a famous quote where he said, "The belief that there is only one truth and that oneself is in possession of it, seems to me the deepest root of all that is evil in the world."

My whole life I searched for one thing I could believe in, but I couldn't find just one because I believe in possibilities and respect all people's different faiths. I have a real problem with people killing each other for what they believe, so my grandfather's words put it all into perspective for me.

I agree with him.

EIGHTEEN

Magic

If all your hopes survive
Destiny will arrive.
I'll bring all your dreams alive
For you.

In 2008, to raise awareness and garner donations to build the ONJ Cancer Wellness & Research Centre, I was asked to do something rather extraordinary: walk the Great Wall of China. The idea was to make it a media spectacular and invite as many celebrities as possible to join me. Someone had approached director of fund-raising Peter Dalton at the Austin Hospital with the idea four years earlier and it took that long to get permission from the Chinese government. I thought it was a wonderfully inspired idea, and, with Peter, began to plan it.

The whole thing was pretty complicated from the get-go, but we were determined. This trip would be the first major fund-raiser for the ONJ Centre and I was thrilled to participate both on the ground and in the planning stages. Before we "got out there," though, we had to be totally organized, and there were times when I thought, *Oh no, this will never happen*. But each little stop was followed by a start, and the plan to walk gradually moved on.

As part of this big project, I released *The Great Walk to Beijing: A Celebration in Song* to raise further proceeds. Artists like Sir Cliff Richard, Keith Urban, Richard Marx, and Barry Gibb all signed on to do duets. I just called my friends, and they were so generous with their time and their efforts.

It was particularly lovely to reunite with Cliff Richard because we went so far back. He was so quick to come on board.

"Anything you need, Liv. And I can't wait to walk," he told me.

And it really touched my heart singing with my talented friends, including singer/songwriter Jann Arden from Canada, who I'm singling out because she's a fellow cancer thriver, and Aussie singer Belinda Emmett, who sadly passed away before we could record. We made sure to feature one of her tracks on the CD in her memory.

In the lead-up to the walk, each day I would receive delicious and goose-bump-causing messages asking the most exciting things: "Hey Olivia, wondering if you're good with camping in the Gobi Desert? Because there aren't any hotels there." My response: "It will be a big adventure. Sign me up!"

The mission would take twenty days of walking the 159 miles along portions of the Great Wall. We would begin on April 7 and end up in Beijing on April 28. Best of all, I would be joined by incredible friends and family; celebrities from the music, acting, and sports worlds; and, most wonderfully, cancer thrivers like myself.

I loved the physical challenge of walking more than a hundred miles (something I had never done) over some really challenging sections of the wall, passing through deserts and mountains while battling through drastic weather changes. I was told that quite often we'd be facing tough conditions and harsh physical challenges, but that felt right. Wasn't it a great metaphor for what we were doing in the first place? This is exactly what cancer patients face as they climb their own personal walls to recovery.

I knew it would be mind-blowing. A once-in-a-lifetime event.

I also knew that I'd better get ready for what promised to be an intense experience. "Physical" actually became my theme song again! Even if I was tired from a show the night before, I dragged myself out of bed and hit the hotel gym as often as I could. I focused on cardio and getting my heart rate up. I couldn't even imagine how much stamina would be necessary for this endeavor but figured I needed as much as possible when I read that the wall is forty-five degrees steep in a lot of places and always uneven.

"How are you going to physically survive this?" a friend asked.

"One day at a time," I replied.

It was amazing how this Walk the Wall project came together— two hundred people quickly agreed to be there with me when I took those steps. In addition to Sir Cliff Richard signing on immediately, we also had the lovely Didi Conn, Dannii Minogue, and TV host Leeza Gibbons (a total sweetheart). Aussie Olympic swimming legend Ian Thorpe showed up, and lost his luggage—including his size 17 (no, that's not a typo) walking shoes. They couldn't find a pair to fit him in China, so he walked the wall barefoot.

Barefoot!

There was someone else walking into my life as well. His name was John Easterling and he was my new . . . everything. We'll get to that in a moment.

The plan was to go to nine different provinces in China. We would fly and bus to different parts of the wall since we couldn't possibly cover the entire Mongolian side on foot during the time period allotted. Each day would be a ten- to twelve-hour endurance test.

Soon I was flying to Shanghai to begin the walk. I wanted to start immediately, and it was so exciting to meet the team. Louise Georgeson had worked hard with Peter Dalton to figure out all the details, and she was there to greet us. Then it was off to bed. The next morning would come soon enough—we were to be up at dawn.

I was awake, ready, and . . . woefully unprepared.

It didn't take long before I found out that there wasn't enough gym time in the world to prepare for this experience. The wall, it turned out, was basically *a straight-up* climb, and the steps were deep, steep, and quite often slippery. You had to be on your game with each step.

We kept walking up, up, up into the clouds. It was one of the most challenging, purely physical moments of my entire life. After the first day, I didn't think I'd ever walk again because the lactic acid buildup made my legs feel as if they were on fire. But all of us pushed through pain to get to the other side.

I ignored the aches and pains, kept huffing and puffing, and then each day found my body getting stronger. After a few days my breathing began to slow down as I walked—my body was quickly adapting. My motivation was our cause, and the panoramic views were stunning—it was a once-in-a-lifetime way to experience something so breathtaking. It became exhilarating to push myself to new heights, literally. As I walked, I imagined all the workers who built the wall and the blood, sweat, and sacrifice that went into creating something for the ages.

They couldn't possibly know that so many years later those same steps would be used to help people around the globe regain their health and lives.

It's stunning when you think of how everything is connected.

What we were doing for cancer awareness was groundbreaking and the press from all over the world was following us. There were reports in newspapers and magazines, but they only told part of an unraveling story. For me, the joy in this trek came from the small magical moments, like Cliff singing to us on the bus, or the day my *Grease* costar and good friend Didi arrived to walk with me and reminisce about the happy days of filming the movie. And walking across the Gobi Desert is something I will never forget.

The days required so much stamina, and I had to really bring it, since I was leading the others. What I lacked in physical strength, though, I made up for with the determination gene I got from Mum. She was a strong woman who loved the outdoors and she used to hike the mountains of Europe with her father, Max Born. How I wished she could have walked the Great Wall with me. She would have loved it!

One of the days, we hiked for about eight hours, going straight up—no joke. Oh, how I ached at night! That next morning I was practically crawling out of the bed and toward breakfast.

I groaned silently (and then not so quietly) while my legs wobbled. But then I shook it off, brushed my teeth, and pulled on my sweatshirt.

Soon I was out the door and facing the wall.

Every morning we would hold hands and sing "Magic." It was life-affirming as we made our way toward that first step.

You have to believe we are magic.
Nothing will stand in our way.

One of the most memorable moments was when Joan Rivers arrived to "walk." Her manager, Billy Sammeth, a dear friend of mine who we've just sadly lost to cancer, had also been my manager for a while.

He made the call to Joan who quickly said yes.

One morning, I stepped off the bus in Beijing and Joan was right there in perfect makeup with that big smile, wearing black pants, a black shirt, a hot-pink trench coat—and sky-high red pumps. *Wait, what? There is no way she could make it up even two stairs in shoes that high!*

"You've got your heels on, Joan!" I said in an amazed voice.

I'll never forget her words to me.

Joan said, "Olivia, when you invited me, I thought you said the Great Mall of China!"

She followed this by walking up a few stairs, turning around, and asking, "Where's the ladies' room?"

Later she told Martha Stewart on her show, "There was so much wind on the wall, I could have skipped my last two face lifts." She also remarked, "The wall was built and rebuilt over the centuries. It's had more work done on it than I've had on my face."

God love her.

Joan changed her shoes and we gave her walking poles to help with the climb, and we were off. She and Billy were there with me for a full day. "I was the only one there on a walker," Joan later joked.

Joan brought spades of wonderful and much-needed humor to our journey. I'm so grateful she came all that way for me and so sad that she left us much too soon. I miss her warmth and kindness.

On we walked through every climate and condition: hot, cold, rain, burning sun, and snow.

There were other practical concerns along the way as well. I was honestly worried about how anyone would go to the bathroom. That problem was solved by taking along a red tent with a toilet inside. Boy, that red tent was a beacon of relief for us all (in more ways than one). Our guides were kind enough to carry this contraption, which wasn't easy.

One day we were walking along a freezing-cold stretch with several inches of snow on the ground. We had a mile and a half to go to reach the next village, which, when you're walking along the wall, might as well be a thousand miles. We had two amazing local helpers who carried certain supplies, along with a donkey helper. That day, they set up the red tent in the middle of a barren field where the wind was so fierce that I was doing some tent business and the actual tent was almost whipped away. (Just imagine that photo hitting the internet!)

Each day, we did what we had to do. No matter what. Weak but determined is how I felt one morning when I woke up with a raging fever and a throat that was red and raw. I couldn't skip a day for any reason whatsoever because I was the leader, so I put a scarf around my neck, hid my illness from everyone else, and hit the stairs.

One foot in front of the other. Climbing, climbing, climbing. My bones ached from the fever, and I could barely swallow, but there was no choice but to trudge on. People were depending upon us to raise this money.

Never give in.

One day we were walking through the snow in a little town when a young girl ran right by me in a red sweater with something wiggling in her hands. I saw that she was on her way to a pond that was in front of us—and then I heard a loud splash. "What is that?" I said to the young man walking with me.

He ran to the pond and fished out a little ball of fur. It was a kitten, a tiny baby about five weeks old, soaking wet, understandably frightened, and cold beyond belief.

I was wearing a bumbag (fanny pack) and frantically looked through it for something so this little kitten wouldn't freeze to death. I found my warm red scarf and wrapped him in it, rubbing his wet fur dry until the shaking little creature began to relax. Then I tucked him into my bumbag, which was against my warm body. We were close to our bus—we had no milk or food for him, but at least there was heat. Luckily, I managed to find some condensed milk in the next town. I poured some on my fingers and put it in the mouth of this precious little kitten whose eyes were still closed. He was a ginger tom and, of course, I called him Magic.

I carried him with me for the rest of the walk and let him sleep on my heart at night. I adored him and he became our trip mascot.

Magic had a standing order of fresh milk at each one of our stops and slept with me at night. He walked the wall with me every day in my bumbag. I was so desperate to bring him back to the United States to live with me, but I knew I couldn't bring a live animal through customs, and certainly not one that young that didn't have its shots yet.

One of our cameramen offered to keep Magic, promising he would be well loved. It broke my heart to give him up, but at least I knew he was going to a good home. I think it was Magic who helped me get through the last days of the walk, with his tiny meows making me smile each step of the way.

I was so attached to him and I still cry when I see photos of him. He died a few days after I left China. I missed him and knew he missed me. I think my love kept him alive. He was too young to have been away from his mom and needed her milk and nurturing to stay alive. I tried to be all that for him, but we just ran out of time.

The last two days on the wall, Magic opened his eyes and I stared into them. This little creature had helped me so much and given me so much comfort, especially after John got a call from his brother, Don, in North Carolina. Don's wife, Vivian, who had struggled with brain cancer for two years, was dying. John immediately began the long trip back and arrived half an hour before she passed. As for the kitten, I'm glad that he could stare into the face of one who loved him during his brief life. Our little mascot was in my bumbag the day we crossed the finish line in Beijing. Years later, I would adopt a cat in the United States and name him Magic #2.

I'll always be grateful to all who took part in this adventure.

NINETEEN
Pearls on a Chain

Remember I said someone else was also walking with me on the wall? Well, it was the love of my life: John Easterling.

True love found me when I wasn't looking.

I first met John through my dear friends Nancy and Jim. John is an environmentalist, a treasure hunter, a plant-medicine expert, and a businessman. He spent forty-two years working with plants in the Amazon rain forest in Peru, which is why he is known as Amazon John. We had crossed paths over the years at charity events and talks he gave on plants and botanicals, and I found him very interesting.

Apparently, he didn't feel the same way about me. As John will tell you, "I thought anyone from Hollywood and involved in the things she was involved with must be some kind of nutcase!" (Maybe he was right!)

John will also say that he knew of me, but that was it. "I didn't know any of the details. I didn't have any of her albums. I hadn't seen any of her movies. It just wasn't in my orbit." His "orbit" was treasure hunting in the Amazon. There was no room there for a trip to the multiplex to see *Xanadu*!

Nancy and Jim had met John at the Anaheim Health Expo in 1992 and quickly developed a friendship. Nancy was actually in line for an ice cream and saw this man giving people samples of his herbs. "I listened to John speak about how he has been to the Amazon over sixty times," Nancy told me. "His mission is to help people live healthier lives."

"My dream," John told the crowd, "is to see millions of people experience these life-changing herbs."

Nancy had taken her mother, Lenore, then in her early eighties, to the expo that day. Lenore tried the herbs and felt so good and had so much energy that she stayed up half the night and cleaned out all her closets.

Nancy joked, "I'll have what she's having!"

Lenore asked to go back to the expo the next day to stock up on more herbs from "that nice, handsome man." Nancy and Jim loved the products as well, and they found them so life-changing that Jim ended up becoming an independent distributor for John's company, Amazon Herb.

Over the years, I saw John with Nancy and Jim several times, and we always chatted for a few minutes. Then one day he came to Malibu to do a special talk about the rain forest. At the time, I was living there with Chloe, who was about nine. We were coping with the divorce.

John gave his speech that evening, which was fascinating. I was one of the many who gathered afterward to talk to him, and we shared a few words. He had to leave early the next morning—but then the unimaginable happened.

On the way to the airport, he was blinded by the sunlight and suddenly his car careened off the road and fell fifty feet down onto another road, totaling the rented Lexus. This could have been a fatal accident, but he was very, very lucky. The car somehow found solid ground below. The impact of the crash to earth was jolting for poor John, though, who was strapped to a gurney and rushed by ambulance to the hospital in Santa Monica in agonizing pain.

Doctors told him that he had almost certainly broken something in his back and the X-ray showed a fractured T12 in his spine. They wanted to put him on painkillers, but John refused to take anything but his own herbs. "I knew what the best material was for relieving pain," he said. And they didn't have it at the hospital.

After the adrenaline of the accident began to subside, the real pain set in. He made a phone call to Jim and Nancy, who were living in my guesthouse at the time. Jim brought him a bottle of his Recovazon (one of John's Amazon Herb products for recovery from injury or physical exertion), and soon John had clearance to actually leave the hospital, despite his fractured back.

John didn't know anyone locally, except for Nancy, Jim, and me. Since they were living with me, all of us made an anxious trek to the hospital.

We picked up a very apologetic and stoic John, who hid his pain, insisting that he hated to bother any of us. We drove him back to my house to rest and recoup. I got him settled on the couch, reminded him that this was no bother at all, and got ready to jump back into my car.

"I'll run to the pharmacy to get your painkillers," I told him.

"I refuse to take them," said the man who could barely stand.

What?

"I'm very confident in the botanicals I'm doing. But I do need a little help," he insisted.

There I was at my house rubbing his back, arms, and legs with Recovazon. Chloe wandered downstairs to see what was going on. It's funny what you remember, but I can still hear him telling my daughter that she had healing hands. Chloe was fascinated and quickly signed up to become my assistant nurse.

"Olivia and Chloe laid their hands on my back and it was a big relief," John recalls. "They had some really powerful healing energy between them."

The "patient" insisted that he didn't need anything else (beside his herbs and maybe a glass of water) and then went to sleep on my couch. The last thing I remember from that night was John calling his girlfriend to tell her what happened. Later, I wandered downstairs to check on him and smiled when I saw Scarlett, my Irish setter, sleeping by John's feet. Dogs always seem to know when someone is in pain.

I was shocked when John insisted he would leave the next day.

"But you can barely walk! Why don't you take a few days and just relax?" I asked.

He wouldn't hear of it. A warrior-type, he forced himself to stand, thanked us profusely, gave Scarlett a pat, and called a cab. I will never be sure how he did it. When I called a few days later to check on him, he said he was fine. With a fractured back. That's my boy!

I didn't even have a chance to see for myself how he'd healed because I wouldn't see him again. Not for years.

John and I did talk occasionally on the phone, though, and during one of our chats I mentioned that our darling Scarlett was pregnant. "Can I have one of the puppies?" John asked me. So I sent Duke, the largest of the golden pups, to him, plus another pitch-black pup named Seal to his friend Charlie. I was just thrilled that they were going to great homes and I wouldn't need to worry about two of the nine new additions.

Even after this, I still didn't see John for a long time, except for a brief encounter at a charity event. Out of the blue one day, I called him to check on Duke and ask a business question. I was thinking of doing a skin-care line for one of the major chains and wanted to see if we could rebottle his own skin-care products (that I loved) and rename them for this possible deal. We could easily get them into a lot of stores.

"John, I have been asked to do this . . . ," I began.

I described the idea to him and he said, "Why would I want to do that?"

I reminded him that it would be a great way to expand his distribution to the entire world. "But if it's a major-chain store, they're going to want to cheapen my product and put it in toxic plastic bottles," he said. "It's not something I'm interested in."

That was that.

I'd be lying if I said it didn't hurt my feelings. On the other hand, I really respected John and how he stuck to his ideals of producing pure products based on his deep knowledge of health and healing. He was so proud of his line and personally sourced every ingredient from the Amazon. It wasn't about the money for him. It was about the product and not diminishing the quality of it—even a tiny bit—despite the fact that he was being offered store placement around the globe. Frankly, there aren't many others I know who would have said no to that kind of deal. At the very least they would have thought about it, wrestling with the pros and cons for a few days.

John took about zero seconds to decide.

My goodness, I thought. *He has principles.*

I'd be lying if I didn't say I liked that. Very much.

After that business idea went bust, we still kept in touch on a personal level.

"I found the real person," John says now. "Olivia was so friendly, engaging, sincere, and genuine. I began to learn that she is such a caring person. It was very meaningful to me."

He would occasionally send me pictures of his dog, whom he renamed Sherlock. He told me that he tried different names, but nothing stuck. Then he was at his brother Don's house one day and saw the dog sniffing around. Don said, "Hey, Sherlock, what are you doing?" Ears suddenly perked up. The name was perfect, and Sherlock confirmed this by answering to it.

Eight years later, I was performing near John's hometown in Florida. I called home to check on things and told my assistant, Dana, "I think John lives somewhere near here in Florida. Why don't you call him and invite him and his girlfriend to the show?"

He actually showed up with another "date." He arrived backstage the next night with Sherlock! I hadn't seen the pup in so many years, yet he remembered me. A flurry of kisses and licks followed—and I'm talking about what happened between Sherlock and me.

John and I chatted a bit about what was going on in our busy lives. The interesting thing was he knew so little about my career.

"I've never seen *Grease*," John confessed.

I don't presume everyone has heard me sing, but it seemed like the entire world had seen *Grease*.

"Never," he said with a smile.

In fact, he knew very little about my music, although he was really interested in my album called *Grace and Gratitude*. I listened as he told me why the music touched his heart. We continued to talk about the deeper messages of the music we loved, and John confessed that he previously thought I was just this "Hollywood chick" but now he was seeing me in a different light.

Oh, and one more thing: he didn't have a girlfriend anymore.

He loved the concert, especially when I opened the show with "Pearls on a Chain." He told me everyone in the audience was deeply moved. Later, John said that the moment hit him especially hard, piercing him right in the heart, as the song starts with a Peruvian flute.

"I felt this wave of healing go through the audience," John recalls. "Everyone was crying. It was a big movement of healing moving through an entire auditorium. It came to me instantly. I knew who she was in that moment. I thought to myself, *This woman is a healer. Music and song is just a medium of her healing.* And all I could think about was connecting with the *curanderos* and healers I work with in the Amazon."

This was the song that started it all.

Every day my sun rise will dawn where you are.
Every night we sleep underneath the same stars.
And if we stand face to face
You will see love's amazing grace.
We are pearls.

We are pearls.
We are pearls on a chain.

Looking back now, I see that John and I are on the same strand.

The next day, John came to visit me at my hotel. I was at the pool in a bikini with wet hair stuck to my face and no makeup. Embarrassed doesn't begin to cover it! (John now says, "I thought you looked radiant." No wonder I married him!) Sometimes you just have to live in the moment, though, so we had lunch and continued our conversation. He was a fascinating man who was consumed with health, wellness, and doing greater good. Just like me.

We talked about my mission when it came to the ONJ Centre and how I was determined to find a cure for cancer. Hollywood chick? Please!

At the end of the day, he suggested something that sounded extraordinary and a bit frightening.

"I'd really like to take you to the Amazon," John said. "I want to take you to Peru to meet the *curandero* healers. I go every June. I'd like to take you next June."

Wait—what? That's a hell of a first date!

"That's . . . interesting," I said.

He even had a calendar date in mind, but it was six months away! This was serious.

"At that moment, I knew I had to connect her with the healers I work with in the Amazon," John recalls. "She said yes and I thought, *I'm taking Olivia Newton-John into the rain forest. Now what?*"

After John left, I rang Nancy and she made this trip to the Amazon more of a reality. "We're going next June with John to Peru," she said. "It's going to be a celebration of my sixtieth birthday. You must come with us and celebrate."

Were they all in cahoots? Did I really say yes?

John came to Los Angeles on business one more time and we decided to go to Nancy and Jim's for dinner (she's a great cook) to discuss the trip. In the car on our way to dinner, he played the most beautiful music that was native to the Amazon, complete with that pure flute sound.

"I'm working on a special drink I want you to taste," he said.

He had this new Amazon herb concoction in a beautiful Peruvian cup specially created by his dear friend Pablo Seminario from the sacred valley of the Incas.

"Was it a love potion?" I asked him later.

What I couldn't know at this moment is that Nancy and Jim always felt that John and I would be a match. They believed that if they could get us to the Amazon, we would fall madly in love with each other for life.

I wish someone had told me this was the plan! I thought I was just going on an adventure. . . . But then again, isn't that what love really is?

As the time approached to travel with my friends and John to Peru, I was still hesitant. I had just been to Hong Kong on a concert tour and I returned home only two days before I would have to fly to the Amazon. Frankly, I didn't have it in me to embark on another enormous trip.

It's funny when I think about it now. My life could have been very different if I didn't summon something from deep within and push past my exhaustion.

I'm so tired, my body shouted.

But it's Nancy's birthday, my mind countered. *You have to go.*

I shudder now to think I might have missed it.

John met us at the airport in Lima, but that wasn't the end of our air travel. The next morning, we were packing up again to catch a small plane that would fly us over the Andes and into the heart of the jungle.

On that early-morning flight over the snow-covered mountains, the view was so magnificent that I found myself holding my breath. I watched as the sun rose over untouched blankets of snow that sparkled like they were covered with millions of diamonds.

All of a sudden, any tiredness on my part seemed to pass. There was a surge of adrenaline that made me feel like anything was possible.

We disembarked at a tiny airport in the town of Pucallpa. We were met on the tarmac by an indigenous chief dressed in ceremonial brown-and-white hand-painted *cushma* (robes) and an elaborate beaded headdress. As we made our way through the airport, I began to realize that John was like the Godfather there! The locals adored, respected, and honored him. He had always given some of the proceeds from his herbal formulas to help with local education and health. In turn, the people found ways to make his trips easier and celebrated his returns.

Heavenly blue skies with wispy white clouds drifted above as we puttered downstream on a *peki-peki* boat on the Yarinacocha Lagoon near the headwaters of the legendary Amazon River. We went all the way to a small boatel (like a hotel, but you could only get there by boat) on the banks of a tributary of the Amazon. Each room was a thatched hut with screens for windows. Yes, it was basic, but so beautiful, as the huts blended into the environment. It was clean and gorgeous in its simplicity.

"We had a generator and running water. It wasn't hot water, but we had water. When the generator was on, it powered the lights and the water in those screened-in little cabanas. It was actually quite lovely," John remembers now.

"Tomorrow, I'm going to take you upriver to my property," John promised us. Nancy, Jim, and I couldn't wait to make the trek.

Nancy would later tell me, "I saw the chemistry between you two from the start."

John told me that he had several hundred acres there on the banks of the river where he grew *camu camu*, a special fruit mostly grown in Peru and Brazil, where it's always been used for health purposes. John told me that the fruit, the size of a large grape, starts out as green and then changes to red when mature. It's filled with vitamin C, potassium, and leucine to help with muscle and bone-tissue growth while also acting as a natural energy booster and antioxidant.

I was fascinated as I listened to him talk about his life's work. He wasn't just there to tell me. He would *show* me what he did as we embarked on a journey through the rain forest together.

I had been to the rain forest before when I'd traveled to Belize to film a program about saving the native howler monkey. That didn't prepare me for the splendor of spending time with John in the jungle that day, though. Everything about it was extraordinary. This was a private trek with the best personal tour guide.

We took a small boat to his plantation. This was a new location for me, but John was the perfect tour guide and pointed out various surrounding sights, including the Ucayali River. It wasn't long before we were met by Alicia, a *curandero*. We hiked deeper into the rain forest with Alicia and her husband, Alberto. She waved a smoking device as we walked and had bells attached to both of her ankles.

"What is she doing?" I asked.

"Keeping the big snakes away," John told me. "The number one cause of death here is poisonous snakebite."

We sat down on a log, and John launched into a story about another visit during which he'd also rested on a log—and then it moved.

"Moved?" I said, swallowing hard.

"It was dark. I sat on an anaconda," he said with a laugh.

John had talked to me about doing an ayahuasca ceremony involving drinking a hallucinatory plant/vine blend under the guidance of an experienced shaman. "It's a very special medicine and quite revered," John said. "It can create a mind-altering experience if you do a full-on ceremony with it and drink more of the vine mixed with the Psychotria leaf that's boiled down to a concentrate.

"Prayers are said over this medicine," he told me.

This process ensures a long night connecting with your higher self. At the time, I said I wasn't interested.

The truth was, I was afraid to do anything with mind-altering results.

"I understand. This is not enough for a full experience. This is just a taste so your body can receive the energetic imprint of this important medicine," John said.

I was offered a small capful of the liquid, poured out of a water bottle.

"Oh, John," I said, sipping the thick, dark liquid. "It tastes really good."

"I just wanted Olivia to taste it, which should have had a minimal effect on her," he says now. "I knew her body would understand what it was, and it could be quite clearing for her, which is why I gave her just a little capful."

The ayahuasca explanation continued with Alicia singing a beautiful *icaro*, a deep and seductive Shipibo song of connection. John asked me to also sing a song and I felt the perfect one was "Grace and Gratitude" because I had so much in life for which I was grateful.

There I was singing the song of gratitude in the middle of the Amazon rain forest!

Definitely a highlight of my life.

> *Thank you for life.*
> *Thank you for everything.*
> *I stand here in grace and gratitude*
> *And I thank you.*

*

We spent a little more time in the rain forest and hiked back to the river where indigenous Shipibo artisans were waiting with their wares to sell, including beautiful hand-painted clothing and table-cloths, artwork, pottery, and jewelry made of shells and beads. After

this wondrous day, we went back to the boatel by the river for a delicious dinner of fresh fruit and fish cooked on an open fire because
there was no gas or electricity. We ate by the amber light of the
candles on our table and talked about the day and what it meant to
each one of us. I told my friends how amazing it was for me to truly
experience a place that was so wild, free, and in balance with nature.

Of course, all good things must come to an end, and by ten
that night, I was yawning. I needed to get some rest. John walked
us back to our huts, which were perched right on the edge of the
river. Nancy and Jim were right next to me, and John opted for a
hut about 100 feet away, behind us in the jungle area. The hum of
the gas-powered generators went silent and the lights blinked out.

I drifted off quickly, only to wake up around midnight feeling
so sick that my eyes couldn't focus and I could barely stand.

We were supposed to leave at four in the morning for a river
trip to a Shipibo village to meet up with John's indigenous friends.
I knew John had planned a predawn breakfast for us, but even
the thought of food was making my stomach churn. *Feasts! Boats!
River! Someone make it stop.*

I raced to the bathroom to throw up. Thank goodness my hut
had a working toilet.

What is happening to me?

Somehow, my feet forced my flip-flopping stomach and hazy
brain out into the open in the middle of the night. It was so dark,
and I could barely summon the energy to knock on Nancy and
Jim's hut door.

"Oh, guys, I don't feel well," I told them. "Would you please go
tell John that I can't go on this trip down the river? I'm really sorry.
But you guys should go and just leave me here."

I crawled back to my hut, and it wasn't long before John was knocking on my door and his hand was on my forehead. I knew that Nancy had run to get him.

"I know what's going on," he said.

I didn't know. But I wanted whatever was happening to, please, God, stop.

"I feel so sick, John," I moaned.

"It's not that you're sick," he promised me. "You're just so sensitive that you're integrating with the rain forest and the animals."

"I'm not integrating," I groaned. "I'm disintegrating!"

"Wait here," he said in the predawn darkness. Where in the world did he think I could go? I could barely make it back to the bed without the room spinning.

John raced to his hut and came back with a portable record player and some of his favorite healing music. I'd always thought that music was my medicine and now that theory was really on the line, in the middle of the rain forest, in a hut.

John kept the deep chanting music on low and lay gently next to me in the bed. I wish I could say it was romantic, but I was on the verge of kneeling in front of the toilet. When he put his arms around me, though, it did feel really good to be held in the strong embrace of this adventurous and mysterious Amazon man. But then I had to detangle myself to jump out of bed and throw up again. It was so horrendous and I was so weak, but I still mustered up the voice to tell him, "You really need to go. Just leave me here." I was so embarrassed.

"I'm not going anywhere," he said.

*

It wasn't long before I started seeing very odd visions. "I really don't know what's going on with me," I said as these strange sights continued to play in my mind.

"Tell me what you're seeing," John said calmly. We were back on the bed and he was holding me again in those supportive arms.

"I'm seeing you," I cried. "What do you mean?"

"You are standing above me," I continued, "and I'm on the ground. It feels like I'm in the inside of something like a pyramid. There is stone behind you and you're standing on a platform. There are big chunks of stone everywhere. And you have this robe on. . . . I might be losing my mind!"

I waited for him to tell me I was indeed crazy.

"What color is the robe?" he asked. "Describe it to me."

"Well," I said, "it has geometric patterns. It's dark with a red pattern on it. And you have an unusual hat on. And you're commanding your people."

He fell off the bed. Literally. What I said freaked him out.

"I did fall on the floor when she described me in that tunic," John says. "That night, we just tumbled back in time and space."

John proceeded to tell me a story about his life.

He had been on several archaeological digs. One such dig, at a pre–Inca Chimu site, yielded an ancient tunic. He kept it for a time and considered giving it to the Smithsonian Institution, who were quite interested in purchasing a piece of history. He showed the piece at galleries in New York and at the pre-Columbian show in Santa Fe. John wasn't sure what to do with this textile because each time he'd unravel it to show it to someone, he would get feverish and his heart would race.

"My hands would shake, and I'd just have to lie down," he said. "I felt like I had the worst fever."

My own hands were trembling and I felt freezing cold as he told his tale.

"There was just something about this textile that made me ill," he said.

Then he told me that he had a realization that he needed to bring it back to Peru and rebury it. The only solution was to allow it to rest where it wanted to remain eternally. This wasn't an easy task. John had to basically smuggle the tunic back into the country, and that was just the first step. He had to retrace his journey back to a remote place and bury it again. Since the original site was now an official archaeological dig, he had to find another site to bury the tunic.

"There are certain things on earth that should never be disturbed," he said.

That wasn't the end of the story.

"Something happened after I put the textile in the ground again," he told me.

I was so engrossed that I forgot about throwing up.

"After I buried it again, I was leaning over to put the earth back in place and a condor flew over me. The shadow of his wings touched my shoulder and then it flew up off again," he said. "When I looked up, it was gone.

"I've never had that sickness again," he told me.

Cut to me lying on that bed with my teeth chattering. For some reason, I was having visions of John wearing that exact textile that he buried.

"Now, I'm seeing an opening in the stones," I told him, describing my continuing vision. "I can see a blue pool of water below me." I had the feeling I would be thrown into that water.

"I can see it, too," he said.

"It feels like we've had a life experience before—together," John said.

It felt so real.

Because it was.

That night, in this faraway place, deep in the Peruvian rain forest, John didn't leave my side. He held me gently, played soft music, and took care of me. He stayed the entire night. By morning, I felt not just better, but clearheaded, too.

It's hard to describe the feeling, but it was as if someone had lifted a gray veil that had been hanging over me and I finally shook off all the stress and self-doubt that had been plaguing me for a long time. I had been on antidepressants for about six months prior, but from that day on I didn't need them anymore.

All that weight had suddenly evaporated and my brain felt crystal clear. My entire body was at peace. It was amazing that someone could go from sick as a dog, throwing up all night, to a feeling of euphoria. When I stopped to think about it, it was abundantly clear that I had indeed purged much more than what was in my stomach.

As I began to feel better, John and I decided to sit outside. We watched the sun rise and talked for a long time.

I knew that there was something much deeper here. I thought he was feeling it, too.

We literally missed the boat that morning and John sent everyone away. I felt badly that he missed seeing his friends in the tribe, but John was fine with it. Instead, he planned for us to spend the day together quietly resonating, our frequencies melding into one, deep in the womb of the rain forest.

I knew this was a new beginning. As the sun was setting, he promised to take me into the Andean highlands to a special Inca site where he buried the ancient textile robe.

The next day, we flew out to Cuzco and John took me to a place he said was very special to him. We drove quite a way out of town and hiked out to a rocky perch where two hills met. We sat high up, overlooking the beautiful ruins of an Incan tambo (place of rest and renewal) complete with fresh water from an underground spring gushing out of a stone wall.

"This has always been a special place for me," John said. "It's where I come to make my annual decisions and affirmations for what the next year will bring."

"Can I be a part of that?" I heard myself say.

"Yes," he said without any hesitation. (Later he would tell me that he was shocked to say it, too.)

We sat, meditated, and prayed. Words weren't necessary, because there was a sudden knowing between us. At one point, John asked me what I wanted from my future. I talked about my precious Chloe and how what I wanted most in my life was for her health and happiness.

"I also need to raise major funds to open a cancer center in Australia," I told him.

As we sat with sweet hummingbirds singing in the background and a gentle breeze caressing my face, I knew that this was right—and I was in the perfect space and with the right person at my side. You always hear stories of how people connect and from that day forward, they're together. I never believed that would happen to me.

"I want health and happiness—and love," I said, finally telling him what I wanted for my own life.

His affirmation was he wanted to get his herbs into millions of bodies and heal them. We had much in common.

It was a beautiful thing to sit with someone so special and discuss our deepest hopes.

"We fell deeply in love and committed to supporting each other," John recalls. "As I was seeing my next year, Olivia said, 'Can I be a part of that?' I said, 'Yes.' We looked at each other and then out at this big blue Andean sky. Although we were very far from home, we *were* home."

In the peace of the mountaintop, so far away from city noise and distractions, we just knew we were meant to be together. I fell in love with this incredibly smart and compassionate man who says yes to everything.

He says yes to life.

By the time we went back to our hotel, I knew that I wasn't just falling in love with John. I had a flash that I didn't share with him until much later.

I knew we would be back here in a year to be married on that ledge.

We had already started the beginning of our life together in the most sacred way—with shared hopes and dreams.

Six months later, we were attending a conference in Arizona, where John was speaking. By this time, we were inseparable. It was Valentine's Day, and we had the entire day off. Joy! John kept taking me to these power places in the Red Rocks around Sedona. Each was interesting and included a church filled with people and a mountaintop with people hiking all around us. We stopped at a long trail by a stream and then went up cliffs to a towering bluff overlooking miles of canyon. He seemed a bit anxious. (He later admitted he was looking for the right spot to propose, but at each opportune moment someone would appear on the trail and inter- rupt.)

Finally, we went to dinner, and I kept waiting for something to happen because we had spent the day at some pretty amazing proposal spots! We had also just returned from a romantic trip to Prague and I had a feeling that a proposal was the next step. I knew we were going to end up together.

At dinner, we started some impromptu charades.

First two words: WILL—YOU. Then he ran his hands through his hair.

"Hairy?" I said.

He made the "sounds like" motion.

"Harry, dairy—marry," I said with a big smile.

He pointed at me.

I spoke the words "Will You Marry Me?"

He laughed and pretended to be surprised.

He always says I proposed to him, but he set it up!

We didn't have a ring, but he hollowed out the dinner roll and put it on my finger.

It was absolutely perfect.

It was us.

Of course, the first person I told was my daughter, who gave us her blessing.

"I just want you to be happy, Mum," she said.

So much of my life had been lived out in public, and we wanted to keep our relationship very private. It was precious to us, something we wanted to savor with each other, to enjoy without the rumors and the inevitable stories. For the wedding, I didn't need a big song and dance. I wanted to do something private, sacred, and special. I wanted our ceremony to reflect that it was just a beginning and we were vowing to make each day a celebration. I loved when John said that we had the rest of our lives to be on a honeymoon.

A year later to the day, John was in Peru on an expedition with his good friend and photographer Gregg Woodward. I flew down and met him in Lima. John asked Gregg to stay on a few days to record something special. The next day, we were back up to Cuzco, the old Inca capital.

We spent the night before the wedding wandering down cobblestone streets looking for treasures. John found an amazing formal wedding poncho, and I found a pair of locally made boots with the thickest and warmest wool inside. I also discovered a marriage shawl that complemented my little white dress that had traveled with me. I couldn't have planned it any better.

I married John Easterling on the winter solstice, June 21, 2008, on that same Peruvian mountaintop where we had first sat. It was exactly one year since we were on this ledge, visioning our future. Our altar was our ledge. The ceremony took place on this sacred site at six in the morning as the full moon began to yield to the sun climbing the Andean peaks and brightening a new day and a new future.

A local shaman named Odan officiated, accompanied by two musicians, one playing a conch shell and another on a Peruvian flute, the quena. The music was gorgeous, haunting and absolutely perfect. We thought about asking friends to make the trip but decided we wanted this to be private. And anyway, we couldn't fit any more people on the ledge! It was our moment.

On the way up the mountain, I realized I hadn't thought of a bouquet. I started picking wildflowers. By the time I got to the top, I had the most beautiful bouquet any bride could ever want.

"It was an extraordinary, beautiful, wonderful thing," John remembers.

We spent our honeymoon in Peru for a week. Afterward, we returned to John's home on Jupiter Island in Florida. Nine days later, we had a beachfront ceremony in Jupiter Island to make it legal, although to me the ceremony in Peru would always mark our real wedding. We were married by John's dear friend Bill, an Episcopalian minister.

We even kept that a secret for a few days and didn't tell our friends until we surprised them with a celebration at a July Fourth barbecue at our house in Malibu.

Mum always said to me, "Darling, you need to marry a businessman."

I used to say back to her, "A businessman? What on earth would I have in common with a businessman?"

She was so right, though. And John is so much more than just an amazing businessman. He's incredibly compassionate, caring, and kind, and a brilliant human being. He's funny and interested in the world and in healing it.

I'm so lucky to have a wonderful, beautiful husband who is so loving, and who loves me for me. John is also very patient and calming, which is perfect for me, because he's someone who really thinks things through, whereas I can be impulsive. He helps me see the steps I need to take.

We have so much in common, including our quest to stay healthy and our love of animals. He'll greet our dog and cat, which is exactly what I do, the moment we step through the door. I could never be with someone who didn't love animals.

My husband has so many ways that he shows me love, including writing me beautiful poetry. I love his sensitivity and concern for his family—his brother, Don, and sister, Nancy, and the respect he shows his father, Tom, who just turned ninety-four. Sadly, I never met his mother.

I always tell my friends that you're never too old to find love.

I found the love of my life at fifty-nine going on sixty.

Lucky me.

No one could believe that even after we were married, John still hadn't seen *Grease*.

Around this time, my good friend John Travolta invited my new husband and me to dinner at his home. John graciously sent a plane to pick us up, and we landed in his backyard. It was always his dream to have planes at his home and to be able to take off and land on his property—and he made it come true. Even when we were filming *Grease*, he told me, "One day, I'll have a house with a runway." I knew he would do it.

So, my husband and I landed at the Travoltas' beautiful home. John and his wonderful wife, Kelly, had an amazing dinner ready for us. Halfway through that dinner, John T said something about the movie *Grease*, and my John told him, "Never seen it."

"Seriously?" said John Travolta. "Were you living under a rock?"

Everyone laughed.

"No, I was in a canoe up the Amazon when the film came out," my husband said with a smile.

I could see the wheels turning in John T's mind. When we left the dinner table, he suggested we have dessert on one of his planes, which had just come back from being refurbished. My husband is also a pilot and loves anything to do with aviation, so he said he would love to see the plane. We wandered over to this sleek, magnificent machine parked on John T's very own runway, and dessert was served. As we sat down, *Grease* starting playing on the television screens scattered about the cabin.

Here we were watching *Grease* on a plane with John Travolta!

It was such a fantastic night, and when the film was over, my John said to us, "That was a really good movie. But one thing. Olivia looks better now."

Another reason to love him!

TWENTY

Silent Ruin

And if I close my eyes to the wild silent ruin
Then I'm just like everyone else.

Long before my marriage to John, I was driven to travel the world in the name of saving our creatures and environment. When I was asked to host a TV series called *Human Nature* in 1995, I said a quick yes because it was right up my alley. The idea was to explore the relationships between humans and animals around the globe. For fifteen glorious episodes, I traveled the world zeroing in on topics that were so close to my heart.

One of my favorite episodes featured Margaret Owings, a wonderful woman who dedicated her life to helping save mountain lions and sea otters from extinction. I didn't need to travel far to meet her in Monterey, California, where she had a magnificent house on the cliffs. From the moment we first hugged, I felt like she was a mother figure for me. She was intuitive to the point where she would say, "I knew you were going to call before the phone rang." It wasn't long before I would tell her, "I want to be you when I grow up." I was in my forties when I said this! (And I'm still waiting to be like her when I grow up!)

I respected Margaret's commitment to saving animals and reveled in her life force. We became fast friends, and soon I was staying at her house, built high on a cliff above the wild Pacific Ocean. From down below you could hear the seals barking. Her home also came with a story. She told me that a man wanted to marry her and told her so while they were sitting on a cliff top. "I told him, 'I'll marry you if you build me a house here,'" she said. Then she turned to me and said, "You're standing in that house."

She had other animal causes in addition to her work with the mountain lions. One day, she suggested that I go with her to a meeting with marine biologists from the local area. We arrived and suddenly Margaret said, "Liv, I'm not feeling well. Would you speak for me?"

I knew very little about the underwater experiments involving sonars she was there to talk about. In the deepest parts of the ocean, scientists were experimenting with sound waves and this was seriously affecting the hearing of dolphins and whales. It was horrific for those gorgeous creatures that depended upon sonar for survival. Margaret was there to explain why she was trying to put a moratorium on this type of "experiment." Once she told me the basics, I stood up and spoke from my heart about the subject and how the dolphins and whales deserved to exist in peace. I can still remember the serious looks on the faces of all those marine biologists who thought that I had been an expert in this area for many years!

Fooled 'em!

For another episode of the series, I made the trek to Alaska to record the plight of eagles that were rescued and rehabilitated after the horrendous *Exxon Valdez* oil spill that occurred in Prince William Sound in Alaska. We landed by plane and then took a train and a boat to film a scene where I would release an injured eagle back into the wild.

We arrived at a large-bird rescue aviary where the former "patient" was waiting to spread his wings again. We had to capture him from the air as he was practicing flying back and forth with his newly healed wing. The bird expert helping me was holding a huge burlap bag, which he tossed in the air up over the eagle to bring him down. It worked—except the eagle landed right on the top of my head and dug those large claws into my scalp.

"How *fantastic*," I said, wincing back the pain. "How many people can say they have an eagle scar on the top of their head?" (I wasn't badly hurt and consider this one of my life trophies.)

Soon Matt, little Chloe, and I were out on a boat in the middle of Prince William Sound, where I would eventually release the bird on camera. I went down the stairs and so did Chloe, who put her hand out to steady herself and burned it on the stove. We were out in the middle of nowhere without medical help and the day was just beginning! I went into mom mode, bandaged my poor little girl's hand and explained to her, "There is good and bad in everything. We just had some of the bad, and now it's time for the good." (I hoped!) I felt so badly for her because we couldn't go back right away.

We could only release the bird once, which meant we had only one camera take for this shot. "When you let him go, throw him upward," I was told. Aiming the bird was going to be quite a trick. I was a little afraid of him since he was very heavy, extremely powerful, and wild. He could also see the massive glacier in the distance and was feeling his freedom. It's funny how creatures, human or not, refuse to be daunted when they can smell and taste possibility.

As the time neared for the release, I stood closer to the bird, who was being held by a handler. All of a sudden, the moment was upon us and I was given this raptor. I held him firmly in my arms. I could hear our hearts pounding in tandem. I was reminded to throw him upward and suddenly released him into the air. You could hear the rush of his feathers being taken by the wind as the sky became his home again.

It was one of the most unusual, interesting, and life-affirming moments I've ever experienced.

My cameraman was thrilled because we got it all on tape in one incredible shot that became a defining moment of the series. And thank goodness Chloe's hand wasn't seriously burned. Phew!

One of the most tragic pieces we filmed for *Human Nature* was on an assignment in Greece, where we examined the plight of circus dancing bears. The sheer horror of it is something I will never be able to push out of my mind. The reasons that these bears lift their feet, or "dance," is that they're being tortured. They actually stand on electronic plates and are shocked into moving that way.

It hurt my heart to find out that some of the shocked bears had to have operations to fix their feet after too many shocks. That some found this "entertaining" made me sick to my stomach— and still does to this day. I couldn't believe that creatures could be treated in such a cruel and inhumane way. But that was the most important part of the show. We could expose these kinds of injustices against animals and hope that decent human beings would find it outrageous and seek change.

This series made sure that I couldn't park my bags too long at home, and soon I was off to Russia with my crew. The assignment was to interview a professor who lived about a four-hour drive from Moscow. The crew members who were traveling with me included our director, Jeff; photographer, Michelle; my makeup and hair artist, whose name was Madonna; and our cameraman, Michael Jackson, an Australian man.

No, you cannot make these things up! The same crew accompanied me during another shoot in Costa Rica, and the hotel we were staying at went bananas because they thought the real Michael Jackson and Madonna were checking in with Olivia Newton-John! When we arrived, we were informed that the hotel was throwing a parade for us. I hope they weren't too disappointed when our very tired and road-weary group rolled in with our suitcases and equipment.

And now we were in Russia, but there was no parade. There was just some cold weather to contend with during a busy shoot that would also take us to Red Square. We wanted to explore the fact that they were losing a lot of falcons in Moscow for industrial and construction reasons. We were there to interview a naturalist who raised falcons to release back into the city.

We were told to arrive in Red Square at six in the morning. I've been to a lot of cold places, but in Russia the temperatures chilled me to the bone and the winds ripped through even the puffiest parkas. It was still so gorgeous as the sun rose over the ornate buildings, though. I love to learn about the customs of new places, and this trip didn't disappoint. Soon a glass was put in front of me, and someone brought out a bottle of Russian vodka.

"It's a little early," I begged off.

My glass was filled to the brim.

Now, I'm not the biggest drinker, but I didn't want to insult anyone. It wouldn't be the last time during this trip that I drank what was put in front of me. You could say I spent my whole time in Russia just a little bit tipsy!

In retrospect, maybe this wasn't such a bad thing, because I was going through a divorce at the time.

Back on the road, we—me, Madonna and Michael Jackson, plus Jeff and Michelle—had to drive to the professor's house in an old van packed with our camera equipment. None of us had been to Russia before or spoke the language, and certainly there weren't any experts in the car when it came to navigating the back roads. This was in the days before GPS, and I'll never forget all of us poring over a complicated map trying to find our way.

As fate would have it, of course, our van broke down in the middle of the Russian countryside, which offered a vast landscape and not much else. We were forced to step outside into the tundra as panic began to set in. I stared at our ramshackle van, which had a flat tire. A short walk later, we found help at a gypsylike caravan that sold mostly . . . vodka! They agreed to change our tire, but it took time to fix it, so we had a few sips to warm up.

Like I said, it was a tipsy trip.

Back in Moscow, I did revel in the cultural marvels of being in this foreign land. All I wanted to do was buy food and give it to people who didn't have much. This was before Russia was more modernized, and its people were suffering from the political climate of the day. I remember going to a supermarket in Moscow, but it wasn't like any shopping experience I've had anywhere else. Large men with machine guns stood at the door of the market, which was intimidating to say the least.

We stocked up on the basics, including boxes and boxes of crackers, which came in handy during our breakdown on the way to the professor's house. Maybe I forgot to mention that we also bought our own bottle of vodka for our travels but couldn't find paper cups, so we used plastic cookie containers. Beggars can't be choosers! I'm not ashamed to say that all of us (minus our driver) drank vodka the entire way to the professor's house. The drink made up for a faulty van heater that only worked on and off.

During this once-in-a-lifetime journey, I found myself wanting to stop all the time and look at the amazing architecture and huge statues of Stalin that stood twenty feet tall in the air. You could say that they left quite an intimidating impression.

And forget about the glamour of five-star hotels. Our accommodations were very basic. At our suburban Moscow hotel, there was a severe-looking lady in a gray uniform with her hair pulled tightly into bun. Announcements in Russian would play over the hotel PA system every twenty minutes, day and night. It was enough to make Madonna, Michelle, and me feel a bit uncomfortable. From the first night on, we decided to sleep in one room together. The bathroom included a rusted-out sink and a toilet and a rusty shower that was dusted with cockroach powder. And there was no need for an alarm clock. At precisely 6:00 a.m., loud music came on through the public-address system indicating it was time for the *whole hotel* to rise and start the day.

No one recognized me in Russia, which was why we thought it would be okay to explore a bit of the nightlife scene. We were taken to an underground nightclub where the music was overwhelmingly loud. Like everything else, it was a bit scary and seemed to be run by the Russian mobsters.

I met so many lovely Russian people who had incredibly simple existences by Western standards. They were warm and welcoming, which wasn't surprising to me—my mother had Russian friends who spent time with us when I was little and I loved their company.

I met more amazing people when we ventured to a Russian farm for part of the shoot to stay with a couple who raised orphaned baby bears after their mothers were shot by hunters. The husband, who was a professor, wouldn't touch the babies, but he would feed them and make sure they were safe, hoping that they would be self-sufficient by the time they were returned to the wild. It made my heart soar to watch these adorable little black bears follow the man around as if they were his own children. Our cameraman even donned the professor's khaki hooded coat, which smelled of him, and the baby bears began to follow him into the forest. I walked behind the little bears, who stopped when we arrived at a tree that contained a honeycomb.

I'll never forget those baby bears running up the tree to get a sweet treat. What we didn't expect was the traumatized bees that came flying out, but they weren't that interested in the bears. Instead, they went inside our cameraman's hood and stung him about thirty times.

Very soon, he went running back to the little farmhouse with the bears in tow. The professor's wife took one look at him and nodded—the idea of needing treatment ASAP wasn't lost in translation. Luckily, he wasn't allergic to bees, but the sting spots felt as if they were on fire.

And what do you think they treat bee stings with in Russia? Why, of course, she reached into the cupboard and pulled out a bottle of vodka! It wasn't long before she was dabbing the vodka on him with a little white rag. Wouldn't you know it? Soon he felt much better!

That night, we sat outside the farmhouse by a roaring fire that reached up to touch the star-filled sky. It was one of those moments in life when you stop and reflect on how far you've come as a human being on the planet. The little Aussie girl was literally on the other side of the world having the most magnificent experience under unknown skies.

I felt invigorated and grateful.

As entertainers, we have a way of starting conversations due to our celebrity. This is one of the best parts of being in the public eye: even world leaders want to meet you. In my case, Mikhail Gorbachev, the leader of the former Soviet Union, consented to do an interview with me for my show.

Diane Meyer Simon, a dear friend of mine who, with Gorbachev, created the environmental organization Global Green, arranged for me to go to a grand Russian hotel to interview him about environmental issues in Russia and the world on camera for the show. I have never been shy in front of power, but this man was a little intimidating. What I remember about Gorbachev was that he had one eye that was kind and compassionate, while the other eye was strong and piercing. Maybe you need both to be a world leader.

There were many times during the interview that I didn't think he was looking at me. He seemed to be looking *through* me. I can't really remember much of our discussion, but when we were finished, he embraced me in a strong bear hug, which was warm and friendly.

What an experience—I'll be forever grateful. I felt like Barbara Walters for a day!

After all of our international adventures, it was only natural that I brought my Madonna and Michael Jackson, plus our director and crew, to my homeland for a little Aussie holiday and corresponding shoot. I knew that this might actually log in as one of our most adventurous stops and made it clear to the director that I had a few caveats when it came to shooting in the wilds of Australia— because things can get pretty dicey.

"I don't do heights or the ocean," I informed him. "In fact, I'm terrified of both."

He reminded me that I had "done heights" before on the show when they'd placed me on the top of some very tall trees in the gorgeous Costa Rican rain forest.

"That was a one-off," I assured him.

The way he smiled and nodded, I knew that he wasn't exactly listening as the wheels in his mind began to turn. What's better than a slightly unsure ONJ in nature? A terrified ONJ! It would make for some great TV!

I had no desire to repeat my day up in the trees in Costa Rica: I'd been shaking in my boots! From my vantage point above the rain forest canopy, in one of those little orange baskets attached to a hoist, I could see where the birds lived and heard them singing from their nests. Every few minutes, there was a rustling that needed immediate defining—I was assured that it was just the local monkeys coming around to see what was happening.

Once I got up there and cameras rolled, I could barely speak, but I finally managed to say a few, very short sentences. When I arrived down firmly on terra firma, I thought the danger was over—but silly me. We went down to the beach for more filming and Matt decided to pick up a snake called a fer-de-lance. This was an extremely venomous little guy who belonged to the viper family. One bite can be fatal to humans. Yes, Matt actually picked up this lovely snake, brown in color with a series of black-edged diamonds on its side.

I reacted the way any woman would under those circumstances.

First, I screamed at the top of my lungs.

Second, I began to run. In the opposite direction.

Matt wasn't the least bit afraid, though, even though he had a history with snakes. When I had my baby shower for our daughter, I was at Pat's house celebrating this wonderful time in my life. Between little sandwiches and presents, I got an emergency call from my brother-in-law saying that Matt had been bitten by a baby rattlesnake. Who knew that the baby ones are more venomous than their bigger family members?

"How does a rattlesnake bite a human being who is biking?" I frantically asked. Oh, what a silly question.

My brother-in-law replied calmly, "Your husband decided to get off his bike and pick one up."

It turns out he was allergic to the antivenom and soon found himself at UCLA Medical Center, where they treated him successfully.

Whew!

But back to our memorable experience taking the *Human Nature* show to Australia. One evening, I glanced at the production schedule for the next day. Many times, I had no idea what we were about to shoot, and that element added to the drama of the series.

This wasn't surprising, though. It was shocking! The one who was afraid of water (and all the creatures in it) would be shot diving into the Great Barrier Reef to feed giant potato cod that called that area home. These fish can weigh between six and thirty kilograms, and they were often fed by divers who loved to photograph them. But their numbers were rapidly declining as the site became more popular and people disturbed their natural habitat. Cod Hole was one of the best-known dive sites in the world and the subject of a heated debate locally over reef management.

There was only one problem. I had never been diving—and it really wasn't something I wanted to do. The only thing worse for me than going to the top of the rain forest would be going under the ocean.

I knew that these gentle fish weren't the only wildlife that frequented this area. Three words struck fear into my heart: shark-feeding frenzy! I was terrified of seeing even one shark, but my director convinced me that it was totally safe. One deep breath, and I decided to take this on as a challenge. A warm sunny morning later and I was sitting on a boat in the Pacific Ocean, with the stunning aqua-blue water giving me a (short-lived) peaceful feeling.

The captain of the boat came out to meet me when we got close to the cod hole.

This is not happening!

I went underwater and fed the cod and still couldn't believe I was doing this. The feeding wasn't uneventful. One of the people in our group was bitten by an eel that had arrived unexpectedly to eat the food. I was told that, although a bit uncomfortable, she would be fine.

I was so proud of myself when the captain pulled me onto the boat. I took off my mask.

"So, what do you think about swimming around Shark Alley?" he asked me.

Shark Alley?

"They're mostly harmless," the captain said.

I was focused on the word "mostly."

When we looked down, a few sharks were swimming around. Luckily, I didn't see any when I was underwater with the cod or I'd still be screaming.

Our delightful captain was only too happy to set the record straight because he said I was one of his favorite singers and he didn't want me to be otherwise known as shark food. It turns out the Great Barrier Reef is home to numerous species of sharks, including bottom-dwellers known as wobbegongs, and larger, even more terrifying ones like tiger and hammerhead sharks. There are even sharks named for the place, called white-tip and black-tip reef sharks.

"The good news," the captain said with a smile, "is that the white- and black-tips feed on fish and pose no danger to divers. They're even considered quite timid."

I would have to take his word for it.

As the boat lurched back toward shore, I saw even more sharks.

Back on dry land, I had to laugh. Because of this show, I had faced and conquered two of my biggest fears: heights and water. I did it, and I was proud of myself.

I learned to face my fears and do it anyway.

Another environmental mission close to my heart took me back to Australia: to fight for the continued existence of the ancient trees. Some of the most pristine forests on the planet are located there, and this is where some of the tallest, primordial, and most treasured trees in the entire world can be found. Some of these trees are more than five hundred years old and up to three hundred feet high. They're filled with nooks, holes, and crannies that are like a history book. These ancient trees are not just majestic, sturdy, and awe-inspiring, though. On a very practical level, they are also the place many species of local animals and birds call home.

I strongly encourage anyone to spend a few hours getting lost in the trees. A sense of tranquility and peace will come over you, providing a welcome relief from your daily stresses. The sad part is that tree logging is still a flourishing industry in Australia.

I returned home to tour these ancient trees, including one major stretch of forest that had been hacked down. The devastation was frightening and sad. This once thriving, lush, and untouched area actually looked like a war zone. Instead of being a place of life with a canopy of trees reaching skyward, indigenous plants, and an animal habitat, there were just piles of rotting wood left over from the chopped-down trees. It brought tears to my eyes as I toured these former wonderlands, knowing I wouldn't ever be able to take my daughter to see these five-hundred-year-old treasures. And future generations of Aussies had forever lost such a life-affirming part of their culture.

The stats were not good. More than half of the Australian forests had already fallen victim to this kind of deforestation.

What could I do to help? I joined forces with environmentalist Jon Dee of Planet Ark to bring attention to the plight of the forests there, and even worked to plant one million new trees on National Tree Day to help replace those that were lost. Jon and I began to spread the word that the trees needed to be saved. "There is more money to be made from Australian tourism and people visiting the trees than the pennies brought in from the wood chips," Jon said, adding, "I'll forever be grateful to Olivia for shedding light on this subject. We exposed this issue and saved so many of the ancient trees for generations to come."

I've planted more than ten thousand trees on my property in Australia. When I wander among my trees, it's almost a spiritual experience for me. It's going to nature's church.

I'm proud to say our efforts resulted in planting many millions of trees.

One of my favorite moments on my global travels to save the planet was in the seventies, long before I was married or had Chloe. I was invited to take part in a TV show that would take cheetahs back to Namibia in Africa. The numbers were quite devastating. Only a hundred years ago, there were one hundred thousand cheetahs on earth, but by the mid 1970s, more than 90 percent of these amazing cats, the fastest land animal, were gone.

A dedicated woman named Laurie Marker was working on a

plan to save them by repopulating a part of the world where their survival was more likely. The cheetahs Laurie brought were born in captivity in Oregon and were used to being fed, so the experiment was to bring them back into the wild to teach them how to hunt for their own food, breed, and replenish the species.

My mom had come along with me to Namibia because she loved adventure, animals, and photography. It was the perfect trip for her. It was a long and arduous journey, traveling in planes big and then small, before riding by Jeep across the most beautiful land where hundreds of free species of every kind of wild animal roamed. What a sight!

All of us stayed in a small house that had a pool, but you couldn't just dive in. The first moment we arrived at the house, I casually walked past the pool and saw that there was a cobra snake in it. The cameraman went to film it, got a little too close (as guys like to dare themselves to do), and the cobra responded by hissing and darting in his face. Luckily, we had the camera between him and the venom. He got the shot, but at what risk?

I knew at that moment this was going to be a challenging shoot.

Laurie was there with us. She was a special woman who was a native of Oregon and had moved to Namibia to oversee the Cheetah Conservation Fund. One of the exciting parts of her program was tracking these cheetahs that were being released, so she would know where they were located and if they were still alive. Each morning, to teach them to hunt and survive, we would rig an animal carcass to the back of the Jeep and drag it behind us for two very young cheetahs to chase. This was the way they would learn to hunt in the wild.

Our cheetahs, who were used to being served a few nice meals a day in captivity, didn't want to hunt anything at first, but instead would play with the carcass and chase their friends—us. I would wake up early in the morning and sit by the waterhole with my purring cheetah Khayam while antelope were frolicking nearby. I would say to him, "Go hunt! Look at that antelope over there! Look at that deer! It's called breakfast!" This went against the grain for me, though. I didn't want to watch any beautiful animal kill another one. I love all the animals but had to remember that this was the circle.

Finally, and very slowly, the cheetahs learned to look at the outdoors as their home in every single way. Unfortunately, this was after we left.

Mum loved the trip. I really believe I inherited my love of travel and wildlife from her. Brave and daring, Mum wanted to get out there and see everything.

One night in Africa we were doing a night shoot and driving around in the Jeep when our aide, Adolph, stopped on a dime in the middle of the desert.

"Don't move," he said. I didn't need to be told twice!

I watched as he walked out into the darkness, where anything could be lurking, and used his long nightstick to pick up a snake that was in our way. It was a ten-foot-plus python, but Adolph wasn't concerned. He was used to python roadblocks, and simply put the huge snake in a brown hessian sack and placed it in the back of the truck. The next day we were filming and they wanted something dramatic as I drove past. They put the nonvenomous snake in the tree.

I had a new costar.

We filmed another segment about the white rhinoceros, whose population was and is in serious danger. Farmers in Africa have thousands of acres of land each, and if a rhino ends up on someone's property, they get poached. Our mission that day was to relocate a rhino that had wandered onto the wrong piece of land and was in danger.

Our little group included men on horseback in front, Mum and me in the Jeep with our director, and Adolph driving very cautiously. We not only spotted a very large white rhino, but he also saw us and decided to charge our vehicle. I remember his massive horn butting the lower part of the Jeep and Adolph flooring it so we could take off. I was scared for the horses, who luckily did manage to outrun their rhino "friend." In the end, we did move that rhino back to his rightful home instead of having him drift off into one of the farms to meet his demise.

Animals have been one of the great delights of my life since I was a little girl. I'm drawn to them, sometimes more than I'm actually drawn to people. When we lived in Cambridge, where I was born, the love of my five-year-old life was a beautiful Irish setter called Pauly-Auly that lived next door. (Can't believe I can still remember his name after all these years!) I found any excuse to hang out with him. As a little girl, I was also given a little green tortoise as a pet. My uncle Gustav knew that I had the mumps and brought the little guy to me in a brown paper bag so my dad couldn't see what was happening until it was a done deal. I was allowed to keep him as a pet, but that was it until I was old enough to have my own home.

Funnily enough, he ran away. A tortoise on the lam!

My parents had enough on their plates, without the pets that I was always finding and wanting to live with us. In Melbourne, people would dump animals on the university grounds, figuring they could survive in that place of trees, plants, and openhearted young people who might take them in.

I'd find poor, sweet greyhounds that were considered by the trainers no use to anyone after their racing careers. They had been dumped at Ormond. I'd sneak them food and water and spend time with them. I'm very happy to know now that there are organizations that rehabilitate these beautiful dogs. I'd also remove tiny kittens from paper bags in trash cans where people had literally thrown them away. I'd rescue seven or eight and then take them all to the local RSPCA, hoping and praying that they would find homes where they would be well taken care of and loved.

When my mother made friends with a family in Eltham, the Dattners, who had ponies at their home, I held my breath. "Bring Olivia around on the weekends so she can play with the horses," they said, and my heart soared. I had no idea what I was doing, but I loved each pony as if it were my own. I didn't know how to put tack on, and it took me an hour to figure it out each time. I didn't care. I'd ride and play with them while imagining that I could keep each one.

I remember once seeing a guy being abusive to a horse behind a cart. I was only seven, but I raced right up, grabbed the reins, and yelled at him.

That's how I always felt about animals. Some humans brand animals as stupid, but I don't agree. They have feelings, just like us, and are very sensitive. I believe they have their own language, and it's just that we don't understand it. But it doesn't mean they're stupid.

I love their company, presence, and loyalty and don't feel right unless I have an animal in my life. I simply try to make them safe, comfortable, and happy. No one is happier to see me at the end of a long tour than Raven! (Well, maybe John.)

I love taking care of my animals. That's a good life to me. When I'm not traveling or on the road, I love to get up early and feel the crisp morning air and watch the beautiful California sky. I listen to my rooster crow and then walk across the dewy grounds. Raven is ready to play ball, but we have chores to do first. We go to the barn, feed the horses and then the chickens. I'm a country girl at heart.

The loss of a pet can be as powerful as the loss of any member of your family. I know this from going through it myself and from watching friends who have lost animals and who struggle to function for a long time. Whether it's a pet or a person, grief has no use-by date. Grief goes on, and you carry it around with you. I have a song called "Stone in My Pocket" about this subject. Sometimes grief for a person or a pet feels like you're carrying a boulder around, and at other times it feels like a grain of sand that's always in your pocket.

I will always remember the beautiful animals that have graced my life, and I have loved each one as my family.

The love lives on.

TWENTY-ONE

Trust Yourself

Trust yourself. You know all the answers.
Trust yourself. You know what is right.

I can't believe that I've now been touring for almost five decades. I always say that I love to sing because it's the only thing I'm good at (well, I guess that's a matter of opinion)—but thank goodness I found my passion. I can't imagine any other sort of life.

It's true that touring can be grueling, but it's still so exhilarating. These days I use buses as much as possible to get from point A to point B. What's tiring is all the packing and unpacking and the time spent in airports. If you use a bus, you can avoid a lot of the stress and travel all night long before waking up in a new environment. That's always fun, and I still love that part of it.

I have a great time with John and my band on the bus. We watch movies and unwind as the miles slip by. Some of the most beautiful times are when John and I wake up early to see the sun rising in different parts of the country.

As for the shows, I'm still a little anxious just before I step onto

It was a simple show. I had to convince the powers that I didn't want dancers, bells, and whistles. That's really not me.

I'm so grateful that my voice is as strong as ever thanks to sessions for the last twelve years with my vocal coach, Steve Real. His wife, Martha, also takes wonderful care of me on the road. Steve has helped me keep my instrument in the best shape possible.

The admirer reaction has been so touching to me. One man wrote that he saw the Vegas show *sixty-five times* and he always signed up for the meet and greet afterward. At one of those after-show sessions, he even proposed to his boyfriend on one knee in front of me.

I wished them a lifetime of happiness!

It was often tiring to do a meet and greet each night after the show, but what kept me going is that all the money went to the ONJ Centre, which made any fatigue seem unimportant.

Almost every night, someone would pull me aside and tell me, "Olivia, I'm going through cancer right now." Conversations like this always touch the deepest part of my heart and reinforce that we're all connected. I'll spend a few minutes with that person trying to offer a little support. It makes me feel good to help people.

Remember, we're all in this together.

Now, let's go back to the cinema for a moment.

I have loved Doris Day since I watched her in those wonderful Doris Day–Rock Hudson musicals when I was young. I loved her voice and the spunky characters she portrayed in her films. Her song—"Que Sera, Sera"—was the one I sang all the time growing up, and I still remember the words! When I read her autobiography, I felt a kinship with Doris that went beyond music and movies, as she focused on her love of animals and the hardships she faced and triumphed over in her life. At the time, I seriously inquired to see if I could play Doris in a movie based on her life.

It turns out Doris wasn't interested in having her life portrayed on the screen by me or anyone else. Funny, but I found myself in the same position these last few years, so I totally understand! However, I have acquiesced now, and I am used to the idea.

I must say, though, it was a strange feeling to hear that they were planning to make my life into a miniseries. I thought, *Hang on. Don't those things happen after you're gone?*

Delta Goodrem, who played me in the unauthorized TV movie of my life, is a dear friend, and a talented and beautiful singer/songwriter. She was the perfect person to play me in the Australian production. The fact that Delta has also been on the cancer journey and is a fellow thriver sets her level of compassion and empathy in line with mine.

As I write these words, I haven't seen the movie, and I had nothing to do with its storyline or production. My worry was that the facts of my life were correct, and that the other people in my life were portrayed kindly and fairly. It's not their fault that they were in the public eye because of me.

I've directed that my proceeds from the film go to my Cancer Wellness & Research Centre.

I hope I can watch it one day.

TWENTY-TWO

Live On

We learn how to thrive and then live on.

In 2013, John and I moved from Florida back to California, where we took a temporary house to be near Chloe. My sister Rona helped me move. A month later, she was going to come up to the house again to see how I was putting things together. Rona was always a great decorator, and I needed her input.

I called her the morning she was meant to visit—she was supposed to be driven to my house by my assistant, Dana, but strangely, she hadn't turned up at the meeting point. I was already a little worried, when Rona asked me if it was morning yet. It was 10:00 a.m. and she seemed very confused. She didn't remember that she was coming over, even though we had spoken about it the day before.

I was concerned and called her best friend Maria, who told me she had also received a very confusing phone call from Rona that morning. "Can you go check on her?" I asked.

When Maria went over there, she found Rona in an odd state

and took her to the ER. Maria called me a few hours later and said I should come to LA immediately. Apparently, the doctors were giving Rona some brain tests because my sister seemed to be in another world.

A three-hour drive later, I found my sister in the hospital in a jolly mood. She thought the IV was a champagne cocktail.

The doctor took me aside in the hallway. "We found a mass in her brain," he said.

This was the beginning of a very painful and difficult six weeks.

It was a terrible shock to us when Rona was diagnosed with an aggressive brain tumor at age seventy-two. She was a very healthy, fit person who exercised every day and ate extremely well. And suddenly, almost overnight, she was quite ill and not making sense anymore.

One of my last memories of my wild-child sister is of her sitting up in bed at Saint Joseph Medical Center looking so beautiful and acting very cheerful despite the circumstances, which fortunately she didn't really understand. She would tell people, "I have a brain tumor, but don't worry. I'll get over it."

After doctors did a biopsy of her tumor, we heard the chances of survival weren't good, and the treatment would be aggressive and difficult. I knew my sister's wishes. She had told me what to do in dire circumstances like these. I knew she wouldn't have wanted to have brain surgery that could render her with a wide variety of God-only-knows-what problems. Maria told me that Rona had also expressed to her that she never wanted chemo or surgery.

We took my sister home.

My nieces and nephews live in Australia, and I brought them over to be with their mother during this final time. The beauty of this was that the kids got to be together with Rona and to support one another.

Those were very special days, full of laughter and family, with Rona's children: Emerson, a race car driver and entrepreneur; Tottie, a singer, actress, wedding minister, and goodwill ambassador for the ONJ Centre; Brett, a photographer and fine musician (we recorded the album *Hotel Sessions* together); and Fiona, a yoga and fitness instructor.

Brett brought his guitar and sang to her, which was so moving and Rona loved it. And, amazingly, my brave sister kept us laughing. She was quite happy eating Tottie's and Fiona's meals while Layla, her granddaughter, massaged her feet. Of course, my beautiful Chloe was there to support her auntie, me, and all of us.

The rest of her life was quite peaceful thanks to wonderful hospice services.

I put off my Vegas start date to take care of her. Rona passed after six weeks, on May 24, 2013, in Los Angeles, which was May 25 in Australia—our mother's birthday. It was curious, as our father had died on our brother's birthday, July 3.

Shortly after Rona died, Maria, who is a devout Tibetan Buddhist, arrived. We stood around her bed and John recited the Lord's Prayer. Maria and I put our hands over her body and felt an amazing energy. Our hands kept going up and up until the energy quickly subsided and seemed to fly out the open window on that gorgeous spring day. Maria later told me that her Buddhist teacher had told her that Rona would leave on a wind horse. It gave me a shiver because I believe that she did.

I will forever miss my smart, funny, and brave sister. No one is ever prepared to say goodbye, and a sister is irreplaceable. We shared experiences and memories together that only the two of us understood. It's almost impossible to get used to the idea that I can't just pick up the phone and tell Rona something about my brother or relatives or someone we'd known forever. I miss the knowing and the laughter.

I can hear her great laugh now. Our times together might be in the past, but she lives on within me.

She taught me so much, and she will forever be my chaperone.

Rona's death put me into a spin for about a year. I didn't sing for almost eight months afterward. I wondered if I would ever perform again. I even postponed my *Summer Nights* residency in Vegas for a year as I tried to deal with the loss.

Eventually, though, the show went on.

Going to Vegas for my first residency helped me in an odd way because Rona absolutely loved Vegas. We'd come for fun shopping weekends, see a show, and eat in our favorite restaurants. The moment I stepped off the plane in that city, I felt like Rona was with me.

Time is a wonderful healer, but grief is like an ocean. I found it comes in waves and there are times when you are lost at sea. John was amazing during this time, and music also helped me to get through it. I even wrote a song for Rona and asked Amy Sky to produce it. The idea was to only send it to Rona's family and friends. After it was finished, Amy and I discussed the fact that there wasn't any music made specifically for people who are grieving—which is pretty much anyone at different points of life. It was one of those light bulb moments. Maybe there was a real need for this type of music. Rona's friends and our family certainly thought so, and they kept asking me, "Do you have any other music like this?"

That spurred me on. And I knew that Rona wouldn't ever want me to stop singing—or trying to help people.

Singer-songwriter Beth Nielsen Chapman, a two-time cancer survivor, is a dear friend of mine who wrote an unforgettable song called "Sand and Water" after her husband Ernest died of cancer. We asked if she would be interested in joining Amy and me for this project, and a trio was born! We decided to write the album together, and it was the most nurturing experience. Amy was also raw after the loss of her beloved mother that year. We understood what it meant to say goodbye and wanted to bring those emotions to the music.

We wrote most of the *Liv On* album at my house and recorded it in Vegas. The three of us would sit around in our pajamas with our notepads and cups of tea and tell stories from our own lives. There was much laughter—and many tears. In lots of ways, it was like a giant group-therapy session. The songs these times produced are haunting, beautiful, and heartfelt. They are also timeless.

Loss is loss. It doesn't change.

The song "Live On" is about moving forward through stress and grief to find new life afterward. I love that the whole album has such a positive message about restoring hope as you carry on.

I didn't realize when we were writing the album that the title song would ultimately be a way for me to honor Rona.

Little did I realize that we were also writing it for me.

TWENTY-THREE

Love Is a Gift

I remember when I discovered I had breast cancer back in 1992. My dear Buddhist friend Jim said to me, "Congratulations. Now you will grow." At the time, I wasn't so sure what he meant, but now I know.

The hard truth is, you don't grow in life without difficulties. You can make a decision to get angry or bitter when life's challenges arise, or you can choose to learn and be grateful for the lesson. It's your choice, and I chose and continue to choose to feel grateful that I was given a second and now third chance at life and love.

I'm winning for the third time when it comes to cancer. I feel great and positive. And I feel excited about the possibilities that are coming forward with cancer and cannabis, a healing plant that has been much maligned over the last eighty years. For over three thousand years, people from around the world have continuously used it for medicine. I'm so fortunate that my husband is a plant-medicine expert and is growing his own medicinal strains for me. This has helped me greatly with pain and sleep.

In late 2017, John went on a research trip to Israel, where he met with top scientists studying cannabis. Their work includes examining the cannabis cannabinoids as well as terpenes, or fragrant oils, which give the plant aromatic diversity. "Some smell like citrus, others like skunk. That's the terpenes," John explains. "From a therapeutic standpoint these different smells are proving to have their own therapeutic benefit as well as amplifying the benefits of the cannabinoids like THC and CBD." John has grown thirty different strains and bred some new genetics as well.

"I believe we'll see the most benefit from the combination of different strains including dozens of cannabinoids and terpenes in the extracts," he says.

John designed two formulas especially for me and my pain levels immediately dropped dramatically.

John's work goes far beyond just reducing or eliminating the pain those with cancer have to deal with. The focus now with this plant is its natural ability to go after cancer on several fronts. The primary focus is on compromising cancer growth by interfering with its life cycle, preventing the cancer from developing its own blood supply by stimulating the natural process of cell suicide known as apoptosis, and activating an immune response to kill the cancer. Cannabis works on many levels because it feeds the endocannabinoid system. This system was only recently discovered, in the early nineties, and every human has one. In fact, most animals have cannabinoid receptors on their cells. The endocannabinoid system influences every process—neurological, physiological, immunological response—everything. We have cannabinoid receptor sites in practically every cell in our body.

Although there is no silver bullet, the compelling data on cannabis is driving an unprecedented amount of attention, as the science continues to show its many benefits.

My dream is that it won't be long before everyone has access to this healing medicine.

Going through cancer again, I've had wonderful support from so many. My darling Chloe has been right by my side. It takes me back to that beautiful six-year-old at school, saying, "Why didn't you tell me, Mummy? I would have taken care of you."

This time I told her—and she did.

She has been taking care of me with so much love and grace. I have never been as proud of her as I am now.

"Nothing can stand in your way, Mum," my daughter tells me. She even told the world on her social media, "My mom and best friend is going to be fine! My mom is so powerful and she will beat this in no time. Cancer is the disease of our generation and it is part of me and my mother's quest to beat this."

My happiest moments have been Chloe coming home to check on Mum and just sit and talk. My daughter is a courageous, strong, compassionate, and kind person who makes the world a better place. Her heart is endless and her story is fascinating—and one day I hope she shares it, as it is hers to tell.

And did I mention how gorgeous and talented she is? She has one of the most beautiful singing voices, writes powerful songs, and is a wonderful actress. She and I acted in a couple of TV movies together and had the first mother-daughter number one song in Billboard history with a remake of "Magic" that we called "Got to Believe," released in 2015.

Darling, my dream is for your dreams to come true.

One of the other best medicines is having love in my life. John is the most loving husband and is extremely knowledgeable about herbs, plant medicine, healing, and the human body. Every single day he makes sure that I get the right nutrients and healing herbs. He's constantly researching to find out the latest natural healers and therapies. He's my rock.

He's also the most even-keeled, mellow, kind, and loving person, with a great sense of humor. He makes me laugh so much.

It has been so important for me to get away from the cycle of numbers and statistics. When I found out I had cancer for the third time, a very well-meaning woman wrote to me on Facebook and gave me the likelihood of death from my type of cancer. This was not what I needed to hear. I'm not upset about it—the intentions were probably good—but the execution was a bit questionable.

I'd rather think about a day long ago when I went out with my mom for my birthday lunch to a restaurant outside of Melbourne. At one point, I went to the bathroom and a woman recognized me. (I meet all the best people in bathrooms!)

"Oh, Olivia, love," she said. "I read that you had breast cancer. Well, I had it twenty years ago, and I'm fine."

This was a light bulb moment—and fantastic to hear.

She was the age I am now, telling me she had it so long ago when the treatments weren't even as good.

It was inspiring to me, and now I hope to inspire others.

One of my favorite healing messages from long ago was from Tom Hayden, once married to Jane Fonda, who during my first bout simply wrote, *Thinking of you.*

With this third diagnosis, my first step was to deal with the pain in my lower back, which was becoming debilitating. We decided to mix natural therapies with conventional (intravenous herbal medicine and some photon radiation therapy).

I believe in exploring all the healing options and choosing the best for me. My first go-around with cancer, I had chemotherapy, but I also worked to get my body and mind back in balance with herbs, massage, acupuncture, meditation, and constructive positive thinking. These became the building blocks for my wellness center so many years later.

The second time, I used estrogen-blocker medicine, but it affected my moods and made me depressed, so I had to stop. This time, I did herbal IV treatments at a clinic in Georgia to boost my immune system, and then some photon radiation. Every step was a positive one, and with every step I consulted with my doctors at the ONJ Centre in Melbourne.

During all my treatments, I kept envisioning all the good cells in my body. I would think and even say aloud, "Cancer cells, it's time to allow the good, healthy cells to take your place."

This wasn't a war, but more of a moving over. I felt that if I tried to fight the cancer cells, they would fight back equally hard. Moving them over and winning over them seemed like a far more peaceful solution.

Of course, I'm as guilty as anyone when it comes to allowing a little negative thinking to slip in sometimes. But John is always happy to wake me up and remind me, "Be careful of what's in your head. Your body hears you."

A week into my herbal IV treatments, the pain level went down dramatically and I could begin to walk properly again. I spent the majority of the summer healing, knowing that soon we would take another MRI of my lower back to check on the tumor.

It was a cool autumn day when I went for that second, post-treatment MRI. I went into the test knowing that this MRI would be a long process. I really had to meditate and put myself into a healing place, but it's hard to stay focused with the hammering sounds of that tunnel-like medical machine.

One of my favorite expressions has always been: *this too shall pass.* I wanted it to be over, but we needed to be sure, so they did a brain scan, a spine scan, and then a scan of my sacrum area to see if there was any change in the tumor.

Of course, it was extremely nerve-racking, although a little voice of reason inside shouted that it must be better because the pain level was so good. But there is always a certain level of fear when you put yourself through medical tests, because there's always the possibility that something could be there.

I dismissed those self-defeating thoughts as I lay in that MRI machine. Yes, they would float into my head. I'm human. But I kept reminding myself that I didn't know anything and wouldn't until the doctor called the next day.

*

By morning light, the phone was ringing.

My doctor had looked at the results. In fact, she'd also sent them out to three different oncologists. My brain was clear; my spine was clear; my sacrum tumor was the same. "It's hard to tell if it's active or inactive," the doctor said. "The way we tell is your pain level." And my pain was almost gone.

This was really happy news.

Since then I've continued with my regime of herbs and immune-building supplements, and I have regular meetings with my oncologist and my specialists in Los Angeles.

I spent time last summer in Cancún, Mexico, at a beautiful healing clinic called Hope4cancer. Their treatments are natural and nontoxic, and they investigate the latest protocols from around the world. Dr. Tony and Marcy Jimenez travel the globe in search of the best cancer therapies. I also had great results at Elements for Life Clinic in Bremen, Georgia. They use the latest natural healing modalities including electrodermal screening technology and vitamin and mineral IV therapies.

Cancer is something I will need to stay on top of for the rest of my long life. It's up to me to manage my stress, to eat and rest well, and to continue with the healing protocols. As for working hard, I enjoy it.

Each time my cancer has occurred has been after a stressful time in my life, which shows me, as Louise Hay said, that emotional stress can be a large factor in triggering illness. This is something Hope4Cancer and astute doctors around the world are now recognizing. Addressing your emotional health is a major part of your healing.

*

On the road to wellness, I decided to participate in the Healing Diva Retreat in Cancun, which is also how I discovered Hope4Cancer. The retreat was small, just five women, with Dr. Veronique Desaulniers, who calls herself "Dr. V, Breast Cancer Conqueror." Dr. V is an incredible woman who used natural treatments after she was diagnosed with breast cancer. Her experience led her down a path of research, discovery, and personal transformation. Dr. V even said that she "came to appreciate that cancer was a message of love." I was drawn to Dr. V because her work is evidence-based.

"My body was trying to communicate with me and get my attention," she said. "It was saying, 'If you keep doing things you have always done, you are going to get the same results.'" She changed her emotional patterns, learning to manage stress, set boundaries, and love herself, imperfections and all. I loved how she calls them "my perfect imperfections."

The lovely Dr. V turned this into a very special time for our group, which included three women dealing with breast cancer, one with ovarian cancer, and myself. Cancer is cancer. However it manifests, the fundamental principles of healing your body are the same.

Just spending this time with these strong, amazing women left me feeling so empowered. Women reinforcing women is a powerful healing tool. During our time together, we also worked on emotional healing of our traumas and unexpressed emotions. I think it is very common among women to take care of everyone else first and ourselves last. It's a hard trait to recognize, and it's even tougher to change as we are nurturers by nature.

I thought I had dealt with my issues. I didn't realize that I was still so disconnected from certain feelings and had buried other traumas. Once I expressed them, my tears sprang from nowhere, and I could feel the healing begin.

I loved my experience with Veronique and this group of new friends. The power of women is outstanding. We were able to share with one another very easily in our circle of trust.

It was like my experience in Vegas. Whatever happened in Cancun will stay there forever.

I feel so good now, which is a gift and a relief. Basically, I was in a cocoon of healing for the last part of 2017. I spent that time out of the limelight and at home.

Everyone has to find their own journey to ultimate wellness. My choice is learning about all available options and then doing what feels right to me. Whatever I choose, I believe in and commit to doing. I've continued to receive my healthy anti-inflammatory IV treatments, as inflammation is a major factor of many illnesses. The IVs and supplements I take boost my immune system and help eliminate cancer cells from my body. So many healers have crossed my path, and I'm grateful for their many innovative protocols that I've been exposed to on my journey.

As autumn of 2017 wound to a close, though, I began to fulfill the tour dates I had canceled earlier in the year.

The show went on!

Prior to stepping onstage again, I was nervous because I didn't know how my back would hold up. And I wondered if it would be an emotional experience. Would I be able to sing? But another part of me vowed, "It's okay, no matter what happens. It's real. It's the truth. Just go out there and show the audience what you're feeling."

My first show back was in Evansville, Indiana, with my terrific, supportive band who had been with me for so long. They had my back, of course, and the audience gave me a standing ovation when I walked onstage. It was hard to hold back the happy tears.

The goodwill came at me in waves.

All of this comes together because I have the best team. Dana has been with me for more than forty-one years and is the most loyal, trustworthy, loving, professional woman, and I'm lucky enough to have her as my personal assistant. My brilliant lawyer of over forty years is John Mason. Then there is my talented and hilarious publicist, Michael Caprio, who has been with me for eighteen years.

I met Mark Hartley, my clever and wonderful manager, in Nashville some twenty-one years ago. I appreciate his honesty and his experience over so many years. He has managed acts such as the Jacksons, Toto, Glenn Frey, Brad Paisley, and Vince Gill, among many others.

Figure I would be a breeze!

They're more than just my team. They're my friends.

As for the longevity of our relationships . . . I guess you get a life sentence with me!

I truly believe this will be my final round with cancer. I truly believe it will be like last time and I will go on with my life. (Remember that we create what we believe.)

What has been amazing is the outpouring of love and good wishes from loved ones and total strangers. People I didn't expect to reach out sent me the loveliest words of encouragement. After my last diagnosis, I didn't take many calls because it was just too exhausting, but I read so many notes, letters, and messages sent to me through social media.

Thank you, everybody. I felt your love.

What I focus on now is finding peace during my healing. Part of that is reaching for the positive, but with true intention behind that idea. It's easy to say, "I'm just going to be positive." That's lovely, but you need to back it up in a concrete way.

So be careful what you think. It creates your reality.

As for me, I'm using this time to slow down and really think about what I want in my future. This has reminded me of the importance of true wellness, which includes taking time to stop, breathe, and enjoy.

It has also forced me to remember to simplify whenever possible. I've always found happiness in the most simple and beautiful things, such as walking in nature on a beautiful day, playing with my animals, or even mucking out the horse stalls! I love to sit outdoors and sip tea with my husband as we welcome a new day.

Each moment.

Live it.

EPILOGUE

As I write this, John is standing at the door with one of my special green drinks. My husband brings me my herbs and makes me laugh—a potent combination. Our passion is health and healing—for me, for us, for the world. Everything we do in life revolves around healing of some kind. It not only helps me, but I love that it might also help other people, too. It's our life mission.

"That's my wife," John says. "Her capacity and willingness to genuinely care for people, plants, and animals are amazing."

I'll close my eyes and give him this next paragraph.

"Olivia has a great sense of humor no matter what comes her way. We express gratitude every single day for what we have and for our relationship. We focus on that gratitude. What you focus on is what you manifest."

*

After all my various treatments, John and I took a month and went to our house in Australia to reconnect with nature. It's also where I come to heal. I found myself on the grounds of my precious Gaia in the hinterland of Byron Bay, kicking off my shoes and soaking up the warm spring sunshine that felt so good on my back.

This was the perfect place to contemplate life's constant challenges and changes. My mantra here was simple: live, laugh, love. And, as Gregg tells all our guests at Gaia, *surrender*.

I took moments to celebrate how far I had already come on this recent journey. There were times when it was simply too painful to walk before I had my herbal IV and photon treatments. Then I could walk a bit, but I couldn't walk straight. It was only a few months later and here I was in my beloved homeland, on my own two feet, walking up a hill at Gaia. One foot in front of the other.

Five decades in show business have taught me to have staying power. Maybe that power includes the will to just never give in. My will is iron-strong because I still have so much to do. My dream is that I can see an end to cancer. I'd also love to ride horses and play tennis again.

I will.

My vision is: me and John—a garden—and I'm an old, happy lady. I see Chloe and her husband, James. I see the grandchildren, the horses, chickens, cats, and dogs.

Health and happiness for all.

Thriving.

*

Back on my stone bench in the rose garden, it's early morning and the birds are chirping. John is brewing coffee and I'm giving Raven a quick toss of her ball.

My dog races like the wind. And before I can put my throwing hand down, my husband captures it.

Don't stop believing!

Love and light,
Olivia

AFTERWORD

Overnight Observation

It might be fever, it might be flu
To isolate it, I'll have to hold you.

September–November 2018

I thought I was going to "sail into tomorrow." To put it another way, I planned on gliding into my seventh decade on earth gracefully, without anyone even realizing that I had a major birthday looming on September 26. Little did I realize that, in fact, I would hobble into my seventies on a pair of crutches!

A week before the big day, I was in Australia to partake in my annual Wellness Walk. I had been in some pain for a few weeks in the hip area, but I just chalked it up to too many hills walked and too much exercise to prep for the event.

The wellness and research walk is one of the highlights of my year, and soon John and I were having a lovely time in Oz waiting for the big day, as I continued to silently deal with my pain. The morning of the walk, I woke in agony. My hip was throbbing while my mind raced. My first thought was of all the people who had traveled from around the world to walk with me. I was determined to push past any pain and get out there.

Gritting my teeth, I willed myself upright and managed to start the walk but eventually threw in the proverbial white towel. I couldn't take another step, but I also didn't want everyone to know I was in agony. I started the walkers off at the starting line, wished them luck, and then I hopped into a cart, in which someone drove me from place to place to wave to everyone. I ended up on a balcony overlooking the scene, and it was the most amazing thing to see so many supporters walking with their loved ones, their children, and their dogs, and there were even a couple of policemen on horseback. An animal-food company even made sure that there were bowls for the dogs to get plenty of fresh water. Oh, we had water for the humans, too, of course! Somehow, I managed to forget the pain for a while because it was so inspiring to watch this outpouring of love.

John was beyond concerned.

"Honey, we need to check out this pain," he insisted.

But the show still had to go on. The next day, I was scheduled to do a role in an upcoming film starring my good friend Paul Hogan. I woke up at five in the morning and couldn't walk at all. John lifted me out of the bed and insisted, "You can't do this. We need to go to the doctor."

"But there are so many people on a film set," I insisted. "There is so much money being spent—and they're waiting for me." Somehow, with my husband's help, I managed to get ready and was on the set by seven. On the way, I texted Paul, writing, "Please don't have me in any scenes where I have to move because I'm having an issue. Just stick me someplace where I can stand or lean on something."

Paul was so accommodating about it, and we managed to get through a long day of filming, which was a miracle. What I didn't know then was that I was maneuvering on a fractured pelvis.

If I moved in a certain way, it was torture. After ten hours of standing on my feet on the film set, I agreed with John. We were going to the hospital in the morning, and luckily, I knew the address of one that came highly recommended!

By the way, Paul was so compassionate that day. He shortened the shoot as much as possible and was extremely helpful. He's a longtime friend and such a funny man. Thanks, Paul.

The next morning, I went to the ONJ Centre for an MRI to see what was going on, and it was far more serious than I suspected. "You have a fracture in your pelvis, Olivia," the doctor told me. "I'm admitting you immediately."

I was focused on many different healing modalities, but my bones were weak due to my cancer metastasis. We needed to do something immediately to help prevent further fractures from happening. John and I quickly agreed with the recommendations for my treatment plan at the ONJ.

I was sent directly to a hospital bed, which became my refuge for the next three weeks.

Of course, I retaliated by looking for the humor in the situation. Consider the sheer serendipity of it all: If this had to happen, what were the chances I'd be in Australia and would be admitted into my own hospital?

Gosh, I realized, *I'm going to be able to play the role of undercover boss!*

In all seriousness, it was actually an incredible way to see the

ONJ Centre from the inside out as a patient, rather than just visiting the patients and learning about their treatments and care.

How miraculous was it that I was going to experience life at the ONJ myself?

It was actually a gift.

The truth is, I had never in my almost seventy years spent an extended period of time in a hospital, but the fracture dictated that I needed complete bed rest to start my healing and reduce the inflammation. There was one other matter. It was very important to me that I be treated like everybody else. I wanted no fuss; plus I needed my stay to be totally private. Every single staff member was so respectful, especially those hardworking nurses who took care of me night and day.

It was a lesson in total surrender.

From the first moment, as I was placed on that bed, the care I felt was palpable. I experienced such love that it brings tears to my eyes as I write this passage. I couldn't even wash my hands or take a shower on my own when I was first admitted, let alone deal with the daily bodily functions of life. I'm used to being quite an independent bird and always fought to do things for myself. On one of the first days, while my basic human needs were being cared for by a gentle and patient nurse, I found myself apologizing profusely.

"I'm so sorry. So sorry you have to do this. . . ."

"Don't apologize," she said. "This is what we do."

Independent since I was a teenager, I initially found it extremely difficult to let go and allow people to take care of me. I guess it comes down to one thing: trust. It dawned on me: I was being given the lesson of let go, let God.

My heart soared when I realized that every single patient at the ONJ was being given the same exact care and treatment.

Welcome to my dream . . . come true.

Lying in bed twenty-four hours a day, I realized firsthand how important the wellness programs that I had put into place were for a patient. To have an oncological masseuse—a kind, sensitive person with the gentlest hands—rub my feet, shoulders, and hands in my own room was a luxury I never expected to be so welcome. My favorite days were when I experienced art therapy, again from my bed, where I was given the freedom to sketch or play with watercolors and oils. It opened a new world of discovery courtesy of a lovely trained art therapist who inspired me.

When I felt a bit better, I walked in disguise on crutches through the hospital. I wore my beanie; big, nerdy glasses (actually my own glasses); and a hospital mask because I didn't want to cause a commotion. When we passed a certain ward where a wonderful sing-along was taking place with a talented guitarist, my heart did a leap. Oh, how I wanted to join in! I didn't need a stage and a sold-out auditorium. I just wanted to sing for the joy of it.

But I was the undercover boss!

No singing allowed!

As for the actual healing journey, I made sure to take note of every aspect of what the hospital offered. Remember how earlier I wrote that I spent time with the architect making sure each room had plenty of light? I understood then and now how important light is for your well-being.

As I became mobile on a walker, I experienced the importance of having access to a balcony. How wonderful not to be cut off from fresh air, birds chirping, and the rest of the world. I could take those few, precious steps outside, get a bit of sun and de-stress, which became incredibly important to both my mental and physical health.

People have said, "Didn't you feel frustrated being cooped up in your room for over three weeks?" The truth is I never felt that way. I always felt safe, very comfortable and cozy in my surroundings, deeply comforted by the healing energy of the nurses and doctors who tended to me.

Remember, I was the undercover boss, so I could not take advantage of the group therapy or various support groups that are so important at the ONJ. There is also oncological acupuncture and access to sports therapists who provide exercise programs for you once you leave the ONJ. They give you the tools to help improve your health and fitness levels.

All a win-win.

My Alfred Hitchcock moment happened really late at night toward the end of my stay. That night, the nurses said they wouldn't wake me to do my vitals, but if I needed anything, I could always press my bell. I had just gone to the bathroom by myself (a victory!) when I saw a silhouette standing in my doorframe—much too large to be a nurse . . . and he was a bit hunched over.

"Who is there?" I called out as my heart raced.

The nurses would usually say, "It's just me."

This person said nothing . . . and now he was walking *into the room.*

"Hello? Who is it?" I cried.

He moved one of the curtains open, and in a stream of moon-light, I focused on a little old man standing there in his pajamas.

"Are you lost?" I said.

He mumbled something. By this time, I'd found the call but-ton and I was pressing it madly. The nurses came rushing in, insist-ing, "We're so sorry. He wanders in the night and sometimes ends up in the wrong rooms."

Guess I should be grateful that he didn't try to get into my bed!

There is usually nothing lovely about being woken at six in the morning to go down for a test before breakfast. What made this journey special was that I was on a movable bed in the bowels of the hospital, which is also where they do the laundry. No one knew it was me. I was just another body on a stretcher on her way for tests.

We stopped for a minute, which allowed me to listen. This is what I heard in passing:

"Good morning."

"How are you?"

"How are you doing?"

"Good to see you."

"Have a great day."

This is fantastic, I thought. *Even in the deepest recesses of the ONJ, there is a warmth, kindness, and positive energy between the people who work here. The goodwill at this special place is rising from the ground floor . . . up.*

This is the place.

The place I wanted it to be.

I can't say enough about my wonderful husband, John, during this time. He was fantastically supportive in every way possible, from going out to get me my favorite foods to sleeping on a pullout bed in my room. I encouraged him to go back to our hotel to sleep, but he refused to budge.

That's love.

So back to the big day.

My seventieth birthday.

Prior to my fracture, I had thought of a million ways to spend my big day. At one point, I was going to have a huge party in Los Angeles or maybe a celebration at Gaia. What to do? I racked my brain, trying to figure out how to see all my friends on my birthday—or as many of them as possible. Who could have predicted that I would be a patient in my own cancer and wellness center when I turned seven decades young?

The afternoon of my birthday, it was arranged I'd have my radiation therapy and then go directly to the ONJ Centre. (Funny that I spent the first half of my life trying to get on the radio and the second half of my life trying to get off it.) As I was wheeled on a gurney to have my treatment, it made my heart soar to see colorful balloons and happy birthday signs in the corridor. The nurses came in early that day to decorate. No one knew it was for me.

After my treatment, I was wheeled from radiotherapy on a special chair into the wellness center, where my family and a few dear friends were waiting. In total, there were twelve of us around a one-of-a-kind table that was quite special to me. It was made from a tree grown on my property in Byron Bay that had been drying in my barn for many years. When the hospital was "born," I had this special table made by an exceptional Byron Bay craftsman. It was important to me to have a piece of my farm at the hospital—and I didn't know why at the time.

I ate a delicious seventieth birthday dinner on that one-of-a-kind table in this beautiful wellness center, collecting laughter, sharing stories, and just appreciating how wonderful life is . . . and how grateful I am for the special people surrounding me.

That was my party, and there couldn't have been a more perfect place to usher in a new decade. I welcomed seventy in this healing atmosphere that was my dream—in a mind-set of complete love and peace.

With age, they say, comes wisdom.

If I had to pass along a bit of it: Keep your eyes open for the signs in life.

I was released from the ONJ early on a weekday morning. The car went to pick up John at the hotel, where he gathered our things, and then drove straight to the ONJ, where I was to be transported to the plane.

It was six in the morning, and I was waiting to leave the hospital. As the sun was rising, a beautiful, spiritual man who works in palliative care came to see me. He had something in his hand.

"I didn't know until this morning who this was meant for, but then I realized when I woke up that it was for you," he said.

He opened his palm wide and inside of it was a beautiful cross from Israel. The interesting thing was that my girlfriend Bianca had visited us recently wearing the same exact cross.

"It's so beautiful, Bianca," I'd said. "I've never seen anything like it."

"Oh, we got it from Israel," she'd said.

For some reason, I kept thinking about that cross . . . and thinking about it. I even looked up the meaning of it and read that it had something to do with the idea that when you wore it, you would never be alone.

On the plane ride back to California, I had John close at hand and my new cross around my neck. As time passed, I felt a warm hand settle on my upper back. It stayed there and was comforting in a way that made me want to cry.

I told John about it, and he said, "It's a message. You are never alone."

I've been home for seven weeks now and I'm happy to report that everyone, from the horses to the dog to the cat to the chickens to the humans, are quite happy to see me. Magic, my cat, is usually very moody with me after I return from a trip, as in, "How dare you go away?" He will avoid me for some time until finally we make peace again and I feel a warm nuzzle on my legs. This time was different. He slept on my bed the first night and every night after that one.

Blame my macabre sense of humor for wondering, *Is this a good thing?*

"I had heard that in old people's homes, the cats go into their rooms before they . . ." I joked to John. "I was a bit nervous for a while. In fact, I told Magic, 'Why don't you be just a little bit mad at me? Don't sleep on my bed.' "

I have to look for the humor.

*

Now I'm home again and have finished my radiotherapy and continue with my other protocols. It feels wonderful to be with John; Chloe, who visits to help take care of me; and all our animals. Great friends stop by constantly with the best gift: themselves. I'm getting so much love. Tour again? Not right now. I'm easing into this decade without a mic in my hands. I'm just being.

Dreams shift and morph as we age.

I'm sitting in my yard looking at the setting sun right now as a family of hummingbirds fly low as they dip and weave around our beautiful sage bushes. Their beauty takes my breath away every time I see them. I have a walker (for now) and crutches as I continue my physical therapy with walking and swimming. (I call my walker my little red Corvette.) It makes me see the world from another perspective. I stop now. I sit down. I experience where I am in the moment . . . and I don't rush that moment.

One last thing:

Remember when I said that I wanted to ride horses and play tennis again?

Now I'd be content with table tennis and my miniature horses!

Love and Light,
Olivia

ACKNOWLEDGMENTS

Grace and Gratitude

Thank you, Team ONJ: John Easterling ♥, Dana Sharpe, Mark Hartley, Michael Caprio, Randy Slovacck, John Mason, Bernie Donth, Charles Sussman & Associates.

To my road family, thanks to all my band, singers, and crew over my long career, especially these lovely folks the last twenty years! Madonna Melrose, Martha Real, Steve Real, Matt Real, Marlén Landín, Weston Mays, Mark Beckett, Dane Bryant, Warren Ham, Kerry Marx, Catherine Marx, Matt McKenzie, Steve Nieves, Andy Timmons, Dan Wojciechowski, Dan Waters, Randy Mitchell, Rex Frasier, Cory Stone, Thom Roberts, Kenny Riggs, Lee Hendricks, Liam Russell, and Rick King.

Thank you to my managers throughout the years: Peter Gormley, Peter Hebbes, Lee Kramer, Dan Cleary, Ken Kragen, Roger Davies, Billy Sammeth, Mark Hartley, and all at Fitzgerald/Hartley Management.

Special thanks to Sir Cliff Richard, Gerry Breslauer, Joel Jacobson, Randal Kleiser, Pat Birch, Connie Ortega, Arthur Johns,

Kenny Ortega, Brian Grant, Diane and Gary Heavin, Lee and Dianne Moffitt, David Martin, Morris Diamond, Gavin de Becker, Ulli Haslacher, Frank Assumma, Brian Seth Hurst, Ali Goldman, Sunshine Mulford, Michelle Day, and Denise Truscello.

Thank you to my producers over the years: John Farrar, Bruce Welch, Sir Barry Gibb, Jeff Lynne, David Foster, Phil Ramone, Richard Marx, Chong Lim, Davitt Sigerson, Giorgio Moroder, Amy Sky, Beth Nielsen Chapman, Tony Brown, Gary Burr, Don Cook, Chris Farren, Randy Goodrum, Randy Waldman, Colin Bayley, Murray Burns, Stephan Elliot, Charles Fisher, Dave Audé, Elliot Scheiner, John Shanks, Brett Goldsmith, Dane Bryant, and Steve Real.

Thank you to my amazing team (past and present) who helped to make my dream of the Olivia Newton-John Cancer Wellness & Research Centre a reality: Brendan Murphy, Professor Jonathan Cebon, Jennifer Williams, Peter Dalton, Tanya Carter, Sharon Hillman, Louise Georgeson, Megan Gray, Daryl Jackson, John Brumby, Sue Shilbury, Debbie Shiell, Kim Tsai, Neil Pharaoh and Tottie Goldsmith. Thank you to our committed and caring staff for keeping my dream alive!

Heartfelt thanks to everyone at the ONJ for your exceptional care . . . especially Dr. Belinda Yeo, Dr. Dani Ko, Emma Cohen, and the staff on the seventh floor. Thank you, Dennis, for the meaningful cross!

I am so very grateful to the many people from Australia and all around the world who donate to and fund-raise for the ONJ Centre—your contributions make it possible to continue the special research and wellness programs that make our center so unique. Thank you all so very much.

Thank you to the Home Team: Yvette Nipar, Antonio and

Norma Avila, Autumn Brown, Graeme and Max Fleming, George and Madge Vidler, Rebeca Gonzalez, Mike Stein, Joni Sorita, and Tina Totis Yeager.

To those at Gaia Retreat & Spa: thank you to my dear Gregg Cave, Rod Mickle, Warwick Evans, Ruth Kalnin, Leanne and Jeff Schoen, and the more than sixty other team members and specialty therapists, who all bring magic through the healing cultures of Mother Earth—Gaia!

To my cowriter Cindy Pearlman, whose patience and guidance turned my words and thoughts into a cohesive story! Thank you, my friend!

Thank you to everyone at Penguin Random House Australia and Gallery Books/Simon & Schuster, Inc. (USA).

And, to my wonderful longtime fans and loyal supporters from all over the world—my gratitude for all your kindness and love.

CREDITS

Photographs

James Braund: ONJCRI Board (page 10 of first section)

Kathryn Burke: Olivia and John hugging (page 1 of second section); Raven, Magic, Harry, and Winston (page 5 of second section); back cover photograph

Timothy Clary: Olympics opening ceremony with John Farnham (page 14 of first section)

Nicole Cleary: Olivia in front of ONJ Centre (page 10 of first section)

Benjamin Couprie, Institut International de Physique de Solvay: Born group shot (page 1 of first section)

Michelle Day: Rona Newton-John (page 5 of first section); Olivia with Dr. Ernie Bodai (page 12 of first section); Olivia with eagle (page 6 of second section)

Brett Goldsmith: Olivia and family after AO ceremony (page 6 of first section); Olivia with AO in front of rainbow (page 9 of first section)

Stu Morley: Wellness Walk & Research Run with family and friends (page 11 of first section)

Brin Newton-John: Olivia on her twenty-third birthday (page 1 of first section); family photo (page 2 of first section)

Irene Newton-John: Olivia with baby Chloe and Matt (page 7 of first section); Olivia, Margaret Owings, Nancy and Jim Chuda (page 12 of first section); Olivia with John Travolta and dog (page 11 of second section)

Andrew Raszevski: Great Wall of China walk (page 11 of first section); Olivia and John on the wall (page 3 of second section)

Brittany Scott: Group photo with Dr. Hongdo Do, A/Professor Alex Dobrovic, Professor Matthias Ernst, John, Olivia, Anthony Carbines MP, Profesor Jonathan Cebon, and Kim Tsai (page 10 of first section); La Trobe graduation ceremony and with family and friends (page 15 of first section)

Joe Shalmoni: Olivia and Nancy Chuda (page 7 of second section)

Mark Sullivan-Bradley: Gaia Spa & Retreat photos (page 12 of first section)

Eddie Sung: Performing in Singapore in 2016, Olivia wearing white jacket in bottom row (page 16 of first section)

Denise Truscello: front cover photograph; Olivia and Chloe in white (page 8 of first section); Olivia and Chloe in dotted dress (page 8 of first section); Olivia and Emerson (page 6 of first section); singing onstage against pastel background (page 16 of first section); Olivia in gold dress (page 16 of first section); with *Grease* car (page 16 of first section); Olivia in original *Grease* jacket (page 11 of second section); creating *Liv On* in the recording studio (page 13 of second section); Olivia with Mark, Glenn, John, and Chong in the studio (page 13 of second section); Olivia and Goldie the chicken (page 5 of second section)

Kerryn Westcott: Olivia with Campbell Remess (page 12 of first section)

Gregg Woodward: wedding photos in Peru and Florida (pages 1 and 2 of second section); renewing vows in Peru (page 3 of second section)

Lyrics
Lyrics from "Don't Stop Believin'," "Sail into Tomorrow," "Have You Never Been Mellow," "You're the One That I Want," "Suddenly," and "Magic," by John Farrar, reproduced with kind permission.

Lyrics from "Overnight Observation" by John Farrar and Tom Snow, reproduced with kind permission.

Lyrics from "I Honestly Love You," by Peter Allen and Jeff Barry / Warner / Chappell Music, Inc., reproduced with kind permission.

Lyrics from "Physical," by Steven Kipner and Terry Shaddick / Sony / ATV Music Publishing, reproduced with kind permission.

Lyrics from "We Go Together" and "Summer Nights," by Warren Casey and Jim Jacobs, reproduced with kind permission.

Lyrics from "The Flower That Shattered the Stone" by Joe Henry and John Jarvis, reproduced with kind permission.

Lyrics from "Right Here with You" and "Pearls on a Chain" by Olivia Newton-John, reproduced with kind permission.

GAIA'S MOST OUTSTANDING AND RECENT AWARDS

Winner Overall—World Luxury Hotel Awards—*"2018 Global Hotel of the Year"*

Winner—World Travel Awards—*"World's Leading Retreat"* 2016, 2017, 2018 & 2019, and *"Australasia's Leading Boutique Hotel"* 2015, 2016, 2017 & 2018

Winner—World Spa Awards—*"World's Best Day Spa"* and *"Oceania's Best Day Spa"* 2015, 2016, 2017, 2018 & 2019

Winner—World Luxury Hotel Awards—4 Continent Wins—*"Luxury Spa, Luxury Wellness, Boutique Retreat & Luxury Hotel"* 2015, 2016, 2017, 2018 & 2019

Winner—World Luxury Restaurant Awards—*Global Winner*— *"Health & Wellness Cuisine"* 2017, 2018 & 2019 and *"Luxury Spa Restaurant"* 2018 & 2019

Winner—World Luxury Spa Awards—*Country Winner*—*"Best Luxury Wellness Spa"* 2016 and *"Best Luxury Spa Retreat"* 2017, 2018 & 2019

Winner—Gold List Award—*"Best Luxury Health & Wellness Retreat Australia"* 2019

Winner—Gourmet Traveller—*"Best Health Retreat"* 2011

Winner—Condé Nast Traveller Readers' Choice—*"Favorite Overseas Hotel/Spa"* 2008

CPSIA information can be obtained
at www.ICGtesting.com
Printed in the USA
LVHW042135160922
728349LV00003B/3